TRANSLATING FOOD SOVEREIGNTY

TRANSLATING FOOD SOVEREIGNTY

Cultivating Justice in an Age of Transnational Governance

Matthew C. Canfield

Stanford University Press
Stanford, California

STANFORD UNIVERSITY PRESS
Stanford, California

Portions of chapter 4 were originally published in Matthew C. Canfield, "Banana Brokers: Communicative Labor, Translocal Translation, and Transnational Law," *Public Culture* 31(1): 69–92, © 2019, Duke University Press.

Portions of chapter 5 were originally published in Matthew C. Canfield, "Disputing the Global Land Grab: Claiming Rights and Making Markets Through Collaborative Governance." *Law and Society Review* 52(4): 994–1025, ©2018, Wiley Periodicals, Inc.

Printed in the United States of America on acid-free, archival-quality paper.

Library of Congress Cataloging-in-Publication Data
Names: Canfield, Matthew C., author.
Title: Translating food sovereignty : cultivating justice in an age of transnational
      governance / Matthew C. Canfield.
Description: Stanford, California : Stanford University Press, 2022. |
      Includes bibliographical references and index.
Identifiers: LCCN 2021034819 (print) | LCCN 2021034820 (ebook) |
      ISBN 9781503613447 (cloth) | ISBN 9781503631304 (paperback) |
      ISBN 9781503631311 (ebook)
Subjects: LCSH: Food sovereignty—Northwest, Pacific. | Social movements—
      Northwest, Pacific. | Food supply—Political aspects—Northwest, Pacific.
      | Food sovereignty. | Social movements. | Food supply—Political aspects. |
      Transnationalism—Political aspects.
Classification: LCC HD9007.P33 C46 2022 (print) | LCC HD9007.P33 (ebook)
      | DDC 338.1/909795—dc23
LC record available at https://lccn.loc.gov/2021034819
LC ebook record available at https://lccn.loc.gov/2020455392

Cover art: Luisa Rivera

Cover design: Angela Moody

Typeset by Kevin Barrett Kane in 10.2/14.4 Minion Pro

Table of Contents

Acknowledgments

This book is the product of my education in the global food sovereignty movement. Over the past ten years, activists struggling for more just and sustainable food systems have taught me that food systems are about more than what we eat. My experiences with food sovereignty activists in the United States, Europe, and Africa helped me understand how profoundly the neat rows of corn that made up the agricultural backdrop of my childhood in the American Midwest shaped the lens through which I was taught to see the world. Those fields of industrial agriculture served as a powerful template for social, economic, and ecological organization, a vision of the world that is as monocultured as it is monocropped.

By embracing agroecology, food sovereignty activists seek to transform not only food systems but also existing frameworks of justice. Agroecology takes an integrative approach to food systems, combining practical knowledge, specialist research, and social justice values. It offers a set of principles and a way of engaging the world that nourishes biodiverse and culturally diverse landscapes. As an anthropologist, I was perhaps already primed to take on the holistic lens of agroecology, but my research with food sovereignty movements nonetheless stretched my frames of analysis.

Like agroecology, this book is transdisciplinary. It is informed by knowledge developed by my mentors in the fields of anthropology and sociolegal studies as well as the local knowledge that activists have developed as they have struggled for generations to challenge the industrial food systems that are poisoning humans and the earth. Although you can't eat this book, it is nonetheless the fruit of years of work that I have cultivated with the generous support of many colleagues, friends, and institutions.

The seed for this book was first planted in the office of Sally Engle Merry, my beloved adviser in graduate school. Sally was an extraordinary mentor who inspired and encouraged me to follow my curiosity and commitment to justice with rigor, kindness, and care. Through her hard work, brilliance, and intellectual imagination, she nourished the academic soils in which this project first germinated. Sally's passing in 2020 was a significant personal loss, but like many of us who were mentored by Sally over the years, I have found comfort, support, and new colleagues in the communities she nurtured. At NYU, I was also fortunate to meet Christine Harrington early on. Christine deepened my critical perspective, enriched my interdisciplinary lens, and nourished my activism. My anthropological education was fortified by Bruce Grant, Fred Myers, and Marc Edelman, who offered me productive and critical feedback.

Agroecology depends on the wisdom of Indigenous peoples and small-scale food producers. In my case, I learned from the knowledge produced by generations of food activists. In the Pacific Northwest, Bill Aal, Phil Bereano, Heather Day, Edgar Franks, Rosalinda Guillen, Tomas Madrigal, Mark Musick, Michael and Bobby Righi, and Mary Ann Schroeder welcomed me into their communities and shared their stories of activism and the lessons they have learned through years of struggle. I extend my deepest gratitude to them as well as all of the activists in this book. My hope is that this ethnography serves as an enduring archive of their tireless labor in reconnecting the web of life and rebuilding food systems from the bottom up. I have anonymized the identities of several individuals who did not wish to be named. However, the majority of participants asked that I use their names and affiliations. In addition, a number of activists and researchers guided me as I pursued this project, whether by commenting on my writing or by welcoming me into movement spaces. A special thanks to Faris Ahmed, Molly Anderson, Priscilla Claeys, Michael Fakhri, Nadia Lambek, Nora McKeon, Philip McMichael, Christina Schiavoni, Shiney Varghese, and Nettie Wiebe.

As my preliminary ideas were beginning to sprout, several fellowships provided me with the time, space, and early intellectual "inputs" that fertilized my intellectual imagination and helped me weed out extraneous ideas. At the School of Regulation and Global Governance (RegNet) at Australia National University I met John Braithwaite, Hilary Charlesworth, Peter Drahos, Kate Henne, and Emma Larking, who all welcomed me into an extraordinarily warm and engaging intellectual community. They introduced me to new conceptual frameworks and helped me wrangle my multisited fieldwork into a coherent conceptual framework. At the Department of Law and Anthropology at the Max Planck Institute for Social Anthropology, Professor Marie-Claire Foblets encouraged me to embrace my anthropological contributions and strengthen my arguments. In addition, the Transnational Law Summer Institute at King's College in London forever changed my thinking. I was fortunate to meet lasting friends and mentors Eve Darian-Smith, Manoj Dias-Abey, Priya Gupta, Prabah Kotiswaran, Jothie Rajah, and Peer Zumbansen. There I also met an extraordinary group of junior scholars who inspired me to develop the analytical framework for this book, including Julia Dehm, Marisa Fassi, Ivana Isailović, Emma Nyhan, Phillip Paiement, and Mariana Prandini-Assis. I am especially indebted to Eve, Manoj, and Mariana, who read and commented on chapters and the book proposal.

Like the first planting of new vines, it takes years before anthropological research bears fruit that is ready to be widely consumed. I spent an intense year at the European University Institute's Department of Law as a Max Weber Fellow, where I was lucky to receive support from Nehal Bhutta as well as the feedback and friendship of Per Andersson, Jeanne Commault, León Castellanos-Jankiewicz, Mirjam Dageförde, Ionna Hadjiyianni, Marina Henke, Marta Morvillo, Katya Motyl, Jamil Mouawad, Carolin Schmitz, Anna Wallerman Ghavanini, and Aydin Yildirim. In addition, participants of Harvard Law School's Institute for Global Law and Policy 2018 Thailand Workshop offered helpful feedback.

Throughout my intellectual development and book writing, the Law and Society Association also provided a valuable intellectual community through which to refine my ideas. I was lucky to meet Amy Cohen early on; she has been a generous and brilliant interlocutor. I am indebted to her for reading and commenting on not only my introduction but also so much of my work. The Political and Legal Anthropology Association has also continued to serve as an incredible source of mentoring and support; Erica Bornstein, Susan Coutin, Rosemary Coombe, Bill Maurer, and Mark Schuller have all provided enormous support and mentorship over the years.

Much of the writing for this book took place while I was teaching in the Law, Politics, and Society Program at Drake University, where Renée Cramer has created an extraordinary community of students and scholars. Renée, Godfried Asante, Deb DeLaet, Will Garriott, Michael Haedicke, Nate Holdren, Joseph Schneider, and Daria Trentini were all incredibly supportive. I am especially indebted to the students in the Fall 2020 Senior Seminar of Law, Politics, and Society who commented on my introduction and provided invaluable feedback.

The final sprint of completing this book took place as I took up a new post at the Van Vollenhoven Institute at Leiden Law School. I am deeply grateful to Adriaan Bedner, Janine Ubink, and Pauline Vincenten, who welcomed me into the VVI during a global pandemic in unconventional virtual circumstances. I am thrilled to be a part of this exciting intellectual environment and warm community, and I look forward to contributing to the Institute in the years to come as we collectively cultivate new projects and fields.

The sunshine I needed throughout the years of writing this book was provided by many friends and colleagues, including Narges Bajogli, Alison Baum, Tiana Bakić-Hayden, Carly Benkov, Gabby Berger, Jay Blair, Waqas Butt, Alli Carlisle, Lee Douglas, Lily Drew, Michelle Geller, Sydney Katz, Irina Levin, Mikaela Luttrell-Rowland, Meredith Mann, Alice Manos, Brian Montopoli, Vijayanka Nair, Ram Natarajan, Jesse Paulsen, Levi Pine, Natasha Raheja, Vibhuti Ramachandran, Nick Sainati, Eli Shindelman, Jen Telesca, Andrew Telzak, Jen Trowbridge, and Umut Türem.

I owe a special thanks to Stanford University Press for seeing the value in this project and for supporting it from its early stages. Michelle Lipinski, Marcela Maxfield, and Sunna Juhn helped guide me through the process of publishing my first book.

Funding for this research was provided by a MacCracken Fellowship at New York University, a National Science Foundation Law and Social Science Doctoral Dissertation Improvement Grant (SES 1323743), the Thomas Marchione Food-as-a-Human Right Student Award, and a Graduate Research Initiative Fellowship at New York University's London campus. Portions of the text in this book previously appeared elsewhere, including in the *Law & Society Review* and *Public Culture*.

Finally, my family continues to be my greatest source of love and support. Christopher Baum's spirit has been my light and inspiration while working on this project. His imagination, patience, and resilience motivated me to persist through difficult times. Moving across coasts and continents, he has been a patient listener, critical interlocutor, emotional rock, and constant source of joy. Without the love and support of my mother, Debby, this book would never have been possible. It is she who first seeded the idea of an academic life. She taught me the love of reading and writing and inspired me with her passion for empirical research. I owe everything I am to her, and it is to her that this book is dedicated.

TRANSLATING FOOD SOVEREIGNTY

INTRODUCTION

The Law and Politics of Food Sovereignty

IN 2011, I crowded into the basement of a small church in downtown Oakland, California, with activists from across the country for the first US Food Sovereignty Assembly. It was just three years after a global food and financial crisis had upended the global economy. In a political moment gripped with concern over economic inequality, food was becoming a powerful symbol and site of social change. As people began to arrive at the church, I was immediately struck by those who had been invited. They did not resemble the hippies, hipsters, and affluent white consumers I had come to associate with "food activism." They included the people most marginalized and exploited by the industrial food system: migrant seasonal farmworkers, Indigenous communities, organizations of the urban food insecure, and small family farmers. These were not groups that had typically been politically aligned. In fact, they had often been pitted against one another as competing interest groups in US food and agricultural policy. Yet in the previous three years a small group of US-based activists with links to burgeoning global peasant movements had assembled these groups with the hope of uniting them over their shared grievances. Sitting in the back of the room as a volunteer notetaker, I watched with curiosity, wondering what it would mean for these groups to claim "food sovereignty."

Over the past two decades, millions of people across the world have taken up the claim of food sovereignty. The claim was first articulated in the

1990s by small-scale food producers in the transnational social movement La Vía Campesina, the International Peasants' Movement. Food producers initially united to oppose the threats to their lands, livelihoods, and diets posed by the liberalization of food and agricultural markets through the World Trade Organization. Almost immediately after it was articulated, however, the claim of food sovereignty quickly spread. By the mid-2000s, when skyrocketing food prices caused a global food crisis, other constituencies of food systems, including food-chain workers, fisherfolk, and poor urban consumers, also began to claim food sovereignty to demand local control over their food systems. Food sovereignty alliances now exist in almost every region of the world, making food sovereignty one of the most widely mobilized contemporary social justice claims.

The precipitous rise of movements claiming food sovereignty reflects the state of contemporary food systems. Today there is widespread agreement that our current global food system is socially and ecologically unsustainable. Despite the consistent global consensus of the need to end global hunger, more than 2 billion people in the world lack access to adequate food, including 37 million people in the United States.[1] Beyond food insecurity, malnutrition is also surging. If one combines both of its forms (over- and underconsumption), malnutrition now constitutes the world's number one cause of ill health.[2] Although powerful nations and corporations have consistently pushed the expansion of industrial agriculture, it is clear that this system has not only failed to address hunger but is also responsible for vast ecological devastation. The global food system is one of the largest contributor to global greenhouse gas emissions, deforestation, and the destruction of global biodiversity.[3]

These problems were made even more manifest during the coronavirus pandemic. During the worst of the crisis, newspapers in the United States printed stories of farmers dumping milk and euthanizing livestock alongside pictures of snaking lines of cars waiting outside food banks and workers jammed together at meat processing plants suffering from high infection rates. The US food system—once celebrated as the apotheosis of abundance and efficiency—was revealed to be a shaky structure crippled by corporate consolidation. In the United States we are witnessing growing monopolistic control over the food and farming sector. Four or fewer firms control the market for agro-inputs, beef and grain processing, and many major food commodity chains.[4] Globally, four or fewer firms also control almost all commercial agricultural inputs. Just four companies control 60% of the global commercial seed industry and 90% of the global grain trade, and three companies control 70% of the agrochemical industry.[5] This centralization of control over food systems in the hands of so few is a driving factor in many of the problems that we are seeing today. As the International Panel of Experts on Sustainable Food Systems puts it, the industrial food system is just "too big to feed."[6]

The activists gathered in Oakland were all organizing in response to these issues. Many of them shared these same grievances. But over the course of the day-long meeting it became clear that they also had different priorities. Farmworkers on the West Coast were fighting for fair working conditions in the industrial food system, whereas Indigenous communities were seeking to rebuild their traditional food systems after centuries of settler colonialism and unhealthy donations from the commodity food system. Other groups, such as the Detroit Black Community Food Security Network, were working to dismantle racism in the food system and create consumer cooperatives and urban farms to promote urban food security. Even though the participants of the assembly came up with a long list of rights—from the rights of Mother Earth to the right to access land—none of these claims captured their disparate struggles. In a country in which the language of *rights* has served as the dominant grammar for social justice movements, the activists participating in the US Food Sovereignty Assembly wrestled to consolidate their demands into a single claim that simultaneously respected their diversity and united them into a movement.

As the debate unfolded, it was clear that they faced profound strategic questions: What would it mean to claim *sovereignty* rather than rights? How could they translate food sovereignty across their divergent contexts? And how could a claim that was developed in the global South be adopted and mobilized by activists in the very different political, economic, and agrarian context of the United States?

LAW AND SOCIAL MOVEMENTS IN AN AGE OF NEOLIBERAL GLOBALIZATION

Participants' struggle to reconcile their repertoires of rights claiming with the language of food sovereignty is a product of the way that social movements have constituted social justice claims for the past few generations. In the 1950s and 1960s, rights mobilization became the dominant approach through which individuals and groups articulated claims on society and the state in liberal democracies. The civil rights movement, the women's movement, the LGBTQ movement, and the disability rights movement, among others, all drew on rights-based strategies to seek inclusion into society and demand economic redistribution.[7] By claiming rights, movements consolidated not only their demands but also their collective identities.[8] This "rights revolution" spread globally with the proliferation of human rights as a shared global language of social justice beginning in the 1970s.[9]

Today, however, both scholars and social movements are increasingly recognizing the limits of social and economic rights claims in the face of neoliberal inequalities. Rights-based approaches to social change are constrained by the shifting geographies of power produced by neoliberal globalization. Rights are premised on a vision of the world in which nation-states operate the primary regulatory authority. Since the 1970s, however, the state-centered hierarchical framework of public international law and national economic regulation has been rolled back through deregulation, privatization, and the liberalization of global markets. As Saskia Sassen describes, neoliberalism reorganized the relationship between territory, authority, and rights on a global scale by partly denationalizing some state capacities.[10] Today, as international law grows increasingly fragmented, rights operate as just one normative form through which power operates, amid proliferating forms of governance.

As a result, critical voices are increasingly questioning the emancipatory possibilities inherent in rights discourse. A recent wave of scholarship has revealed how human rights ascended as the primary framework for imagining social justice just as the architects of neoliberalism were institutionalizing the market economy as the principal and governing logic at the national and international level.[11] Analyses tracing the concurrent rise of human rights discourse and neoliberalism build on a long corpus of critical theory that has been skeptical of rights. Feminist and Marxist analyses have consistently argued that rights offer a narrow frame for social justice claims because they remain rooted in "liberal legalism," an ideology of law premised on individual rather than collective rights, private property, and formal equality. Liberal legalism's endeavor to separate the "public" sphere of political equality and the "private" sphere of liberty—the domain of the economy and family—has consistently served as a stumbling block for generations of social movements seeking egalitarian social change.[12]

Postcolonial critics also challenge the transnational culture of modernity that human rights language often reproduces.[13] Rights discourses emerged from the European Enlightenment and colonial project and today still carry the values of Eurocentric modernity. They remain premised on a universal, secular vision of human nature and atomistic worldview that separates humans from nonhuman nature and privileges the individual as the primary legal subject.[14] Human rights have consistently been mobilized by powerful states in the global North to distinguish between "traditional" and "modern," "savage" and "savior," thereby reproducing a Northern-centered world order that maintains colonial hierarchies of power.[15] Although rights remain an important legal and symbolic resource, both social movements and sociolegal scholars are learning that rights are "not enough," as Samuel Moyn puts it, to challenge the overlapping inequalities produced through centuries of colonialism, capitalism, and neoliberalism.[16]

The organizers of the first US Food Sovereignty Assembly seemed to intuitively understand these constraints. Just as the assembly drew to a close and the participants became embroiled in a debate over their priorities, a handful of the assembly's organizers who had more contact with food sovereignty movements outside the United States intervened. One activist who had extensive experience organizing with La Vía Campesina in Latin America explained that food sovereignty did not take what she called a top-down "command and control" approach to political change but rather sought to decentralize control over food and agriculture. Another grassroots activist explained that food sovereignty was best understood through the "three P's"—people, places, and platforms. She said that food sovereignty was mobilized by marginalized peoples, was rooted in specific places and contexts, and offered a shared platform for struggle. At the time, I did not quite comprehend these activists' interventions. Yet over the next seven years, I began to understand that these activists were radically recalibrating their horizons of social justice and developing new practices of mobilization in response to the metamorphosis of capitalism and regulation in an era of neoliberal globalization.

CULTIVATING TRANSNATIONAL
GOVERNANCE FROM BELOW

In this book I analyze how activists in the United States frame, claim, and mobilize food sovereignty. Food sovereignty movements combine rights claims with an expansive demand for "sovereignty," or control, over the social, economic, and ecological relations involved in food production and provisioning. This claim, I argue, cannot be understood outside the mutating global political and legal order of transnational governance, a global regulatory order that has emerged alongside neoliberalism and the spread of global capitalism.[17]

Over the past three decades, as neoliberalism has ascended to become the dominant ideology, it has transformed the legal and regulatory order across local, regional, and global levels. Although neoliberalism is often associated with the weakening of regulation, scholars have observed quite the opposite—more capitalism necessitates *more* rules and regulations.[18] Yet the forms that regulation takes have been reconfigured and rescaled. Through a suite of regulatory reforms promoted by states and international institutions in the global North, state-dominated approaches to national economic regulation have been increasingly replaced with *governance* through networks. States are now embedded in transnational networks that include a variety of nonstate actors—from transnational corporations to social movements—that compete to set nonbinding norms, rules, and standards through which political, social, and economic relations are ordered. The proliferation of governance through networks has reshaped the form, exercise, and operation of global power.[19]

Critical observers have described how the rise of transnational governance is reordering power and authority through the economic logics of the market and producing a new era of corporate rule, but few have attended to the ways that activists are responding to the changing cultural and symbolic politics of this regulatory order by producing new social justice claims and conditions of possibility. Indeed, as transnational governance blurs the boundaries once established by liberal legalism to establish constraints on power, it offers both new opportunities and constraints. On the one hand, transnational governance draws on symbols that appeal to social movements. The networked form of transnational governance implies horizontal relations and social ties. It relies on collaboration, participation, and inclusion of actors beyond the state. By constituting claims in relation to transnational governance, food sovereignty activists demand the inclusion of those most marginalized in public policymaking. Moreover, they are able to articulate food sovereignty as a holistic social justice claim that transcends the divisions between public and private imposed by liberal legalism and Euro-modernism.[20] On the other hand, however, transnational governance is often initiated from the top down, by elites who seek to extend market logics and manage their "externalities," not radically upend them. For neoliberals the networked form of transnational governance provides a framework for the dissemination of neoliberal reason and market values.[21] As a result, transnational governance also enables the deeper domination by powerful market actors by dismantling previous institutional and symbolic forms of regulation that have endeavored to set limits on power.

Food sovereignty activists are well aware of this paradox. They encounter it continuously as they engage in multistakeholder and collaborative arenas of governance that produce the voluntary guidelines, private certifications, and codes of conduct through which transnational governance operates—all of which they are deeply skeptical of. Yet by dialectically constituting claims for food sovereignty in relation to these emerging forms of governance, I argue that they are cultivating decentralized, democratic networks through which they are reconfiguring relations between communities, nature, and markets. In doing so, they are producing what I call *governance from below*.

My analysis builds on sociolegal scholarship on law and social movements. Sociolegal scholars and anthropologists have illuminated how claiming rights generates culturally constitutive processes of meaning making, the effects of which often far exceed the outcomes produced through judicial or legislative arenas.[22] However, although sociolegal scholars have recognized that social movements frame their claims in relation to dominant legal forms,[23] studies of law and social change have curiously remained focused on state law. I therefore examine the mutually constitutive relationship between transnational governance and social movements. By accompanying food sovereignty activists as they made claims across local, national, and transnational arenas of governance and within different forms of governance, I show how they are constructing new practices of mobilization, or what I term *social practices of translation*, to leverage this new order. In doing so,

I offer a new methodological lens through which to examine how power and influence operate through the ethnography of governance networks.

My analysis is based on ethnographic fieldwork that I undertook with food sovereignty activists in western Washington State. Since the late 2000s the Puget Sound region has become home to one of the densest concentrations of food sovereignty activists in the United States. Drawing on my fieldwork, I describe how activists have developed a set of social practices through which they translate food sovereignty across these various geographic scales, contexts, and institutional arenas. Through these shared social practices of translation, food sovereignty activists cultivate governance networks that build new cross-sectoral, cross-territorial relations. By deploying these prefigurative practices of translation and legal mobilization, I show how food sovereignty activists are shaping the standards, values, and relations produced through transnational governance in powerful ways.

FOOD, LAW, AND SOVEREIGNTY

I first grew interested in the politics of food and agriculture not because of an agrarian upbringing but rather as a result of my first job. At age 14 I worked as a runner on the floor of the Chicago Board of Trade. For a few months over the summer, I donned a drab khaki and teal mesh vest and ran orders for commodity futures on the exchange floor. As brokers watched weather patterns over the Midwest corn belt, they would scribble coded orders on tickets for "July corn" or "August soy," which I then ran to traders who stood packed together in multilevel "pits" where they screamed over one another until someone fulfilled the trade. I was perplexed by the whole system. It seemed deeply disconnected from the actual object that they were trading—food.

In 2007 I was reminded of this experience when prices of rice, wheat, and maize—the three staple cereal crops on which much of the world depends—more than doubled and caused a global food crisis. Over 150 million people were suddenly forced into hunger, causing food riots in more than thirty countries.[24] The crisis was the confluence of many causes, including the increasing use of agricultural land for fuel crops, the volatility produced through trade liberalization, and speculation by the very grain traders for whom I had once worked.[25] It also coincided with a global financial crisis, leading to one of the greatest global recessions, the fallout of which we are still managing today. In the aftermath of these converging crises, food not only emerged as a symbolic and material battleground over neoliberalism but also seemed to offer a practical way to build alternatives to it.

The 2007–2008 food crisis exposed the precarity of the industrial food system. It undermined the narrative that industrial food production—by which I mean the large-scale, input-intensive production of crops and animals that rely on commercially produced agrochemicals, antibiotics, and other inputs[26]—is indispensable to feed the world. Since then, contention around the global food system has only grown. Although agribusiness has sought to deepen its grip on global agriculture by forging past geographic and biophysical frontiers through new technologies and by promoting a Malthusian narrative about the need to expand global food production, small-scale food producers, rural workers, and urban consumers have increasingly coalesced around the claim of food sovereignty as a path toward just and sustainable food systems.

However, struggles over food are not unique to neoliberalism. The dual status of food as both a basic need and an economic good on which millions of people depend for their livelihoods has made it a unique object through which generations of people have assessed dominant regulatory systems. Attempts to assimilate food production and provisioning into the market-based values of capitalism have long motivated collective resistance. To protect their autonomy and livelihoods, peasants and small-scale food producers have unfailingly mobilized to oppose processes of enclosure and incorporation into capitalist markets. High grain and food prices for urban consumers have also unseated political regimes from the French Revolution to the Arab Spring. The historian E. P. Thompson famously argued that hunger engenders struggles in which popular classes articulate the proper balance between market and communal forms of provisioning—what he called "moral economies."[27] Food systems have always served as symbolic and material arenas of struggle through which societies have questioned, contested, and reconstructed dominant regulatory arrangements.

These struggles are not only about the price of food. Anthropologists emphasize the central role of food in people's everyday lives. Food is intimately connected to people's value systems. It reflects people's ties to place and to one another. As Heather Paxson describes, food is an object of value that "transcends quantitative measures, whether of kilocalories or grams of fat, or in dollars and cents. . . . Through food, people solidify a sense of self and connectedness to (or distance from) others."[28] In short, food is deeply cultural. Food is profoundly bound up with people's conceptions of justice, whether that stems from peasants' beliefs about fair provisioning for their labor or consumers' expectations about access to fresh, healthy, and traditionally available foodstuffs.

Whereas agrarian scholars and rural sociologists have long been attuned to the central role of food and agriculture in organizing global power relations,[29] sociolegal scholars are only beginning to consider the role of food and agriculture in constructing dominant normative and regulatory orders. Recently, scholars have started to explore the cultural significance of food and agriculture as an underlying cultural framework for much liberal legal doctrine. For example, Brenna Bhandar has illuminated how "scientific" practices of commercial agricultural production in England played a critical symbolic role in providing not only the justification for racial and colonial capitalism but also theorizations of liberal sovereignty. As she explains, early liberal theorists, including William Petty and John Locke, rationalized the colonial dispossession of lands from the Irish and Indigenous peoples and justified the necessity of private property based on their failure to comport with English practices of land use.[30] Commercial practices of food production served as the symbolic foundation on which property and sovereignty were constructed based on culturally contingent ideologies of race, nature, and gender.

Drawing on these insights, a growing number of sociolegal scholars are turning to the study of food and agriculture as a legally constitutive site of struggle. I contribute to this emerging scholarship by demonstrating how food sovereignty movements are mounting a fundamental challenge not only to the industrial food system but also to the dominant frameworks through which international law and politics are organized.[31] In doing so, I show how activists claiming food *sovereignty* are challenging the culturally contingent visions of society, nature, and the market on which liberal sovereignty has been constructed over the past three centuries.[32]

TRANSNATIONAL GOVERNANCE AND THE
NEW LEGALITY OF FOOD SOVEREIGNTY

When La Vía Campesina (LVC) originally developed the claim of food sovereignty in 1996, they did so to protest the incorporation of food and agriculture into the agreements of the World Trade Organization and to demand the renationalization of food and agricultural policies. Yet, although LVC initially targeted the World Trade Organization, given its role in setting the legal rules for the liberalization of food and agriculture, LVC's claims for food sovereignty began to mutate alongside shifts in transnational governance. As neoliberalism transformed political and legal space, food sovereignty activists found themselves embroiled in a variety of arenas of governance constructed to develop regulations for food systems at the local and global levels.

As described earlier, the rise of transnational governance is a product of global capitalist expansion. The term *governance* signifies a shift away from the top-down forms of command-and-control state-led regulation that predominated during the mid-twentieth century toward more inclusive and voluntary forms of regulation, or "soft" law.[33] The proliferation of governance not only heralded the transformation of the state toward a more facilitative function in which it too was embedded in relational processes of governance but also led to the blurring of boundaries on which liberalism was premised. I use the term *transnational governance* to refer to a variety of regulatory processes at the sub- and supranational levels in which public and private actors collaborate in setting voluntary, nonbinding standards, including transnational private governance constituted through value chains[34] and market-driven forms of regulation through labeling and certifications.[35]

Although the concept of transnational governance includes different forms and arenas of regulation, they share a common form: the network. The construction of networked forms of transnational governance is the product of shifting cultural representations of socioeconomic organization that arose in the 1980s and 1990s.[36] Social scientists have long drawn on the concept of social networks as a descriptive framework to analyze human relations and social ties, but the aesthetic properties of networked structures—their horizontal, flexible, and open-ended features—became an organizational form that appealed to competing actors. Luc Boltanski and Eve Chiapello contend that the rise of networks is attributable not simply to the development of new information and communications technologies but also to the convergence of critiques on both the left and the right of the hierarchical Fordist mode of regulation.[37] By the late 1990s, scholars proclaimed networks as "the new social morphology of our societies" and the "new world order."[38]

Boltanski and Chiapello's insight is instructive for understanding strug-gles over transnational governance. In drawing on the networked form, contemporary forms of regulation and governance are premised on a set of cultural symbols that are mobilized by rival actors to both legitimate and resist neoliberalism. In their study of disputing arenas in the United States, Sally Merry and Christine Harrington describe how legal and regulatory "ideologies are formed through the mobilization of symbolic resources by groups promoting different projects."[39] In the context of transnational gover-nance, the networked form is imbued with different meanings by competing actors. For transnational corporations, networks offer a representation of a boundaryless world of global markets and flexible specialization, whereas for transnational activists, networks provide a model for an egalitarian, de-centralized system of participatory democracy. These competing meanings have enabled the network to ascend as both the dominant representation of social and economic life and the organizational form of transnational governance.[40] Transnational governance is thus not simply a set of institu-tional structures and practices; it is a site of social struggle. Hegemonic and counterhegemonic actors may embrace the networked *form* of governance, but they imbue networks with competing cultural meanings and practices through which they ultimately seek to instill networks with different rules and standards.

In the years after it was first articulated by LVC, social movements re-defined food sovereignty in light of the rolling-out of transnational gov-ernance. In 2003 LVC redefined food sovereignty as "the right of *peoples* to define their own food and agricultural policies."[41] This definition not only offered a more inclusive framing but also expanded the meaning of sovereignty beyond the territorial Westphalian frame of sovereignty that privileges the nation-state. This redefinition of food *sovereignty* reflected changes in the way sovereignty was effectively exercised. Indeed, although sovereignty has been primarily understood as a claim to absolute authority over a political community—which in the Westphalian frame has corre-sponded to the nation—many scholars have acknowledged that sovereignty today effectively operates relationally, through global networks.[42]

Because activists reframed their demands to control food and agricul-tural systems through the language of food *sovereignty* rather than as a right to be granted by sovereign nation-states, some scholars suggest that food sovereignty has produced a "new rights framework."[43] Priscilla Claeys describes how food sovereignty activists have purposefully framed their primary claim as *people's right to food sovereignty* rather than the human right to food because activists see the human rights framework as too individualistic and state-centered. Food sovereignty, she argues, is more radical because it allows movements to reclaim control over food and agriculture and promote egalitarian social change from the bottom up.[44] In making this argument, she cites an internal LVC document from 2008 that called for "a new legality and a new institutionality at the national and international levels."[45]

Although LVC activists were unlikely referring to the concept of "legality" developed by sociolegal theorists, their use of this term nonetheless resonates with the way that law and society scholars have understood the production of law, power, and authority. Patricia Ewick and Susan Silbey elaborated the concept of legality to describe the "meanings, sources of authority, and cultural practices that are commonly recognized as legal, regardless of who enacts them or for what ends."[46] They developed this term to emphasize the role of law as an emergent feature of social life and to show how law is constituted through everyday engagements and understandings of law, or what they call *legal consciousness*. As they explain, legality operates "as both an interpretive framework and a set of resources with which the social world (including that part known as the law) is constituted."[47] Although they first articulated the concept of legality in the domestic context, Ewick and Silbey's notion of legality is useful in the context of transnational governance because in this emerging neoliberal political and legal landscape, law no longer bears the authority that it did in the Westphalian liberal legal context.[48] As rival actors struggle to produce authority and deference, they do so by seeking to promote shared meanings, practices, and values—what Ewick and Silbey refer to as legality.

In addition to resignifying the claim of food sovereignty to reflect a democratic vision of transnational governance, LVC also took on a networked organizational structure to resist neoliberalism. Paul Nicholson, a farmer from the Basque Country and a leader in LVC, explains that LVC developed a "new organizational vision" that had intentionally weakened its international secretariat by moving it every four years to a new location. The aim in this was to emphasize the autonomy of movements at the grassroots level: "The struggle for food sovereignty, which is common to all LVC organizations, requires a different strategy of alliances right from the local level, with horizontal decision-making in one's own organization. Food sovereignty is clearly a new democratic demand of citizens."[49]

Because food sovereignty activists prefigure the networked form of transnational governance, they imbue networks with distinct meanings and practices. Anthropologist Jeffrey Juris argues that the "alter-globalization" or "anticorporate globalization" movement was the first social movement to adopt a "cultural logic of networking," based on its veneration of digital networks as the technology, form, and political norm through which they imagined global justice.[50] Food sovereignty activists draw on a different model of connectivity: *agroecology*. Food sovereignty activists see agroecology as "the essential alternative to [the industrial model of food production], and as the means of transforming how we produce and consume food into something better for humanity and our Mother Earth."[51] The importance of agroecology as a symbolic template for food sovereignty activists' vision of political and legal organization was made clear by one activist who described to me the challenge that food sovereignty activists now face. Sitting in a café in Rome after a long week of negotiations in the UN Committee on World Food Security, he explained how the dominant socioeconomic forms of organization through which power has been constructed and contested are inadequate for food sovereignty movements. "The formats of social organization that we have in front of us are political parties, religious sects, and social networks, none of which is a format for people dealing with nature." Peasant movements, he said, are shaped by their desires for autonomy to determine their own agricultural practices; they seek to make their own decisions and speak their own languages. "But they are not a sector. They are dynamic and moving, because they are people in the field with nature."

His comments emphasized that agroecology has deeply shaped food sovereignty activists' visions of social transformation and modes of political organization.[52] Agroecology is not simply a technology of production; it is a transdisciplinary science, social movement, and practice.[53] It incorporates political and social values as well as ecological approaches to food system design to promote sustainable and equitable development.[54] For activists, food sovereignty and agroecology are two sides of the same coin. Their interconnectedness is captured by a mantra I often heard repeated by activists:

"Food sovereignty without agroecology is a political slogan, and agroecology without food sovereignty is only a technology of production." By drawing on agroecology rather than networked forms of technology, food sovereignty activists provide an alternative political representation through which to build new forms of governance, premised on their relationship with nature. Moreover, by drawing on agroecology, they also challenge the ideals of commercial agriculture that formed the symbolic and material foundations of liberal sovereignty. In contrast to both the forms of agriculture on which liberal sovereignty was premised and the digitalized networks that inspired alter-globalization movements' vision of global governance, food sovereignty activists draw on agroecology to offer a fundamentally different vision of global social organization rooted in decentralized, democratic practices of food production and provisioning.

MOBILIZING FOOD SOVEREIGNTY:
FROM CLAIMS TO PRACTICES

Understanding how food sovereignty activists seek to institutionalize their claims in the polycentric landscape of transnational governance requires that we reassess how we understand the relationship between law and social change. In studying how social movements have responded to neoliberal globalization, Boaventura de Sousa Santos and Cesar Rodríguez-Garavito implore us to dispatch the distinction between law and politics and the focus on rights that has shaped the literature on legal mobilization. Maintaining this distinction, they argue, not only reproduces the boundaries constructed by liberal legalism but also fails to reflect how contemporary movements approach law as part of a broader political strategy for social and political transformation.[55]

Building on this approach, global sociolegal scholars have suggested that the focus on rights has also elided the critical relationship between rights and regulation.[56] The division between rights mobilization and regulatory struggles stems from liberal legalism's distinction between law and politics and from the way this has been reflected in the disciplinary division of labor between legal scholars and political science. However, transnational governance has reconfigured the relationship between rights and regulation. In her pioneering study of the water justice movement, Bronwen Morgan argues that the dominant framework through which sociolegal scholars have approached disputes and legal mobilization—"naming, blaming, and claiming"—needs to be reworked in the context of transnational governance. She proposes that movements engaged in redistributive struggles must also engage in "rulemaking, monitoring, and enforcement." Although rights "frame basic value conflicts," she argues that the operational reality of provisioning takes place in the context of regulatory governance.[57] Movements seeking redistributive justice must therefore engage in both rights *and* regulation in their social struggles.

Scholars in other fields have framed the limitations of rights-based approaches to transnational governance in different terms. In his study of network power, political scientist David Grewal argues that rights have limited efficacy in the context of networked forms of governance because networks are based on relations. He suggests a relational approach to rights, which requires those promoting social change to ask more nuanced questions about distribution, such as "*who* is free, *from* what restraint (or *because of* what enabling condition), to perform which action."[58]

These analyses provide critical insights into the claim of food sovereignty and why activists have articulated justice claims beyond rights. In contrast to the atomistic view of society endemic to liberal legality, food sovereignty is a relational practice. In their analysis of the Potato Park of the Peruvian Andes, Alastair Iles and Maywa Montenegro de Wit describe how food sovereignty activists use a "'relational' ontology . . . in their work to unseat dominant institutions." They argue that food sovereignty "is not an extraneously existing object but is a living process[;] it foregrounds the conscientious building and maintaining of relationships between people, institutions, technologies, ecosystems, and landscapes across multiple scales."[59] Similarly, based on her fieldwork among Venezuelan food sovereignty activists, Christina Schiavoni describes how activists approach food sovereignty as a *process*, one that is constantly being reshaped over time.[60]

But how do food sovereignty activists construct these relations? And with whom? How do they decide when to strategically mobilize rights language and when to mobilize food sovereignty? And how do they institutionalize their values? In her analysis of the water justice movement, Bronwen Morgan suggests that the processes through which activists engage in rights and regulation are best understood as a set of *social practices* through which activists articulate "generalized claims upon the social

order."[61] Approaching claims as social practices not only offers a more realistic understanding of the ways that claims are made meaningful across
different contexts—as anthropologists have revealed about the practice of
human rights mobilization[62]—but also suggests that we must pay attention
to the specific practices through which social movements seek to influence
the norms and standards constituted across plural and overlapping governance networks.

TRANSLATION AS SOCIAL PRACTICE

Building on this scholarship and my ethnographic fieldwork with activists
in the Pacific Northwest of the United States, in this book I argue that we
can understand food sovereignty as a set of *social practices of translation*.
Sociolegal scholars have increasingly turned to the metaphor of translation to describe how power is constructed and contested across divergent
meaning worlds and local contexts. Food sovereignty scholars have also
embraced the concept of translation, acknowledging that food sovereignty
"is *always* in the process of translation."[63] The growing salience of this
metaphor is a product of the networked form of transnational legality;
networks are, after all, communicative structures woven together through
shared interpretive frameworks and meanings.[64] Rival actors compete to
exercise control in this context by translating their ideas and values across
several overlapping regimes of governance. As John Braithwaite and Peter
Drahos explain in their study of transnational business regulation, "Power
in global regulatory systems arises from enrolling organizational power,
rarely from commanding it. The enrolling occurs through webs of dialogue and persuasion, not through webs of reward and punishment."[65]

   Sociolegal scholars have developed a variety of different theories of translation to explain how actors assemble networks and construct constituencies around shared norms. For example, in the context of human rights
mobilization Sally Merry draws on linguistic approaches to translation
to describe how activists mediate the meaning of rights claims between
global and local contexts to make them salient for local populations.[66] Her
approach to translation is particularly attentive to the actors—their backgrounds, ideologies, and resources—that mediate meaning. In the context
of regulatory governance scholars have drawn on a different approach to
translation by building on actor-network theory and Foucauldian theories

of governmentality.[67] This framework draws on a more abstract notion of translation to describe the ways in which actors are enrolled in networks based on shared knowledge, norms, and standards.[68] Combined, these two approaches illuminate how translation operates as an interpretive process in which individuals and communities exercise power by constituting networks based on shared meanings, knowledge, and relations.

Yet, even though scholars recognize that translation is a legally constitutive process, they do not distinguish between different *practices* of translation. Attending to these differences is critical because translation is not a singular practice. Subaltern and feminist scholars emphasize that translation is always an act of power—that "any process of description, interpretation, and dissemination of ideas and worldviews is always already caught up in relations of power and asymmetries between languages, regions, and peoples."[69] Building on these insights, linguistic anthropologist Susan Gal notes that translation is a metaphor that refers to a variety of metasemiotic processes through which actors aim to create equivalences across meaning worlds.[70] Equivalences, she explains, can be subsumed and interpreted by actors as a universal or a "general equivalent" among diverse contexts, or they can be recognized by translators as a contingent and unstable articulation.[71] Put more simply, how translation configures different meanings—whether by subsuming difference or acknowledging it—has profound political implications.[72]

Moreover, scholars of social movements and globalization have also suggested that counterhegemonic activists have developed particular practices of translation. Based on his observations at the World Social Forums, de Sousa Santos argues that without a shared consensus of social transformation, social movements have turned to translation to build alternative social and economic structures. Translation, he argues, "is the procedure we are left with to give coherence and generate coalitions among the enormous diversity of struggles against neo-liberal globalization when there is no . . . general theory of progressive social transformation."[73] By engaging in translation, social movements "create intelligibility, coherence, and articulation in a world that sees itself enriched by multiplicity and diversity."[74]

These insights suggest that actors develop specific *social practices of translation* in their efforts to cultivate social relations and influence institutional arenas. By elaborating the counterhegemonic "translocal" practices of translation developed by food sovereignty movements, I demonstrate how these practices serve as a form of mobilization in the blurred boundaries of transnational governance. I show that social practices of translation operate as a form of metagovernance—the governance of governance[75]—through which social movements and other actors constitute shared networks, meanings, and norms and seek to encode them within institutional arenas.[76]

In chapter 1, I elaborate the practices of *translocal translation* of food sovereignty activists. These practices are shaped by three values of food sovereignty: a demand for self-representation by people's movements, a commitment to local and Indigenous forms of knowledge, and a desire to promote the autonomy of different peoples and constituencies of food systems. I argue that these values are operationalized as semiotic practices of translocal translation through what I describe as representational practices, epistemologies, and practices of commensuration. In each of the coming chapters I examine how food sovereignty movements deploy these practices of translation to constitute governance networks and influence institutional arenas of governance from below.

THE ETHNOGRAPHY OF GOVERNANCE NETWORKS

This is a transdisciplinary book. I draw on scholarship from legal anthropology, sociolegal studies, and agrarian studies to examine how food sovereignty movements have constituted new visions of social justice and practices of mobilization in dialectical relation with changing forms of transnational governance. I build on a tradition of critical, interpretive sociolegal research that has focused not on legal institutions as the primary unit of analysis but on everyday experiences and engagement with legality.[77] Analyzing how activists conceptualize and engage in struggles for social change reveals how law and governance emerge from the everyday practices of people. This tradition of research is increasingly important for understanding transnational governance as public international law becomes increasingly fragmented.

Methodologically, the book develops what I describe as the ethnography of governance networks: an empirical transcalar approach for analyzing the formation and constitution of global legality through networks. Networks are therefore both the unit of analysis in this book and the method of study. To understand how activists articulated and strategically mobilized claims for food sovereignty, I needed to participate directly in activist networks. I chose to ground this study in the United States to examine how the nascent food sovereignty movement is uniting with larger transnational activist networks to challenge the US dominance of the global food system. This book joins a small but growing number of empirical studies on food sovereignty in the United States.[78] More specifically, I decided to focus on the Puget Sound region of Washington State as the base for this research because of its historical role as the birthplace of the alter-globalization movement in 1999, when hundreds of activists from across the world flooded Seattle to protest the World Trade Organization. The region remains deeply connected to transnational networks. Today, it is home to the densest concentration of food sovereignty activists and organizations in the country.

The bulk of the research for this book was conducted over twenty months of intensive ethnographic fieldwork from 2013 to 2015 in the Pacific Northwest of the United States, but my research is ongoing. The ethnographic component of this research comprised three activities. First, I engaged in participant observation in two local food sovereignty organizations, by volunteering with them and conducting more than sixty interviews with food activists in the Puget Sound region. Second, I observed how food sovereignty activists engage in food governance at the local, regional, and global levels. This included monthly meetings that I observed, recorded, and transcribed in Seattle as well as annual meetings of the UN Committee on World Food Security in Rome—a critical convergence point for transnational food sovereignty activists. Finally, I participated in transnational food sovereignty networks by attending movement convergences and by participating in online networks in which strategic mobilization was coordinated. Participating in and observing food sovereignty networks from local, national, and transnational vantage points revealed how activists' unique networking practices became embedded in the very claim of food sovereignty.

This approach to studying social movements, which involves direct participation in them, might strike some social scientists as odd. However, anthropologists have shown how such forms of engaged research can yield important insights. Jeffrey Juris and Alex Khasnabish argue that ethnographic analysis that is undertaken "*within* rather than outside grassroots movements for social change, is able to uncover important empirical issues and generate critical theoretical insights that are simply not accessible through traditional objectivist methods."[79] They highlight a crucial feature of anthropological research that distinguishes it from other disciplines, namely, that anthropology's critical and reflexive stance toward knowledge production is based on the understanding that knowledge always reflects particular positionalities, politics, and relations of power. Although this epistemic humility is a product of the discipline's dubious history as a hand-maiden to colonialism, today it serves to challenge the epistemic domination that is often naturalized by claims to objectivity and authority. Moreover, as de Sousa Santos emphasizes, objectivist approaches to research can re-produce the "cognitive empire" of the global North. He calls on scholars to draw on "epistemologies of the South," in which knowledge is born from social struggles.[80] It is this knowledge that I sought to attend to through my ethnography of governance networks.

PRECARITY, PARTIALITY, AND POWER IN TRANSNATIONAL GOVERNANCE

By using the network as the method of research, I encountered many of the same challenges as those confronted by activists engaged in translocal translation, namely, the partial perspective that is endemic to the network. This partiality inherent in the networked form has motivated some critical political theorists to suggest that the networked vision of justice emergent in contemporary transnational movements is flawed. For example, Luc Boltanski and Eve Chiapello argue that because networked perspectives are always partial, "there is very little chance of it providing acceptable solutions in terms of social justice on its own, precisely because the net-work does not offer an overarching position allowing for consideration of those who find themselves on its margins, or even disconnected."[81] In other words, the network has no outside that serves as a horizon for social justice.[82]

A similar perspective has led some analysts to critique the rise of net-worked and transnational governance as postdemocratic or postpolitical. Critical geographers and political theorists such as Eric Swyngedouw and Wendy Brown have argued that, even though new forms of transnational governance create the veneer of democracy through more opportunities to participate in governance and policymaking processes, these forms of governance in fact serve to deepen neoliberal hegemony by suppressing political dissensus and by privatizing the public interest.[83] This account of the postpolitics of network governance suggests that networked forms of governance transform political conflicts into problems that can be managed technocratically, effectively reproducing the status quo.[84] These critiques of neoliberalism and transnational governance offer important insights into the potential of governance to reproduce entrenched asymmetries of power. They often do.

However, these theoretical accounts also offer overdetermined critiques of the networked representation of society and economy and of capitalism's power. As feminist geographers J. K. Gibson-Graham ask in their study of postcapitalist possibilities, "Why [would] anyone who opposed capitalism . . . theorize it as all-embracing, leaving nothing outside?"[85] Building on these insights, I argue that we must be careful not to reproduce the totalizing modernist assumptions that underlie much critical political and legal analysis. Food sovereignty activists reject these values and challenge the mechanistic worldview that has driven universalizing claims of both science and jurisprudence.[86] They offer a new vision of social and environmental relations that opposes decontextualized visions of social transformation and instead embraces a relational ontology of egalitarian plurality.

As food sovereignty activists enter the postliberal landscape of transnational governance, however, the precarity of this vision of social justice becomes clear. In dismantling liberal walls of separation, they enter a terrain of political struggle that at once allows for deeper visions of democratic social transformation and may also facilitate more profound forms of domination. Yet from this precarity emerges new visions of justice and collective social life. As Anne Allison points out in her study of postindustrial Japan, there is "an emergent potential in attempts to humanely and collectively survive precarity: a new form of commonwealth (commonly remaking the wealth of sociality), a biopolitics from below."[87]

Just as food sovereignty activists have cultivated new emancipatory claims and practices from the economic and ecological precarity endemic to our contemporary era, sociolegal analysis too must recognize this contemporary condition. Precarity is "*the* condition of our time," Anna Tsing argues. She urges us to think *with* this precarity: "Thinking through precarity changes social analysis. A precarious world is a world without teleology. Indeterminacy, the unplanned nature of time, is frightening, but thinking through precarity makes it evident that indeterminacy also makes life possible."[88] Acknowledging precarity, ontological humility, and epistemological diversity while at the same time holding onto the differential distribution of privilege and precarity requires new ways of thinking about law, governance, and justice.

Sociolegal scholars have often adopted the modernist and universalizing assumptions endemic to Western jurisprudence in analyzing projects of resistance. When confronted with popular or alternative legalities, they have often critiqued them for resting in the shadow of state law. Yet sociolegal scholars are beginning to recognize that such a perspective also blinds us to their emergent potentialities. Simon Halliday and Bronwen Morgan remind us that oppositional legal consciousness and the forms of legality produced through political and legal disputes are just that—a *struggle*.[89] These conflicts have the ability to promote collective feelings of agency that can have a profound effect on structures of legality when viewed beyond the limited temporalities of most academic studies. These interventions emphasize that as scholars and students, our analyses of these movements and representations of law are also constitutive. After all, we are embedded in the construction of the legal fields that we seek to study.

And what better object through which to reimagine law, society, and economy than food? We all need to eat. Few would oppose creating food systems that promote environmental resilience, treat animals more humanely, provide livable wages to those who produce food, and enhance the collective well-being of humanity by ensuring access to healthy, fresh, and culturally appropriate food for all. As the poet and agrarian writer Wendell Berry writes, "Eating with the fullest pleasure—pleasure, that is, that does not depend on ignorance—is perhaps the profoundest enactment of our connection with the world."[90] In a time of profound economic inequalities and existential threats to planetary health, rebuilding these relations based on the pleasure of mutual solidarity is necessary now more than ever. Ultimately, it is through this empirical study of food sovereignty activism that I demonstrate how food sovereignty activists are doing just that—culturally constituting these relations and new practices of governance from the bottom up. By mobilizing food sovereignty in relation to new forms of transnational governance, activists are producing new political constituencies, values, and forms of knowledge that are necessary for a political and legal order rooted in more just social and ecological relations.

THE CHAPTERS AHEAD

In the chapters ahead I analyze how food sovereignty activists translate food sovereignty across different constituencies, sectors, and geographic scales and thereby shape governance from the bottom up. In chapter 1 I situate the rise of food sovereignty networks in the Pacific Northwest and elaborate the concept of translocal translation. I describe how activists in the Pacific Northwest first began to develop social practices of networking in the 1970s with the emergence of the alternative agriculture movement, but a new generation rekindled the holistic vision of radically transforming food and agricultural systems by drawing on the practices and repertoires developed by peasant movements in the global South. From there, chapters 2 through 5 examine how food sovereignty activists deploy different dimensions of translocal translation in relation to a variety of forms and arenas of transnational governance—from multistakeholder standard setting to private governance through global value chains to transnational regulatory networks. Chapter 2 focuses on the local level, examining the ways activists leveraged an arena of collaborative local food governance to redefine the local through their networking practices. Chapters 3, 4, and 5 scale upward from the local to the global. These chapters detail how activists are engaging in governance to revalue agricultural labor, protect people's knowledge, and, finally, democratize institutions of global governance.

Chapters 2 through 5 also dwell on the paradoxes that activists face as they engage in different forms of governance. Activists consistently face the challenge that the forms of governance in which they engage sit in the shadow of neoliberal legalities—regimes of international and state law that have been constructed to facilitate market-based forms of social and political organization. Indeed, local arenas of collaborative food governance, global value chains, transnational regulatory networks, and multistakeholder governance have all been born from regulatory rollbacks and market liberalization. As a result, they often reflect the power asymmetries produced by neoliberalism. Corporations, philanthropies, and Northern governments all attempt to mobilize mechanisms of governance to set standards to ultimately stabilize and enhance market coordination.

Yet transnational governance cannot be reduced to neoliberalism. As described earlier, transnational governance is a terrain of struggle constituted through the convergence of critiques of former models of regulation. Its networked structure may serve to entrench market-driven inequalities, or it may deepen democratic claims and spaces of freedom once walled off by liberal legalism. Ethnographically attending to the ways that North American and transnational food sovereignty activists are translating food sovereignty in relation to a multiplicity of arenas of transnational governance reveals how food sovereignty activists are productively engaging in these arenas. I show how they are producing political constituencies and relations, undermining the forms of value supposed by global value chains, opposing the dominant forms of agricultural knowledge that have historically constituted private property and liberal sovereignty, and ultimately reimagining global governance by centering the voices of those most marginalized. Put in other terms, through their interactive and dialectical practices of engagement with transnational governance, they are actively transforming regulation to reflect their vision of decentralized, diverse, and democratic systems of food governance. As food sovereignty movements continue to spread La Vía Campesina's message to "Globalize Hope! Globalize Struggle!" they are not just revealing that another world is possible. They are actively building it.

1 Translocal Translation and the Practice of Networks

IN THE EARLY AFTERNOON of Thursday, December 2, 1999, about 5,000 activists gathered outside the iconic Pike Place Market in Seattle. In the crowd were farmers and food activists not only from the United States but also from India, France, South Korea, Mexico, and other countries. The market, which is a hub of the region's vibrant and diverse local food systems, was a powerful symbol of their demands. Over the previous three days, activists from across the world had converged in Seattle to protest the liberalization of global markets through the World Trade Organization. During a week of raucous protests, activists with radically different agendas and visions of social justice not only effectively shut down the final World Trade Organization meetings of the millennium but also inaugurated a repertoire of contention and claims for global justice that would form the basis for a new era of transnational activism.

The Battle in Seattle, as it is now called, is most famous for the alliances it spawned between "teamsters and turtles"—labor and environmental activists—but the meeting of local and global food activists led to what would turn out to be a more enduring transnational movement. Each day of the protests was dedicated to a different theme. The fourth day was entirely focused on food and agriculture. Planned by an organizer of a regional sustainable food network, the day began with a panel at the old United Methodist Church in downtown Seattle. It included local small-scale food producers as well as emerging leaders of the nascent movement La Vía Campesina. Following a panel discussion, the attendees marched to the Pike Place Market and protested outside the grain terminal of Cargill, a major global grain trader. Reflecting on the day to a reporter from the *Capital Press*, a local farmer explained, "There was a clear feeling that agriculture is going in the wrong direction. We should be going toward helping small local farms survive because they offer so many economic and environmental benefits toward rural communities—not toward vertically integrated enterprises controlled by a few."[1]

The Battle in Seattle was the first time that many US-based activists encountered La Vía Campesina and their message to "Globalize Struggle! Globalize Hope!" but it was not the first time that activists in the Pacific Northwest had attempted to challenge the dominant industrial food system. The Pacific Northwest has long been a major center of alternative food activism and agitation, a fact evidenced by the market in front of which the protestors at the Battle for Seattle rallied. In fact, some of those in the crowd had been working to localize food systems since the early 1970s, when the Pacific Northwest began feeling the first pangs of economic globalization and the world experienced a major global food crisis. The alternative agriculture movement, as it is often called, inaugurated a new set of social movement repertoires that sought to radically reorganize social, economic, and political life.

This earlier generation of food activists was not unlike the food sovereignty movement.[2] They too embraced network practices of activism inspired by new models and images of socio-ecological relations. But by approaching the network simply as a means or tool through which to transform food production, the alternative agriculture movement inadvertently ended up reproducing the consolidated corporate food markets that their movement had united to contest. Today, as a growing number of activists in the Pacific Northwest turn to the claim of food sovereignty, they approach the network not simply as a means for collective action but as a model for decentralized democratic governance.

In this chapter I examine how different generations of food activists in the Pacific Northwest and beyond have envisioned and practiced the network as a form of social movement organization. As communicative structures that enable activists to express and disseminate social values, networks are a form of organization that sits between hierarchies and markets;[3] networks can be constructed to build political constituencies as well as to produce new markets. The instability inherent to networked forms of organization means that the visions and practices that movements adopt determine what kind of impact they will ultimately have. Alternative food activists were among the first to adopt the networking form. For this reason, scholars often draw on this movement as a case study to analyze how social movements transform markets through new forms of regulatory governance.[4] Although they have offered different accounts as to how the alternative agriculture movement transformed into the contemporary organic food industry, I draw on ethnographic fieldwork, including life histories and archival research, to show how internal struggles between competing constituencies in the alternative agriculture movement of the Pacific Northwest led commercial farmers to sideline the social justice values of other constituencies in the movement and turn to the state to adopt a narrow definition of food focused only on allowable agricultural inputs. My account of this process emphasizes both the internal politics of networking and the external regulatory context of the alternative food movement. Today, as food sovereignty movements seek to avoid what is often described as the co-optation or mainstreaming of the alternative agriculture movement, I show how they have developed a radical new social justice claim that is inextricably bound to their egalitarian networking practices and emerging forms of governance.

This chapter therefore provides both the historical context for the formation of food sovereignty movements in the Pacific Northwest and the theoretical framework through which I analyze food sovereignty movements' novel practices of mobilization in the rest of the book. As activists translate food sovereignty across the world, I argue that they are not simply mediating meanings between different social and ecological contexts. Rather, they are constituting networks through specific social practices and protocols. This approach to translation, which combines insights from anthropology, sociolegal studies, and science and technology studies, understands acts of translation as semiotic practices through which individuals and groups construct new social relations and negotiate relations of power. As I describe later in this chapter, food sovereignty movements have developed creative new tools of mobilization, or what I refer to as *translocal translation*, through which they assemble food sovereignty movements. These practices, I explain, are premised on three key values and aims of food sovereignty: (1) demanding direct representation by those most marginalized and affected by the food system, (2) democratizing knowledge, and (3) insisting on the autonomy of communities and peoples. By drawing on these values, activists enact and claim food sovereignty as a process of translation through which they prefigure democratic forms of transnational governance.

This chapter is based on interviews, archival fieldwork, participant observation, and secondary literature on the history of food sovereignty movements. In the Pacific Northwest I spent about two years collecting life stories of food activism and conducted research in the personal archives of food activists and at Washington State University. The activists I encountered as I went through minutes of past meetings, binders of old directories, and pictures in these activists' homes offered me the opportunity to excavate these networking practices and compare them to contemporary food sovereignty activism in the United States. By analyzing these movements alongside one another, I show how food sovereignty activists in the Pacific Northwest are rekindling the radical roots of the alternative agriculture movement.

NEOLIBERALISM AND THE RISE OF FOOD
POLITICS IN THE PACIFIC NORTHWEST

In the 1970s the Pacific Northwest experienced the first spasms of economic contraction that laid the foundation for neoliberalism. During this period, the region emerged as a national hub of food activism. Although the United States has a long history of agrarian struggles, this turn to food was different from past movements.[5] A generation of mostly young middle-class activists critical of US foreign and domestic policies turned to food as a symbol of community, countercultural identity, and resistance to economic imperialism. For many of these activists, food had not been on their radar. But after a slew of books and articles were published that sought to bring public attention to the politics of food—most famously, Frances Moore Lappé's *Diet for a Small Planet*—a young generation began to reckon with the effects of industrial agricultural production on both the United States and the rest of the world.[6] Some newfound food activists in the 1960s and 1970s decided to go back to the land to engage in ecological and organic food production and to build new rural communities. Others remained in cities to form urban food cooperatives and alternative

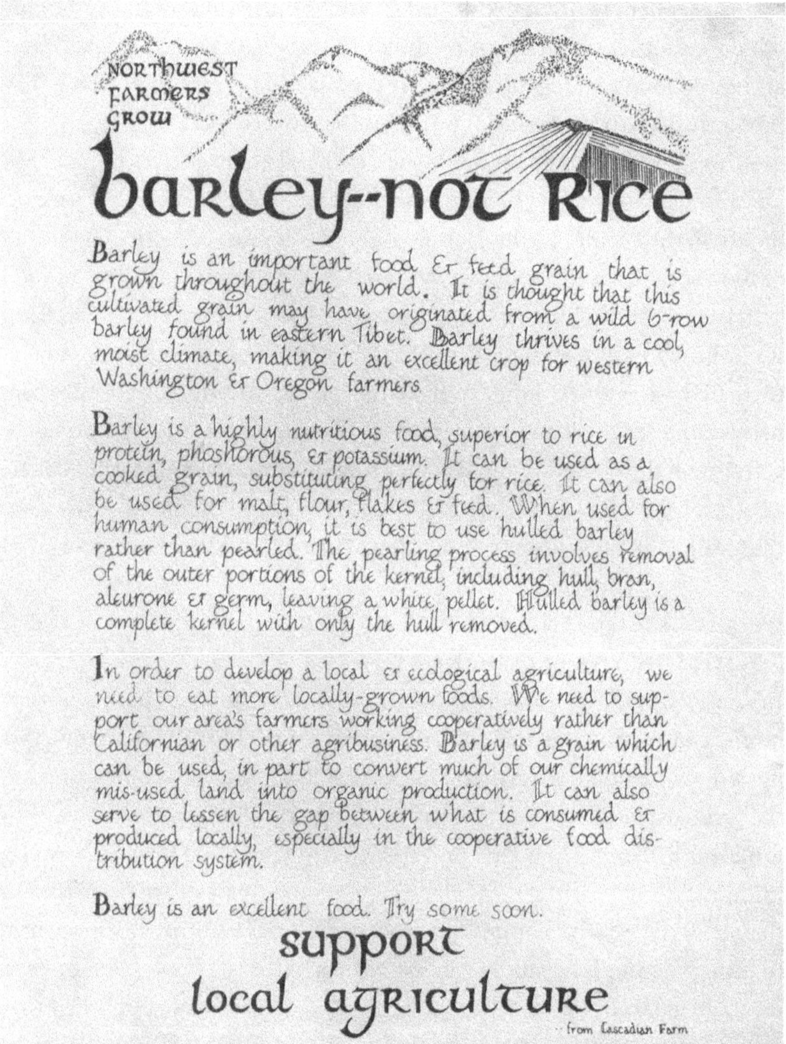

FIGURE 1 Poster supporting Cascadian Farm. Source: Tilth Association Papers, Manuscripts, Archives, and Special Collections, Washington State University Libraries.

agrifood networks. Through their activism, food became a site of symbolic and material struggle for alternative forms of social and economic organization. As food studies scholar Warren Belasco jests, "Brown rice became the symbol of anti-modernity."[7] In the Pacific Northwest, however, rural homesteaders preferred barley, not brown rice.

In the 1970s the debate over food and agriculture was about more than production methods or government subsidies; it was as a proxy for discussions about the future of American power in a global context. In the preceding five decades the United States had emerged as the dominant power in what Harriett Friedmann and Philip McMichael describe as a global food regime.[8] But beginning in the 1970s, twin global crises—food and oil—precipitated major political and economic transformations, domestically and globally. The 1972–1973 world food crisis, which resulted from skyrocketing grain prices, claimed 5 million lives.[9] It was as a wake-up call to everyone from world leaders to small-scale food producers that food systems were being upended by the political and economic realities of the day: increasing global market integration, competition, and subaltern struggles for self-determination and control over natural resources.

For the United States, diminishing economic power and dwindling political hegemony precipitated a wholesale reappraisal of its political strategies, economic endeavors, and core values. No longer able to maintain the dominance it had established in the postwar period, policymakers and the public were faced with profound questions, and agriculture was at the forefront. "Food power" became a new watchword among foreign policy elites and domestic social movements over the future of US global power. As historian Emma Rothschild explained in a 1976 article for *Foreign Policy*:

> The issues and illusions of food power suggest more general questions about the politics of US economic power. The use of economic power has appeared to require a diminution of US power in general. "Food power," that is, is conceivable only in a situation of agricultural transition, where the United States is engaged in retreat from the power it exercised during the 20 years when the world food economy was American-ordered and American-secured. This paradox explains the fallacy in the CIA analysts' view of food and power. They see food as restoring the "primacy" of the United States: yet the use of food as power is founded on the diminution of that primacy.[10]

Food power and food politics thus became a contentious arena in which foreign policy experts, domestic agricultural interest groups, and emerging social movements struggled not just over domestic agricultural policy but also over American political and economic dominance more broadly.

Although the United States was in many ways to blame for the global food crisis, it nonetheless played a central role in responding to it. After Algerian president Houari Boumédiéne called for a global conference to address the crisis at a conference of nonaligned nations, the United States helped to organize the World Food Conference. During the conference there was significant disagreement within the US government over how to respond. On one side, then secretary of state Henry Kissinger sought to maintain an aid-based policy as a show of goodwill to uphold the US's global political dominance. Kissinger saw food as an important political tool and "one of the few weapons we have to deal with oil prices."[11] On the other hand, Secretary of Agriculture Earl Butz, along with the agribusiness lobby, sought to take advantage of the high food prices. Butz argued that with the recent economic recession, the United States no longer needed to subsidize what he saw as inefficient family farms. He pushed for a more market-driven national food and agricultural policy, which he argued would relieve financial strain on the government and incentivize more "efficient" forms of industrial agriculture. Now identified with the mantra "Get big or get out," Butz promoted an agenda to remake American agriculture that centered on expanding production, increasing exports, and lowering food prices for American consumers. He contended that this would be a win-win situation for domestic policy goals. Butz was supported by the immensely powerful commercial farm lobby and by consumers who were reeling from inflation and the rise of food prices.[12]

For an emerging cadre of leftist activists concerned with food politics, both positions were deeply problematic. Whereas Kissinger advocated using food as a weapon against its adversaries (or "for peace," as the administration put it), Butz sought to ensure American dominance by shifting from aid to trade and expanding the production of cheap American grains by ending policies of supply management, which had been in place since the New Deal. In other words, Kissinger sought to maintain American political hegemony through political means, whereas Butz saw the future of American power through markets. Food politics therefore became an arena of social struggle that linked everyday consumption and culture with larger questions of global political and economic power. This concern with both the domestic and foreign politics of food led a new generation of communalist and countercultural activists not just to oppose the US's food and agricultural policy but also to use food to build alternative political and economic relations.

THE RISE OF THE ALTERNATIVE
AGRICULTURE MOVEMENT

In the same year that world leaders were meeting at the World Food Conference in Rome to discuss the global food crisis, environmental activists gathered in Spokane, Washington, for Expo '74, the International Exposition on the Environment. There, then little-known farmer and writer Wendell Berry spoke in a symposium titled "Agriculture for a Small Planet." In his speech Berry lambasted the policies of Earl Butz. He told the audience that Butz's "get big or get out" philosophy would lead to "disintegration of the culture and the communities of farming" and "involved the forcible displacement of millions of people." For Berry, this policy destroyed communities, their systems of social value, and the "practical possibility of survival." Food and agriculture were more than just systems of production, Berry told the audience; they were symbols of cultural value. The social organization of agriculture, the ecology of cultivation, the forms of provisioning, and everyday acts of eating all reflected people's relationships between each other and the earth. Reducing these relationships to mere inputs and outputs, he declared, augured the destruction of core American values: democracy, neighborliness, and, in a word, community.[13]

Listening to Berry's speech that day, Mark Musick, a young activist, was captivated. Musick was recording and editing the speech as part of the symposium documentation staff. A few days after returning home from the conference, Berry wrote a letter to the young people he had met in Spokane in which he described what he saw as "the constituency for a better kind of agriculture." He encouraged them to organize "another kind of symposium" to "bring together the various branches of agricultural dissidence and heresy . . . representatives of farm workers unions, NFO [National Farmers Organization] and any other such groups, family farmers, urban consumer cooperatives, small farm co-ops, organic farming and gardening co-ops and organizations, the publications of dissident agriculture, and the conservation organizations, wilderness societies, etc."[14] Just four months later, Musick and small group of friends organized the Northwest Conference on Alternative Agriculture in Ellensburg, Washington, with more than 700 people in attendance. Over the next year the conference inspired attendees to organize additional conferences across the Pacific Northwest. These included the Politics of Food and Land conference in Port Townsend, which was "a conference to develop strategies for the transformation of the Puget Sound Region into a community of people who are sensitive to both the ecosystem and to cooperative ways of living and working together";[15] the Nooksack River Encampment in Whatcom County; the Natural Living and Agriculture Conference in Pendleton, Oregon; the Montana Alternative Agriculture Conference; and Living the Revolution, a conference on Whidbey Island. Through these gatherings, Musick and his friends created a network of different constituencies—what was emerging as the alternative agriculture movement.

As he recounted tales of building the movement over lunch one day at his home, Musick chuckled at the "heroic" titles of the conferences. He emphasized what a truly transformational moment people believed they were living in. "People were really grasping, they were imagining . . . we were really expecting the collapse of the culture. With the oil embargo everything was going to contract and become radically decentralized and people were going to be self-reliant." Musick devoted the next decade of his life to building the constituency that Berry first suggested. He moved to a cooperative farm and began several years of farming. During that time, he and others formed the Tilth Association, an organization dedicated to connecting the different groups of activists of the burgeoning alternative agriculture movement.

In organizing Tilth, Musick drew on a new vision of networking influenced by the countercultural bible, *The Whole Earth Catalog*. Published by Stewart Brand between 1968 and 1972, the catalog provided a visual stimulus for reimagining the world. By offering a new vision of the "information society," the catalog produced a zeitgeist of do-it-yourself attitudes toward social and environmental reinvention. Drawing on the work of theorist Norbert Wiener, the catalog declared, "Society, from organism, to community, to civilization, is the domain of cybernetics."[16] For Wiener, society was composed of overlapping domains of informational systems.[17] The image of the network, which was at the heart of these theories, suggested that systems and societies were self-regulating and could be transformed with better information and communication.

As we drove to visit the Tilth Archive in Pullman, Washington, Musick explained to me that the forms of organizing and social change he encountered in the catalog offered an attractive alternative to what he had experienced as a limited model of organizing while working as a volunteer in the VISTA program on the Paiute Reservation. The community organizing model he had been trained in depended on mobilizing existing communities. But in an era of increased mobility, economic instability, and ecological devastation, this model had its limits. By organizing information, Musick found that he did not need to simply focus on existing communities; he could build new ones. For activists like Musick, the network evoked an appealing vision of society. Egalitarian and nonhierarchical, it was a form of political organization that was based on collective decision making rather than hierarchical political authority. Cooperative, but not bounded, networks offered a form of community that did not demand either rigid conformism or complete autonomy. Moreover, in contrast to the hierarchical and mechanistic metaphors of society that dominated their parents' generation, the image of the network offered a holistic approach to social change drawn from the ecological consciousness of the countercultural generation.

In assembling these new networks, Musick also drew on new technologies. To compile the directory for the Northwest Conference on Alternative Agriculture, he used edge-notched cards as a manual "computer" to compile geographic and interest-area indexes for the hundreds of attendees. The directory's 32-page subject index listed the participants under 192 interest areas, including composting, dryland farming, homesteading, seeds, and land reform. The introduction to the directory, which was mailed out to all conference participants, emphasized that it was to be used as a tool, an implement itself in creating new social groups around shared interests and values. Over the next several years, Musick worked to further develop this network through the *Tilth Newsletter* and other publications. By sharing information about politics, farming, and food, Musick was working to build networks that could transform the economy and society.

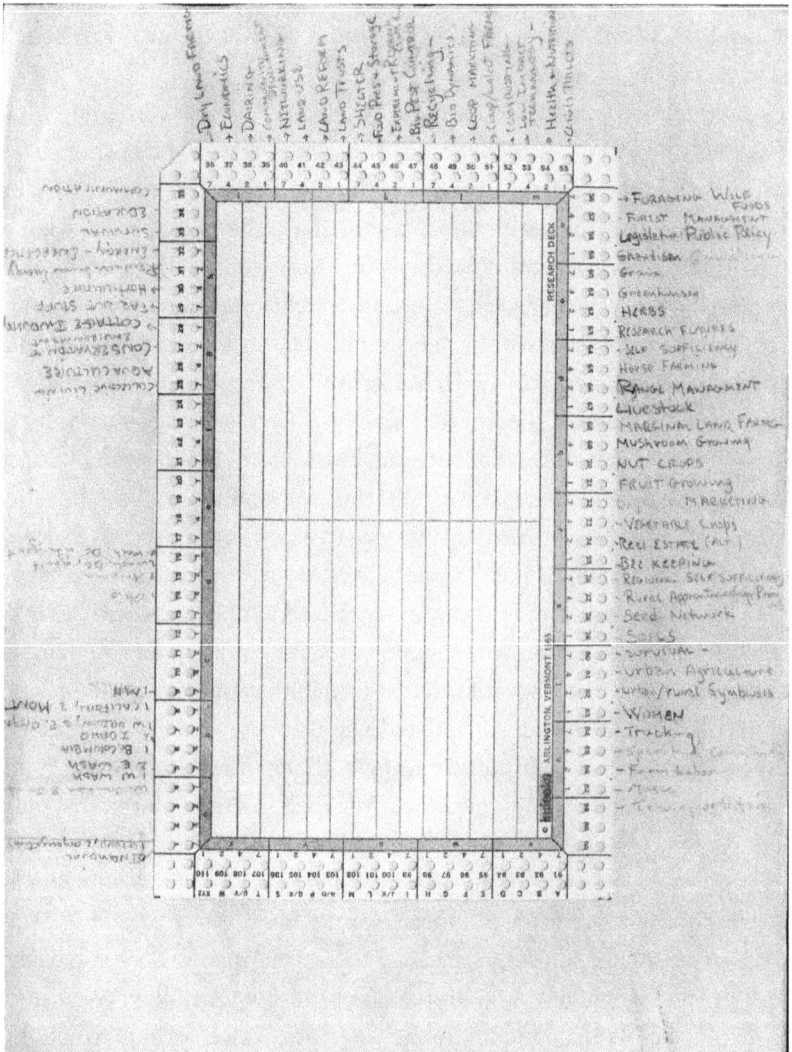

FIGURE 2 Example of an edge-notched card. Source: Tilth Association Papers, Manuscripts, Archives, and Special Collections, Washington State University Libraries.

FROM ALTERNATIVE TO ORGANIC

Soon after the formation of the Tilth Association, activists found themselves facing tensions over strategies for how to move forward. A new sub-
group led by Gene Kahn was formed. Kahn was the founder of Cascadian
Farm in the Skagit Valley near the North Cascades. He had founded Cascadian Farm in 1972 after moving to the Pacific Northwest from Chicago
to pursue a graduate degree at the University of Washington. In his early
days, Kahn was a back-to-the-lander with similar ideals to others in Tilth.
He told me that when he began farming, he thought that it was more of
a "food political movement. . . . The core of it was that we were going to
change America and we were going to do that by following a new paradigm." Yet as Kahn engaged in the difficult labor of farming in upper
Skagit Valley, he became increasingly passionate about "the notion [that]
to be a real farmer required scale." By the late 1970s, Cascadian Farm had
become one of the premier organic farms, quickly expanding into food
processing and other organic products.

Along with other farmers, Kahn began to believe that organic farmers needed their own organization to promote their interests. He did not
think that they shared the same interests as the urban gardeners and food
activists that Musick had brought together through Tilth. In early 1977
Kahn joined with other commercial organic farmers in organizing the
Tilth Producers Cooperative, which was created "primarily to assist in
the economic development of farm-scale organic food production."[18] The
cooperative was focused first and foremost on the economic survival of
farmers. Musick himself was unclear of the relationship between the two
organizations and worried that fissures between urban and rural were
already beginning to appear. In a letter to a friend, Musick wrote that he
and another founding member of the Tilth Association "argued for the
creation of a broad-based organization that would include everyone in the
alternative agriculture movement. . . . Our reasoning was that such an organization would provide a constituency to support small scale farmers."[19]
But Kahn argued that "what was really needed was an organization by and
for commercial farmers, that farmers had historically been ripped off too
many times by people with other interests and they needed to form and
control their own organization."[20]

The Tilth Newsletter

Rt. 2, Box 190-A, Arlington, WA 98223

WINTER, 1977   NUMBER 15

CONTENTS

A New Beginning

Early arrivals to Pragtree Farm were recruited to help pound in the final nails on the end walls of the large new "Roadhouse" where the meeting was to be held. The long spell of hot weather that had baked Western Washington for weeks had been broken a few days before by torrential August rains and familiar cloudy skies.

The morning of the meeting was cold and misty, but the weather didn't prevent a much larger than anticipated crowd from gathering at the farm. The sound of banging hammers ended about an hour before the meeting was to begin, and everyone was able to gather inside the Roadhouse, protected from the wind and a brief downpour which finally hit later in the afternoon. Aside from the thunderous noise of rain on the roof, the meeting continued on without pause.

As an outgrowth of discussions which led to the formation of the Tilth Producers' Co-operative, a Planning Meeting was held at Pragtree Farm on August 27th to discuss the formation of a new general membership organization for the alternative agriculture movement in the region.

At the Planning Meeting, "Tilth" was adopted as the name for the new educational and research organization,which is being initiated for the purpose of conducting and promoting a biologically sound and socially equitable agriculture in the Pacific Northwest. Beginning this winter local chapters will be established to bring together people throughout the region who are seeking to create a new agriculture.

Over 70 people attended the Planning Meeting; people from Idaho, Washington, Oregon and Northern California. Following a tour of the farm and a pot luck lunch, the group worked throughout the afternoon to discuss the needs that they felt as small farmers, new homesteaders and home gardeners who were seeking to understand and practice new approaches to agriculture.

The meeting began with personal introductions. Then Elaine Davenport, a long-time home gardener from Seattle, described her experiences on a recent tour of European organic farms which led her to the idea of forming a new organization here in the Northwest.

Last fall Elaine had joined a tour of organic farms in England, Germany, Austria and Switzerland in conjunction with a major conference of the International Federation of Organic Agriculture Movements. One of the things that impressed her most, she said, was the number of large and very active organic agriculture organizations that she discovered in Europe. Involving people from all walks of life, they sponsored very effective educational, marketing and research programs.

While on the tour Elaine also got to know several people involved with the Maine Organic Gardeners and Farmers Association, which is one of the largest and most effective organic agriculture organizations in this country, with over 1,000 active members in local chapters throughout the state. From the wide range of programs these groups offered, Elaine said she realized that we in the Northwest were really lacking an organization that could bring together and support all facets of the organic agriculture movement in our region.

Upon her return from Europe, Elaine began sharing with others her enthusiasm for what she had learned. At an early meeting of the Tilth Producers' Cooperative back in February, Elaine stressed the need for an organization in which both farmers and home gardeners could

(continued page 2)

FIGURE 3 (AND OPPOSITE)   A few pages from an issue of the *Tilth Newsletter*. Source: Tilth Association Papers, Manuscripts, Archives, and Special Collections, Washington State University Libraries.

photographs by Jef Jaisun

Structure and Name

Once there was a general sense of what the organization might do, the discussion turned to how it would be structured. It was agreed that the focus of the organization should be on independent local chapters in which people could join in sharing, learning and working together. Local groups would be empowered to define their own geographic areas and set their own membership fees. Local chapters would also be involved in determining regional policy.

The regional level of the organization would work on developing programs and on maintaining communications between members through publications such as the newsletter and research reports. The regional level of the organization would be responsible to and supportive of the local chapters.

Now that there was a general understanding of the purposes and structure of the organization, it was time for us to come up with a name.

Woody Deryckx suggested that the group adopt "Tilth" as the name of the new organization. When asked what the word meant, Becky Deryckx said that it had two meanings---the word "tilth" is used to refer to the quality of the soil and, in an older meaning, tilth was also used to refer to the cultivation of knowledge and wisdom.

Becky Deryckx

Becky explained how the word was chosen for the group which organized the first Northwest Conference on Alternative Agriculture, held in Ellensburg, Washington back in November, 1974. That conference brought together for the first time all aspects of the alternative agriculture movement in the Northwest region.

However, although Tilth has been involved since that time in several other conferences, it has never been formally incorporated and has never had an official membership. Now, a new organization was finally coming together, and, after further discussion, it was agreed that it would be appropriate to adopt the name Tilth.

Getting Started

Following the completion of the first day of the Planning Meeting, a Steering Committee was formed to carry out the nuts and bolts of legally incorporating the new organization. This group stayed overnight at Pragtree Farm and met the next morning to establish Tilth's first Board of Trustees and begin the process of drafting Articles of Incorporation and By-Laws, and securing Federal tax exempt status. People on the initial Board of Trustees are Joyce Schowalter of Ellensburg, Mike Maki of South Bend, Carl Woestendiek and Elaine Davenport of Seattle, Tom Thornton of Ferndale, Binda Colebrook of Arlington, and Michael Pilarski (Skeeter) of Marcus, Washington, and Marshall Landmann and D.J. Lougheed of Eugene, Oregon.

The next meeting of the Board of Trustees will be at the Barter Fair. At that time a final set of By-Laws and Articles of Incorporation will be completed and the organization should be legally incorporated by the end of November. Once that is accomplished, local chapters can be initiated. Meanwhile, a lot of other groundwork is already underway.

Elaine Davenport proposed that, as one of our first activities, Tilth sponsor a conference on Urban Agriculture in Seattle next February. A group has already been set up to work on the idea. Communications and Research Committees are being established. Mark Musick will coordinate the Communications group, and Woody Deryckx has taken on the responsibility of initiating the Research program. More details on these activities, and details on how to set up local Tilth chapters will be published in future issues of The Tilth Newsletter.

It was surprising that so many people showed up on such a blustery day to talk about the idea of forming a new organic agriculture organization, and it was gratifying that so much was accomplished in such a short time. Many of the people attending the Planning Meeting had first met each other three years ago at the Northwest Conference on Alternative Agriculture. Others had been keeping in touch through publications such as The Tilth Newsletter and Organic Gardening and Farming Magazine, so in a very real sense a regional organic community has already existed.

What was needed to give it form was for people to commit themselves to begin creating the organization together. Although much was accomplished, it was clear that there is still much to be done over the next few months and in the years ahead.

-Mark Musick

The Tilth Producers Cooperative quickly turned its attention to the issue of certification. By the late 1970s the cooperative had two examples of organic laws to look toward: Oregon passed the nation's first organic regulation in 1973, and California passed the California Organic Foods Act in 1979. In forming an association of farmers intent on having a Washington State law passed, the Tilth Producers Cooperative further solidified their own identity as professional commercial farmers, not just back-to-the-landers. "Certification was really important," Kahn explained to me, because "it was to gain legitimacy and confidence in the eyes of the consumer that we had a definition and that we weren't just making it up as we go." After several years spent developing a definition of organic production, the group began submitting legislation to the Washington State legislature for an organic labeling law that would enable the Washington State Department of Agriculture to certify organically produced food. By 1985 Washington State enacted the Washington Organic Food Products Act.

Although Musick was supportive of certification, it was clear that the Tilth Producers Cooperative and the Tilth Association were premised on different social values and visions of social change. For Kahn, organic certification offered an incentive for individual farmers to engage in environmental stewardship. By creating a legal definition and set of standards for the organic market, he sought to make organic products more intelligible for consumers and prevent others from claiming their produce was organic without using regulated production methods. On the other hand, Musick embraced network building as a form of organization to promote the holistic objectives of the alternative agriculture movement that included supporting small-scale farmers, farmworkers, and local economies.

Eventually, the definition of *organic* through state and, later, national regulation stripped the alternative agriculture movement of its momentum and its more radical ambitions. In the negotiations over the standards in the National Organic Program, issues related to social justice, including farm size and farm labor, were excluded from the definition of *organic*.[21] As Patricia Allen and Martin Kovach describe, "The original holistic paradigm of organic agriculture [was] dissected into component parts."[22] Michael Haedicke contends that this was a product of different organizational logics in the negotiation of the standards, during which the transformative and holistic vision of food systems change was replaced by an expansionary and technical vision of developing organic food markets.[23]

Years later the food writer Michael Pollan lambasted Kahn for seeking to create commercial markets for organic food: "Gene Kahn makes the case that the scale of a farm has no bearing on its fidelity to organic principles and that unless organic 'scales up' it will 'never be anything more than yuppie food.'" For Pollan, "Organic is nothing if not a set of values (this is better than that), and to the extent that the future of those values is in the hands of companies that are finally indifferent to them, that future will be precarious."[24] Pollan, of course, was not the first to make this critique. It is the same critique that Musick had voiced in his letter. Musick, like Pollan, sought to create communities based on collectivist values—environmental stewardship, social justice, small-scale food production, and local economies. Kahn, however, adopted a different approach, one centered on market-incentivized environmentalism. After many years of farming, Musick went on to manage the farm program at the Pike Place Market, helping to revive it into Seattle's symbol of local agriculture. Kahn grew Cascadian Farm into a national brand, eventually selling it to Welch's and later to General Mills.

The story of the Tilth movement reveals the complex politics of the network. For Musick, the network served as a form of organization for activists committed to social and political transformation. Less concerned with defining *organic*, he sought to build networks built around shared values of social justice. For Kahn, however, the network served as a form of economic organization for goods whose meanings and values had not yet been quantified. By defining *organic* through state and federal regulation, he hoped to create legitimacy for organic production and expand into new, less relationship-dependent markets.

Sociologists have captured this tension by describing networks as forms of organization situated "between" markets and hierarchies. As Walter Powell explains, networks "are especially useful for the exchange of commodities whose value is not easily measured."[25] Networks therefore provide a structure for the formation of both movements and markets.[26] The difference between them is shaped by the *practices* of participants in the network. Quantifying and institutionalizing value, subordinating contentious political values, and eschewing the holistic framework, as Kahn promoted, are a few of the ways that the values of networks can be hierarchically prioritized and made intelligible for larger markets.

The struggle over Tilth therefore reflects the hazards that networked movements face as they blur the boundaries between society and economy. Although the organic food industry ultimately undermined the more radical goals of the alternative agriculture movement, these values did not disappear; food sovereignty movements would eventually provide a new set of relational value practices and repertoires of contention that would reinvigorate network-based movements for social transformation that Musick helped to cultivate.

LA VÍA CAMPESINA AND AGRARIAN STRUGGLES IN THE GLOBAL SOUTH

Given that transformative social and political changes in the United States have often been led by people of color and the working class, it is unsurprising that activists in the United States would need to look to conceptual frameworks and strategies developed by marginalized peoples in the global South to challenge US food and agricultural policy.[27] Although food producers and consumers in the United States certainly felt the effects of neoliberal globalization through volatile crop prices and declining support from the government, the effects of neoliberalism were experienced more profoundly by small-scale food producers in the global South. Beginning in the 1980s, nations across the global South faced mounting debt from private international banks. International finance institutions offered loans conditioned on adopting "structural adjustment policies," which required borrowers to privatize nationally owned enterprises, reduce public expenditure, and liberalize trade. The result was a major crisis in the agricultural sectors of the global South. Low crop prices, government austerity, formalization and expropriation of land tenure rights, and integration into global markets led to 146 food riots in 39 of the 80 debtor countries between 1976 and 1992.[28] As a result of these crises, a new generation of transnational agrarian movements emerged to challenge neoliberal policies.[29]

Latin America became a central hub of resistance. In 1981 the Continental Conference on Agrarian Reform and Peasant Movements held in Managua brought together peasant organizations from around the continent and took place every year until 1989. As national peasant and farmer organizations assembled transnational movements to challenge neoliberalism, they struggled to articulate justice claims that recognized their diverse identities and class locations. To do so, they experimented with a variety of new rights claims. As María Martinez-Torres and Peter Rosset describe, these movements "were involved in struggles to establish rights: rights to livelihood, to one's body, to land, and rights to have human rights."[30] These new claims reflected the organizations' efforts to challenge the power imbalances that existed both in their countries and globally.

Peasants in Latin America were not the only ones forming transnational networks.[31] The 1980s witnessed the birth of many movements of Indigenous and rural peoples. In India the Narmada Bachao Andolan (Save the Narmada Movement) organized to oppose the construction of a dam financed by the World Bank that was poised to displace thousands of Indigenous peoples.[32] Around the same time, the Movimento dos Trabalhadores Rurais Sem Terra (Landless Workers Movement) formally organized to support large-scale land occupations by landless farmers. In Europe small-scale producers formed the Coordination Paysanne Européenne. These movements were constructing international links to support their movements in order to challenge the transnational actors and institutions that were increasingly responsible for rural displacement and global market coordination.[33] Margaret Keck and Kathryn Sikkink described these movements as "transnational advocacy networks." They argue that what was unique about these structures of collective action was that they were transforming the practices of national sovereignty by blurring the boundaries between international institutions, states, and citizens.[34]

The foundation for what eventually became the International Peasants' Movement, La Vía Campesina (LVC), was laid in the early 1990s, as peasant movements and farm organizations from Central America, Canada, the United States, the Caribbean, and Europe began to meet to affirm their rejection of structural adjustment policies, demand environmental protection, and reject the negotiations over the Global Agreement on Trade and Tariffs (GATT), the international trade negotiations that were planning to liberalize global food and agricultural markets.[35] By 1993 movements from these world regions met in Mons, Belgium, and formally founded LVC. In the Mons Declaration, they defined three shared claims that united their struggle: (1) the rights of small-scale farmers to maintain their livelihoods,

(2) the right to diversified agriculture and quality food, and (3) the right of countries to define their own agricultural policies.[36] These claims built on the internal and external rights that peasant organizations across Latin America and around the world were beginning to articulate in response to the shifting locus of decision making to supranational authorities.

Through their experimentation with new types of claims and alliances, these movements produced two important political innovations. First, they challenged previous grammars of social justice. As Nancy Fraser describes, transnational movements such as LVC make claims not just for redistribution and recognition but to challenge existing structures of *representation*. LVC makes claims for the recognition of the cultural significance of food and rural ways of life, for the redistribution of resources to respect and protect their livelihoods, and for food producers and food-chain workers to have a voice in national and global policies. Through their demands to be included in local, regional, and global decision making, movements challenged the boundaries of the political, which shielded transnational corporations, global governance structures, and powerful states from justice. In doing so, they produced claims for what Fraser calls "post-Westphalian democratic justice."[37]

Second, LVC developed new methods of coordination and communication to maintain the diversity of those involved in their movement. Although LVC used the language of the peasantry, activists adopted an inclusive understanding of this term. Given the diversity of its members, which included small- and midsize farmers, rural workers, and even small commercial farmers in the global North, LVC developed new tactics to maintain unity.[38] As Annette Desmarais explains, within LVC, "peasant and farm leaders acknowledge differences, move on to establish some common ground, solidify a collective identity and arrive at consensus on strategies and actions, thus effectively building a 'collective will.'"[39] This strategy to maintain diversity was crucial for the growth of the movement.

LVC thus developed new repertoires of contention by articulating new social justice claims and embracing activists from diverse contexts and ideologies. How the movement sought to maintain this diversity, combined with its demands for more democratic food and agricultural systems, would eventually shape the practice of food sovereignty.

THE RISE OF FOOD SOVEREIGNTY

Members of LVC first began to articulate their demands through the claim of food sovereignty at their second international conference in Tlaxcala, Mexico, in the spring of 1996.[40] By that time, neoliberalism had reached its zenith. In 1995 countries around the world signed several agreements that liberalized global food and agricultural systems, including the Agreement on Agriculture and the Agreement on Trade-Related Aspects of Intellectual Property Rights (known as the TRIPS Agreement). The Agreement on Agriculture and the TRIPS Agreement marked a profound shift by incorporating agriculture into a global free trade regime. Supporters of trade liberalization claimed that the Agreement on Agriculture would enable global food security by incentivizing greater global food production, thereby lowering food prices. LVC challenged this neoliberal interpretation of food security by arguing that "food is different." As Peter Rosset puts it, food "is not just any merchandise or commodity. Food means farming, and farming means rural livelihoods, traditions and cultures, and it means preserving, or destroying, rural landscapes. Farming means rural society, agrarian histories; in many cases, rural areas are the repositories of the cultural legacies of nations and peoples."[41] Rather than recognizing the multifunctional role of food and agricultural systems, neoliberalism treats food as a commodity and hunger as a market failure resulting from protectionism or inefficient models of agricultural production.[42]

The language of food sovereignty was mobilized not only to challenge the liberalization of food and agriculture but also, more specifically, to counter the neoliberal interpretation of food security. Developed in the aftermath of the 1970s global food crisis, food security became the primary framework through which international institutions conceptualized the problem of inadequate food access. But in the 1980s, food security was reinterpreted through an individualistic and market dominated framework.[43] Thus, when countries celebrated the liberalization of food and agriculture as a means of achieving food security at the World Food Summit in 1996, LVC was determined to challenge this framework.

It was then that the rest of the world heard about food sovereignty for the first time. During the 1996 summit, the NGO Forum of the World Food Summit issued the statement "Profit for Few or Food for All: Food

Sovereignty and Security to Eliminate the Globalization of Hunger." In the statement, they called for a new model of the global food system.

> We propose a new model for achieving food security that calls into ques-
> tion many of the existing assumptions, policies and practices. This model,
> based on decentralization, challenges the current model, based on a con-
> centration of wealth and power, which now threatens global food security,
> cultural diversity, and the very ecosystems that sustain life on the planet.[44]

By insisting that food insecurity was the result of the globalization of the world economy, the growing power of transnational corporations, and overconsumption, the NGO Forum offered food sovereignty as an alternative framework to food security. However, although food sovereignty was included in the statement, LVC refused to join it, demanding that nongovernmental organizations (NGOs) desist from speaking on behalf of people's organizations and social movements. As Annette Desmarais explains, LVC "challenged not only who would speak, and on whose behalf, but also what would be said and how to arrive at a collective position."[45] The rift between the NGOs and LVC established what would be an ongoing tension between international NGOs and people's movements over the issue of representation and their respective visions of transformation. As more activists and other constituencies began to adopt the language of food sovereignty, these issues would help to shape the meaning and development of this claim.

REDEFINING FOOD SOVEREIGNTY

In the decade and a half since food sovereignty was articulated by LVC, its meaning and definition have shifted in response to both the expansion of the global food sovereignty movement and the development of neoliberal governance. In their 1996 statement, LVC's articulation of food sovereignty remained state centered. This reflected LVC's challenge to the liberalization and governance of food and agriculture through the supranational authority of the World Trade Organization. In their 1996 statement, "The Right to Produce and Access to Land," LVC stated:

> Food is a basic human right. This right can only be realized in a system
> where food sovereignty is guaranteed. Food sovereignty is the right of
> each *nation* to maintain and develop its own capacity to produce its basic

foods respecting cultural and productive diversity. We have the right to produce our own food in our own territory. Food sovereignty is a precondition to genuine food security.[46]

The declaration built on the three rights that LVC had articulated in Mons in 1993. Through this definition, LVC made clear that they saw food sovereignty as a *precondition* rather than as an opposing paradigm for food security. In doing so, LVC grounded the goals of food security in democratic processes that respected the rights of small-scale producers.[47]

By 2003 LVC was no longer focused solely on the state. It expanded the definition to the right of *peoples* to define their own food and agricultural policies.

> Food sovereignty is the right of *peoples* to define their own food and agriculture; to protect and regulate domestic agricultural production and trade in order to achieve sustainable development objectives; to determine the extent to which they want to be self-reliant; to restrict the dumping of products in their markets; and to provide local fisheries-based communities the priority in managing the use of and the rights to aquatic resources. . . . Governments must uphold the rights of all *peoples* to food sovereignty and security, and adopt and implement policies that promote sustainable, family-based production rather than industry-led, high-input and export-oriented production.[48]

This definition expanded the meaning of *sovereignty* beyond the Westphalian framework of territorial nation-states. The subjects of sovereignty in this definition were instead collectively constituted social groups seeking recognition and representation. This definition provided a better description of the marginalization that different rural groups—Indigenous peoples, peasants, and family farmers—were experiencing *within* states. It also reflected the growing number of groups that were mobilizing food sovereignty as a collective action frame. In addition to LVC, the 2003 statement was signed by groups such as the World Forum of Fish Harvesters and Fishworkers. The resonance of food sovereignty thus required that LVC redefine it to incorporate other constituencies.

In 2007, as the world was facing yet another global food crisis, the definition of food sovereignty was expanded once again. During that year, the

International Planning Committee for Food Sovereignty planned a major conference in Mali that brought LVC together with a variety of international organizations and social movement platforms, including World Women's March, the World Forum of Fisher Peoples, and Friends of the Earth International. The Nyéléni International Forum on Food Sovereignty in 2007 drew more than 500 people from 80 countries, during which activists developed the most comprehensive and widely cited definition of food sovereignty.

> Food sovereignty is the right of peoples to healthy and culturally appropriate food produced through ecologically sound and sustainable methods, and their right to define their own food and agriculture systems. It puts the aspirations and needs of those who produce, distribute and consume food at the heart of food systems and policies rather than the demands of markets and corporations. . . . Food sovereignty implies new social relations free of oppression and inequality between men and women, peoples, racial groups, social and economic classes and generations.[49]

This definition reflected a number of changes. First, it clearly linked food sovereignty to sustainable production methods. Second, it not only emphasized the rights of peoples but also identified a specific set of peoples as the primary protagonists in the food system: those engaged in food production and those most affected by food insecurity. In doing so, it incorporated consumers as a constituency for the first time. Finally, it further elaborated food sovereignty as a process of dismantling geopolitical, class, racial, and gendered forms of power and constructing more egalitarian and democratic relations.

MOBILIZING FOOD SOVEREIGNTY: THE PRACTICE OF TRANSLOCAL TRANSLATION

As the definition of food sovereignty was broadened to include new constituencies, it became centered on issues of *control*. Priscilla Claeys contends that the "reclaiming control frame" of food sovereignty became increasingly salient for activists as the movement expanded beyond self-identified "peasant" movements. "At the heart of the reclaiming control frame," she contends, "is reliance on grassroots organizing and mistrust in the capacity of the state and of institutional frameworks to bring social change. The reclaiming control frame highlights alternative 'practices' at the local level and building another world from the bottom-up."[50]

Food sovereignty movements are not alone in turning to *practices* as a result of their diversity. In the absence of any shared theory of social change or singular goal, prefigurative democratic practices enable social movements to envision the world and institutions they wish to build. Prefigurative practices, which were first developed by the New Left in the 1960s, have become common across alter-globalization and anticapitalist movements.[51] In her ethnography of global justice movements, anthropologist Marianne Maeckelbergh explains that "given the alterglobalization movement's affinity for diversity (including as many different voices and goals as possible) and horizontality (a continuous process of challenging the centralization of power to attain as much equality as possible between actors) as the basis for new forms of network democracy, prefiguration is the most effective strategy (perhaps the only strategy) because it allows for goals to be open and multiple."[52] Food sovereignty movements also built on these practices in articulating their vision of food sovereignty.

Thus, although food sovereignty is a *material* process of reorganizing food production and provisioning, it is also a *communicative* process through which activists cultivate their relationships with one another through shared codes and protocols of communication. Because networks are communicative structures, their communicative practices serve to prefigure the governance networks they seek to influence.[53] Rather than "communicative practices," however, I prefer the term *translation*. The term *translation* refers to "conversions of meanings and practices across different national jurisdictions, regimes of value, technical languages, and affective registers."[54] Through translation, activists convert their values into communicative practices. This is why scholars of counterhegemonic movements have begun to describe translation as the primary way in which movements are assembled. "The objective of translation work," Boaventura de Sousa Santos suggests, "is to nurture among progressive social movements and organizations the will to create together knowledges and practices strong enough to provide credible alternatives to neoliberal globalization."[55] In the context of transnational governance, translation refers to the way that activists mediate meanings across arenas and institutions transnationally.

Through translation, activists assemble networks around shared norms and forms of knowledge.

However, transnational activists are not the only actors engaged in translation. Hegemonic actors also engage in translation in an attempt to influence the rules and standards produced across local and global arenas of governance. In describing the practices of translation that food sovereignty activists have cultivated, I draw on the term *translocal translation*, which was first developed by Latin American feminist scholars Claudia de Lima Costa and Sonia Alvarez to describe how feminist movements construct links that recognize both the multiple intersecting forms of domination that activists experience and the uneven geographies of power that they inhabit.[56] Maylei Blackwell defines the concept of translocal translation as a process that "involves actors who, despite being multiply marginalized in their national contexts, create linkages with social actors across locales to build new affiliations, solidarities, and movements."[57] Given that women are a key constituency of food sovereignty movements and make up more than half of the agricultural labor force in nonindustrialized agricultural communities, translocal translation is a fitting term for food sovereignty movements as well.[58] It signals the kinds of relations that food sovereignty movements, as well as other counterhegemonic movements, seek to build across distinct political, social, and agrarian contexts. Food sovereignty activists' translocal practices of translation are shaped around three key dimensions: (1) representation, (2) knowledge, and (3) commensuration. Each of these is tied to specific goals of the food sovereignty movement, as I elaborate.

Representation

Food sovereignty movements are united around their shared value that food producers and those most affected by food security should have a voice in food and agricultural policies. In the definition of food sovereignty created in 2007 at the Nyéléni Forum, activists specifically emphasized the rights of "those who produce, distribute and consume food" to define their own food and agricultural systems.[59] In demanding that *peoples*, whether defined at the subnational or national level, have a right to define food and agricultural policies, food sovereignty is fundamentally concerned with representation.

Representation has dual meanings. First, it refers to the symbolic representations that actors attribute to networks. As described earlier, the network is a symbol that rival actors ascribe with different meanings. Hegemonic actors represent networks with the values of efficiency and pragmatism, framing networks as apolitical processes of problem solving. In contrast, food sovereignty activists represent networks from the perspective of small-scale food producers, as political and ecological relations necessary to sustain life itself. Food sovereignty activists frame networked arenas of governance as political spaces composed of unequal power relations. Rival actors thus struggle to interpret networks through different cultural frames. These frames play a significant role, as sociologist Mayer Zald notes, because they "render or cast behavior and events in an evaluative mode and . . . suggest alternative modes of action."[60] This struggle over symbolic representation is thus a cultural process through which sites of politics are made visible and given meaning.[61]

Second, the symbolic representations that actors attribute to networks shape the concrete processes of inclusion, participation, and decision making within networks. Whereas liberal democracy vested power in "the people," an entity constructed and imagined through the nation-state and thus organized processes of representation through delegation, networks offer a different way of representing the people. As Eva Sørensen argues, "Network governance has transformed the right to represent into a political battle not only between political parties but between multitudes of other actors as well. In a system of network governance, the right to represent the people must be obtained over and over again in ongoing processes of representation."[62] In other words, in the context of transnational governance, representation is both a symbolic struggle to constitute and establish the boundaries of the political, and a concrete struggle over who gets to represent the people or public interest. Through struggles over representation, food sovereignty actors politicize coordination and decision-making processes, make power inequalities visible, and constitute political constituencies.[63]

Knowledge

Food sovereignty activists seek to democratize knowledge and ways of knowing. In the 2007 Nyéléni Declaration, activists declared that they are fighting for a world where "we value, recognize and respect our diversity of

traditional knowledge, food, language and culture, and the way we organize and express ourselves."[64] More specifically, food sovereignty activists
promote agroecology, which is built on local and Indigenous knowledge
or "people's knowledge."[65] Through agroecology, food sovereignty activists share their knowledge through horizontal processes of co-learning,
farmer-to-farmer exchanges, and common rather than private property
regimes.[66] This is captured through the concept of *diálogo de sabers*, which
as Martínez-Torres and Rosset explain, "roughly translates to 'dialogue
among different knowledges and ways of knowing.'" They argue that this
"is key to the durability of the LVC constellation. It is a process whereby
different visions and cosmovisions are shared on a horizontal, equal-
footing basis."[67] This stands in stark contrast to the agro-industrial model
of development, which promotes top-down forms of agricultural development through proprietary knowledge and technologies.

Knowledge practices are also at the heart of transnational governance.
Networks are constituted through knowledge and information. Given
that regulatory expertise is no longer monopolized by bureaucrats in
administrative processes, actors draw on competing knowledge claims
to frame problems, enroll other actors in shared epistemic networks,
and claim interpretive authority. Peter Haas refers to these as "epistemic
communities."[68] Historically, powerful actors have drawn on particular
epistemologies such as "science" as a universal, all-encompassing force
for interpreting the world. By denying the normative foundations of
their worldviews and representing their knowledge as "detached from
interests, universal, and owned in common by the human race," science
has served as a potent epistemic force.[69] Hegemonic actors consistently
draw on the discourse of science to promote proprietary technologies
and productivist models of agriculture systems that neglect questions of
power and distribution.

Food sovereignty activists challenge epistemologies premised on the
mechanistic worldview that has been continuously deployed to reify European colonialism and Western forms of legality.[70] Although agroecology is a science, it values transdisciplinary situated knowledge and is not
disinterested in the economic and political context in which it operates.[71]
In promoting agroecology, food sovereignty activists seek to democratize
knowledge through an "ecology of knowledges."[72]

However, it is important to note that knowledge is not powerful on its own. As global governance scholar Ole Jacob Sending points out, knowledge must be promoted through material or symbolic resources.[73] Wealthy states, multinational corporations, and global philanthropies draw on their vast financial resources by using material incentives to enroll different actors into networks.[74] By contrast, food sovereignty activists rely on their symbolic resources—their demands for democracy, autonomy, and resonant frames of injustice—to construct networks of shared solidarity and social values.

Practices of Commensuration

Finally, food sovereignty is organized around the principle of autonomy and self-determination. As the 2007 Nyéléni Declaration explains, "All peoples that want to be free and independent must produce their own foods. Food sovereignty is more than a right; in order to be able to apply policies that allow autonomy in food production it is necessary to have political conditions that exercise autonomy in all the territorial spaces: countries, regions, cities and rural communities. Food sovereignty is only possible if it takes place at the same time as political sovereignty of peoples."[75] How food sovereignty activists relationally negotiate and respect these differences among multiple and overlapping claims to sovereignty has been a key issue that food sovereignty activists and scholars have sought to navigate.

How difference is valued, accommodated, or effaced is a key component of the politics of translation. As Susan Gal notes, translation is a set of communicative practices that "create equivalences and organize connections among practices. Such processes can also produce incommensurabilities, disjunctures, and power differentials."[76] At the core of these practices is how and whether translators *commensurate* difference. Commensuration is a social and communicative practice that occurs when different qualities, meanings, or values are consolidated into a single term or metric across social contexts for the purpose of comparison and equivalence.[77]

Practices of commensuration are endemic to both capitalism and liberalism. Capitalism requires the commensuration of qualitatively distinct use values into exchange value (or price) in order to enable the purchase and sale of commodities. One of the most important commodities that capitalism commensurates is labor. It is by commensurating labor power that capitalist forms of value are constituted.[78] Liberalism, meanwhile, commensurates people into individuals endowed with formal equality.[79] By contrast, movements that oppose capitalism and neoliberalism construct equivalences in opposition to a shared set of hegemonic actors, but they often refuse to commensurate differences or consolidate into a single struggle. As de Sousa Santos writes, "Through translation work, diversity is celebrated, not as a factor of fragmentation and isolationism, but rather as a condition of sharing and solidarity."[80]

Law is a quintessential tool of commensuration.[81] Hegemonic and counterhegemonic networks therefore use law to translate across arenas of governance in different ways. Corporate agro-industrial networks use law to commensurate diverse social and ecological contexts in order to spread market forms of exchange—they seek to harmonize private legal systems and intellectual property laws to expand global markets and facilitate global investment. By contrast, food sovereignty activists mobilize public and private law to destabilize regulatory arrangements, protect activists' freedom to organize, construct communal property regimes, and promote decentralized autonomy.[82] For food sovereignty activists, legal mobilization is therefore *embedded* in a broader set of networking practices. Law serves as a critical tool rather than as a horizon of social transformation.

BUILDING A FOOD SOVEREIGNTY
MOVEMENT IN THE UNITED STATES

By cultivating shared practices of translation, food sovereignty activists have been able to assemble transnational networks across widely divergent social, political, and agrarian conditions. In the years after the 2007 Nyéléni meeting and the 2007–2008 global food crisis, food sovereignty alliances began to be established in Africa, Australia, and the United States. Although LVC had a presence in all these places, the development of these new alliances reflected the adoption of food sovereignty by new constituencies and a new global reach for food sovereignty movements.

In the United States the food and financial crisis is what first prompted organizations and activists concerned with food systems to adopt the language of food sovereignty. During the crisis, the prices of staple cereals and food skyrocketed. The number of people experiencing food insecurity in the United States alone jumped from 36.2 million to 49.1 million.[83]

Given that 2007 had been a year for record grain harvests, the crisis reflected the profound contradictions of the corporate global food system.[84] Activists in the United States therefore saw the crisis as an opportunity to challenge both the domestic and foreign policies of the US government.

In July 2008, as the world faced a global food crisis, several national coalitions and progressive NGOs allied with LVC decided to build a larger coalition to address the structural causes of the crisis. Together they assembled more than fifty organizations that included antihunger, family farm, food security, environmental, international aid, labor, food justice, and consumer groups. They met in Washington, DC, hoping to influence the 2008 elections, agreeing to jointly issue a call to action on World Food Day in October 2008. The call to action demanded that the US government do three things: (1) stabilize prices for farmers and consumers globally, (2) rebalance power in the food system, and (3) make agriculture environmentally sustainable.[85]

Most of the organizations that attended the July meeting formed the US Working Group on the Food Crisis. The working group combined progressive coalitions working on rural policy, such as the National Family Farm Coalition and the Rural Coalition, along with antihunger groups, international NGOs, and grassroots philanthropies. These groups had not always been politically aligned. The National Family Farm Coalition and the Rural Coalition were both members of LVC and shared a progressive agenda for reconfiguring the global food system by transforming US domestic and foreign policy. They had their roots in the farm crisis of the 1970s and 1980s, when family farmers in the rural heartlands of industrial agriculture were suffering from massive debt as a result of the US's market-driven policies and its attendant boom-and-bust cycles. By contrast, many of the international NGOs were primarily focused on issues of global food security outside the United States and had little experience working on domestic food and agricultural politics. Antihunger groups, meanwhile, were primarily concerned with domestic food politics.

To the activists who put together the working group, the problem was not so much the political differences among the members of the group but the dominance of NGOs and well-funded organizations based in New York City and Washington, DC. Christina Schiavoni, who was then the global movements director at WhyHunger recounted how they had to move quickly because of the crisis. As a result, it was primarily NGOs that were able to attend the working group meetings in Washington, DC. "It was totally skewed towards NGOs and a largely white crowd," she told me. "Some of us immediately identified that was something that we could not move forward with like that." The working group therefore spent the next several months fundraising for a more inclusive meeting to ensure that social movements could attend and represent themselves. In August 2009 the working group organized another meeting that included frontline groups led by Indigenous peoples and people of color, such as the White Earth Land Recovery Project from Minnesota, the Mvskoke Food Sovereignty Initiative in Oklahoma, the Federation of Southern Cooperatives, Growing Power, the Border Agricultural Workers Project, the Farmworker Association of Florida, and Community to Community Development.

Initially, the US Working Group on the Food Crisis mobilized the framework of food sovereignty just as it had been articulated by LVC: as a structural critique of hunger both domestically and internationally. Maria Aguiar, who then worked for the organization Grassroots International, told me that the organizers of the working group saw it "as an opportunity to challenge the whole food bank approach to food insecurity and bring a new perspective." By this Aguiar was referring to the emergency food system in the United States, which emerged in the wake of the rollback of both supply management for farmers and the safety net for consumers. This system, which is run by the voluntary sector, is dependent on the donations of large corporations.[86] As Aguiar explained, "Food banks were working with corporations to just dump a bunch of corporate excess into communities and they weren't really challenging why people are food insecure in the United States." Members of the working group tried to make the link between the issues that communities in the global South were facing as a result of the dumping of cheap US commodities through food aid and trade liberalization, and the experiences of poor communities in the United States.

This position ended up alienating some of the initial participants in the working group. Schiavoni recalled one antihunger group calling her to take their names off a statement that they thought was potentially anticorporate. However, the position also helped consolidate the relationships of those in the working group by naming the problem of food insecurity and blaming those governmental policies and corporate actors that were responsible for it. This process of naming and blaming, which sociolegal scholars describe as the initial steps of constructing disputes, provided a framework through which the working group was able to identify its allies.[87] In doing so, they sought to bring together a diverse set of organizations.

Claiming food sovereignty—the third step in the construction of disputes—turned out to be significantly more difficult. One challenge was the different frames that activists had been using to articulate their demands and visions for change. Activists, including farmworkers, minority farmers, and urban communities of color, had been using the language of food justice to challenge racial inequalities in the food system. Like the discourses of environmental justice and climate justice, the justice frame has been used by communities of color to challenge mainstream movements for agro-environmental change. Other activists drew on the frame of local food or community food security in challenging the industrial food system. These frames, which reflected diverse priorities and concerns, had grown out of efforts to link urban and rural constituencies in the 1990s and had been developed by the Community Food Security Coalition, which operated as a national hub for food activism in the 1990s and early 2000s.[88] Reframing these groups' demands through the language of food sovereignty therefore required activists to cultivate practices of translation that would recognize their different priorities without collapsing their differences.

A second challenge was that many of the NGOs were concerned about using the language of sovereignty. Aguiar told me that for those who had been working with movements from Latin America and the global South, "sovereignty was always about anti-imperialism . . . but it didn't translate much in the US context." In part, this was because many of the NGOs working on issues of food insecurity were focused on hunger outside the United States. However, organizers of the working group thought that using the language of food sovereignty was important to build a broader transnational movement. Activists at the 2009 meeting saw adopting the term *food sovereignty* as a two-way exchange: "to give more strength to movements in the US, while also showing the rest of the world that movements in the US were in solidarity with them too," Schiavoni said.

The US Working Group on the Food Crisis therefore sought to bridge the differences among its participants by translating food sovereignty around two goals: (1) ending poverty by relocalizing food systems and creating jobs and (2) creating healthy food for local communities by giving communities control over their food systems. In other words, activists interpreted food sovereignty through what Claeys called the "reclaiming control frame."[89] This emphasis on *control* was essential for the way that food sovereignty was interpreted not only in the United States but also in other Western industrialized contexts such as Europe. As Aguiar explained, "The easiest way for us to try to translate what [food sovereignty] would look like in the US context was not that it would be a national production program. The easiest way for us to make it palatable and something that people could really imagine happening was in a localized setting. So, we talked about having local control over food production and access to the resources to be able to produce your food and control what kind of food you produce."

In an effort to translate food sovereignty, several "grass-top" organizations worked on a series of materials and publications to translate food sovereignty. The most well circulated material was the pamphlet *Food Sovereignty: Join the Local, National, and International Movement to Regain Control of Our Food and Farm System*, published by Grassroots International and the National Family Farm Coalition, a member of La Vía Campesina. The 16-page pamphlet described food sovereignty as "putting people first."

> All people have the right to decide what they eat and to ensure that food in their community is healthy and accessible for everyone. This is the basic principle behind food sovereignty. If you want to support domestic food security through the production of healthy food at a fair price, and you believe that family farmers and fishers should have the first right to local and regional markets, then food sovereignty is for you.[90]

The pamphlet featured profiles of nine food producers: seven from the United States and two from abroad. The seven US producers were a dairy farmer from Wisconsin, a rancher from Montana, a farmworker organizer from Texas, a vegetable farmer from Mississippi, an Indigenous student organizer from Oklahoma, a fisheries advocate from Maine, and a corn and soybean farmer from Iowa. For each profile, the pamphlet explained "how food sovereignty helps" by focusing primarily on the issue of taking back local control and putting people involved in the food system at the forefront of decision-making processes.

In addition to the pamphlet, Grassroots International and the National Family Farm Coalition also put together a curriculum titled *Food for Thought and Action: A Food Sovereignty Curriculum*. The curriculum was developed with exercises for particular groups, which the authors envisioned would form key components of the US food sovereignty movement: consumers, faith and antihunger groups, environmentalists, and small-scale farmers and farmworkers. One exercise, "Defining Food Sovereignty," asked participants to identify threats to local control of the food system and then asked participants to reflect on different definitions of food sovereignty—the 1996 and 2002 definitions quoted earlier—and on the six principles developed at the Nyéléni Forum in 2007: (1) food for people, (2) valuing food providers, (3) localizing food systems, (4) making decisions locally, (5) building knowledge and skills, and (6) working with nature. These materials played a crucial role in introducing different constituencies across the countries to the claim of food sovereignty.

In 2010 members of the US Working Group on the Food Crisis organized the People's Movement Assembly on Food Sovereignty (PMA) at the US Social Forum in Detroit. At the PMA they issued a statement that committed to "launching a campaign for food sovereignty as the right of the people."[91] The PMA drew on tactics and practices that had been developed at the World Social Forum, which privileged the voices of grassroots organizations over and above middle-class activists and NGOs.[92] The PMA at the US Social Forum helped solidify what would eventually become the US Food Sovereignty Alliance (USFSA) around a set of representational practices that intentionally privileged grassroots organizations and communities of color over both mainstream progressive organizations and international NGOs. In doing so, the organizers of the USFSA challenged middle-class, "reformist" food activism.[93] However, this intentional shift downward was difficult. As one activist explained to me, the United States did not have models of national social movements beyond the labor movement. The challenge was constituting these diverse groups as a *movement*. During the PMA, organizers released the "Statement from the People's Movement Assembly on Food Sovereignty" in which they committed to building a food sovereignty movement in the United States.

A movement for food sovereignty—the people's democratic control of the food system, the right of all people to healthy, culturally appropri-

ate food produced through ecologically sound and sustainable methods, and their right to define their own food and agriculture systems—is
building from every corner of the globe. We find that our work to build a
better food system in the United States is inextricably linked to the struggle for workers' rights, immigrant's rights, women's rights, the fight to
dismantle racism in our communities, and the struggle for sovereignty
in indigenous communities. We find that in order to create a better food
system, we must break up the corporate control of our seeds, land, water
and natural resources. . . . We therefore commit to re-building local food
economies in our own communities, to dismantling structural racism, to
democratizing land access, to building opportunities for the leadership of
our youth, and to working towards food sovereignty in partnership with
social movements around the world.[94]

The statement, which was published in New Orleans on World Food Day in
2010, laid the basis for the formal establishment of the USFSA.

TRANSLATING FOOD SOVEREIGNTY
IN THE PACIFIC NORTHWEST

In the late 2000s the Pacific Northwest emerged as a hub of food sovereignty activism. By the time that the newly founded USFSA held its
first US Food Sovereignty Assembly in 2011—the meeting described in
the introduction to this book—two Pacific Northwest organizations
were already in leadership roles: the Community Alliance for Global
Justice (CAGJ) and Community to Community Development (C2C).
Both organizations had been founded in the 2000s and had adopted
the claim of food sovereignty a few years after. CAGJ was established
after the Battle in Seattle to grow the local networks that had developed
in anticipation of the 1999 Seattle World Trade Organization meetings.
Although it initially focused on challenging free trade agreements, it
turned to food in the late 2000s as the focus for its activism. One of
CAGJ's co-founders, Heather Day, had learned about food sovereignty
not only during the Battle in Seattle but also during several World Social Forums in Latin America that she had attended in graduate school.
In the mid-2000s CAGJ transformed from an organization focused on
global trade to food sovereignty.

C2C was not born during the Battle in Seattle, but it too had its roots in the World Social Forum. Its founder, Rosalinda Guillen, was a farmworker organizer from Northwest Washington who had represented the United Farm Workers (UFW) at the World Social Forum in Porto Alegre, Brazil. Soon after, she left the UFW and founded a small organization in Bellingham, Washington, that was built on the concepts and practices she had learned about in Brazil. Although she originally framed her work in terms of food justice, she soon began to use the language of food sovereignty as the USFSA emerged. Both CAGJ and C2C were founding members of the USFSA and were among its most active members.

CAGJ and C2C are not the only organizations mobilizing the claim of food sovereignty in the Northwest. Several Indigenous tribes also began to adopt the claim of food sovereignty in the 2000s to reclaim control over their tribal fishing and hunting grounds. This struggle is not new. In the 1970s Northwest tribes won a major legal decision that affirmed their tribal fishing rights. But food sovereignty nonetheless has served as a powerful new framework through which tribes across the Northwest, and the United States more broadly, are reviving their Indigenous food systems, contesting the industrial food system, and building solidarity with other movements.

These three groups, which emerged in the late 2000s, represent the diversity of activists and movements claiming food sovereignty not just in the Pacific Northwest but around the country. They include a farmworker-led organization fighting for migrant seasonal farmworkers laboring in the food system, an Indigenous organization working for control over its territories and fishing grounds, and a grassroots organization that consists mostly of urban white activists fighting for local food systems and radical political change.

Like the early alternative agriculture movement, activists from these organizations are attempting to cultivate a movement that combines a variety of constituencies. As each group makes claims for food sovereignty, it inevitably encounters frictions. This is not unique to the Pacific Northwest. Christina Schiavoni emphasizes that food sovereignty activists frequently mobilize claims for multiple, overlapping, and often competing sovereignties.[95] However, whereas different constituencies in the alternative agriculture movement formed rival networks to pursue their priorities, food sovereignty activists have labored to maintain the diversity of their movements by adopting a claim whose very meaning is embedded with practices designed to embrace diverse peoples, knowledge systems, and struggles. As food sovereignty activists in the Pacific Northwest translate food sovereignty, they are constructing networks that, as I describe in the next chapters, are prefiguring decentralized democratic food governance.

CONCLUSIONS

In the Pacific Northwest, activists have long worked to challenge industrial food systems and build local alternatives. Beginning in the 1970s, activists in the alternative agriculture movement drew on new ideas stemming from ecology and systems theory to re-envision social and economic organization through the framework of the network. They were not alone in turning to this holistic image of social organization. As cultural historian Fred Turner notes, "To a generation that had grown up in a world beset by massive armies and by the threat of nuclear holocaust, the cybernetic notion of the globe as a single, interlinked pattern of information was deeply comforting: in the invisible play of information, many thought they could see the possibility of global harmony."[96]

Yet as activists in the alternative agriculture movement found, networks do not necessarily generate harmony. Internal tensions and power struggles among different constituencies emerged soon after the Tilth Association was established. Commercial farmers sought out state regulation to standardize the definition of organic food. The regulation of organic food, first at the state level and then at the federal level, not only omitted the social justice values that many in the alternative agriculture movement had promoted but also led to the dissipation of the alternative agriculture movement altogether. The history of the alternative agriculture movement illuminates how networked-based movements sit precariously between politics and markets. How activists engage in networking practices ultimately shapes their impacts.

As food sovereignty activists in the Pacific Northwest turn to transnational networks to cultivate connections between diverse constituencies and social groups, they draw on networking practices developed by peasants, workers, and small-scale producers in the global South. By constituting practices that express their social values and embedding these practices within the very claim of food sovereignty, activists have developed a new social justice claim and approach to mobilization. Indeed, food sovereignty activists have reinterpreted the meaning of sovereignty not as a fixed set of territorial relations but rather as a set of shared practices of what I have described as translocal translation. These practices are centered on democratizing representation, challenging hegemonic knowledge, and protecting the autonomy of peoples. Through these practices they are building local, regional, and transnational networks.

In the following chapters, I examine how food sovereignty organizations in the Pacific Northwest are deploying these networks to transform food system governance on multiple political and spatial scales. Each of the following chapters explores how activists have cultivated these practices in relation to different forms of transnational governance, from a local arena of collaborative governance, to private value chain governance, to transnational biosafety governance. By analyzing these practices, I demonstrate how food sovereignty activists are creating new constituencies, values, and relations through which they are shaping the formation of transnational governance from below.

2   Constructing and Contesting "Local" Food Governance

IF THERE IS ONE MAJOR CITY in the United States where people take local food seriously, it is surely Seattle. Take a stroll down Broadway, the heart of Seattle's Capitol Hill neighborhood, and the Emerald City's obsession with local food is clear. There, some of the city's finest restaurants offer signature Pacific Northwest fare, from Coho salmon to Penn Cove mussels to Hama Hama oysters—all harvested from the coastal waters of the Puget Sound. Continue a bit further along the street and you'll reach the Capitol Hill farmers market, where neighborhood residents-turned-farmers hawk some of the finest and freshest produce in the city. Further down, at the local Kroger-owned grocery store, the word "LOCAL" is plastered all over the store's walls with images of the Pacific Northwest in the background. In his Seattle travel diary, *New York Times* columnist Frank Bruni affirmed, "I'm hard-pressed to think of another corner or patch of the United States where the locavore sensibilities of the moment are on such florid (and often sweetly funny) display, or where they pay richer dividends."[1] It should be no surprise, then, that in a city whose largest tourist attraction is a farmers market, local food is ubiquitous.

However, travel south of Capitol Hill and local food is not an object of culinary connoisseurship but a symbol of intense inequality. In Seattle a legacy of settler colonialism and redlining has left the city highly segregated and stratified. The city's north is prosperous and white, whereas the south side of the city is poorer and more diverse. In these neighborhoods healthy, fresh, and local food is often inaccessible. In a county with more than forty farmers markets, over 13% of residents and as many as 22% of children were deemed food insecure when I was conducting my research.[2] Across the city marginalized communities have continuously fought for access to local food. In Columbia City, the only neighborhood in South Seattle with a farmers market, residents organized to demand that the City of Seattle expand the buying power of low-income consumers at farmers markets. Further south, the Muckleshoot tribe developed a food sovereignty project to rebuild local food systems decimated by displacement, treaty rights violations, and commercial overfishing.

The emergence of a food sovereignty movement in a city that has come to pride itself on local food is initially what brought me to Seattle. Localizing food systems is one of the primary objectives for food sovereignty activists around the world. Activists' demands for localization are rooted in a desire to develop shorter and more ecologically anchored food chains that are controlled by communities. Yet, although for many food sovereignty activists "local" refers to specific peasant and Indigenous territories in which food sovereignty activists seek greater autonomy and control over their food systems,[3] for activists in the global North the meaning of "local" is often more contested. As the geographer Eric Swyngedouw reminds us, the "local" is "neither an ontologically given and *a priori* definable geographic territory nor a politically neutral discursive strategy in the construction of narratives."[4] Indeed, in the global North constituencies often compete to define the meaning of "local" to support their own goals and interests. As activists and policymakers seek to strengthen local food systems, these debates increasingly take place within new arenas and forms of governance.[5]

Scholars have been skeptical of the potential of localization processes to benefit marginalized communities. Analysts of local food systems have described how mainstream, consumer-centered approaches to localization tend to depoliticize the larger economic structures that determine how food is produced and consumed. As a result, local food movements often reproduce existing inequalities and reinforce neoliberal subjectivities.[6] Similarly, regulatory scholars have raised concerns that local processes of collaborative governance can depoliticize democracy and "responsibilize" individuals for their own self-governing.[7] As a major seat of global capital and a longtime home to progressive social movements, Seattle offers a microcosm to investigate the clashing visions and practices of localization. By analyzing how activists mobilize food sovereignty in the Puget Sound, in this chapter I ask, What does "local" mean for food sovereignty activists? What kinds of socioeconomic, political, and ecological relations do they seek to construct? And how do they seek to institutionalize them through new forms of governance?

My focus in this chapter is not on a single food sovereignty organization but rather on the competing narratives and symbolic representations of localism in one arena of governance: the Puget Sound Regional Food Policy Council (PSRFPC). I center my analysis on the PSRFPC because it allows us to observe how even the meaning of "local" food sovereignty is forged through dialectical practices of translation that activists cultivate through their engagement in new arenas of governance. Through my ethnographic analysis, I describe how the PSRFPC, an arena of network governance developed in response to demands to localize food systems, operated as a constitutive site of struggle through which actors deployed rival *frames* to construct the meaning of the local. Framing food systems, as we will also see in chapter 5, serves as a constitutive cultural process whereby the social relations of food production and provisioning are invested with meanings, values, and representations that render those relations calculable and governable. By examining how different actors' framed local food systems in the PSRFPC, I illustrate how competing frames serve to constitute the political and economic logics that shape how power and control operate through governance. I show how activists mobilized food sovereignty as a frame that politicized local food governance by reimagining the social and ecological ties of food production and provisioning. Through the frame of food sovereignty, I argue, activists developed new meanings of the local through which they reimagined markets and constructed new political constituencies.

I begin this chapter by describing the contested politics of localization in the Puget Sound with the rise of neoliberal globalization. I then move on to chart the development of local food governance in the region, analyzing the competing frames that were mobilized to represent local food networks and shape the practices of the PSRFPC. The chapter ends with an analysis of how these competing frames were mediated in a conflict over farmers markets. Ultimately, although local food governance creates opportunities to deepen market rationalities by embedding local social values and relations in market calculi, I argue that it also provides a relational space through which activists dialectically develop alternative social, political, and ecological relations of local food sovereignty.

NEOLIBERALISM AND THE CONTESTED
POLITICS OF LOCALIZATION

The central location of the Pike Place Market would seem to suggest a consistent demand for local food in the Puget Sound since the market was founded in the early twentieth century. In reality, however, by the early 1970s the Pike Place Market was crumbling because of decades of suburban sprawl. Local food systems had been eroded by national supply chains and the growth of the industrial food system. In the 1970s a young generation of countercultural activists and organic food pioneers breathed new life into the Pike Place Market. But it was only in the 1990s and 2000s that demand for local food shifted from niche countercultural consumption to more mainstream markets. The push for localization emerged as both a product of and a response to capitalist restructuring under neoliberalism. Understanding this contentious dynamic is critical because it has been at the core of debates over the opportunities and limitations of both new forms of governance and local food movements.

Promoters of localization emerged in the context of roll-back neoliberalism. As advanced capitalist countries engaged in competitive deregulation to attract capital in the 1980s and 1990s, governments also lowered their spending. For example, between 1982 and 1985, $12.2 billion less was made available for food stamps because of cuts to welfare assistance by the Reagan administration.[8] At the same time, the federal government also began dismantling New Deal–era supply management programs in agriculture by pursuing Earl Butz's policy of "get big or get out" in agriculture. As governments embraced the self-regulating market, supra- and subnational authorities became increasingly important political arenas for social and economic regulation.[9] As Massimo De Angelis describes, the rise of neoliberal governance emerged from three normative prescriptions: "First, the state, both in the North and in the global South *should* withdraw from the social sector. Second, the market *should* be given open access to all spheres

FIGURE 4 Seattle's Pike Place Market. Source: Wikimedia Commons.

in life. . . . Third, people *should* organize their own socio-economic reproduction instead of depending on the state."[10]

During this period, cities became critical spaces of struggle and strategic political action.[11] Although cities had always been central to capitalist
development, during the late twentieth century neoliberal deregulation and
privatization unbundled their close dynamism with the state, leaving cities
to deal with a host of issues that were no longer addressed through national
regulation.[12] This process of neoliberal devolution led to the development
of new forms of governance, variously described as joined-up governance,
collaborative planning, or collaborative governance, among other terms.
Scholars debated whether the devolution of regulation and governance to
the local level would provide the basis for a new political and economic
formation or would simply entrench neoliberalism.[13] New forms of local
governance therefore became a site of standoff between neoliberal reproduction and resistance. Although some saw in the local the possibility of
constructing a global countermovement rooted in "place-based" resistance,
others cautioned that localization often "dissolve[s] into a kind of primor-
dialism that fixes and romanticizes social relations and identities."[14]

Food became a symbolic and material locus for these contested dynamics. In Seattle local food began to gain broad currency in the 1990s. Farmers markets began spreading across the city from the University District in the north to Columbia City in the south. After the Battle in Seattle, localization took on a new urgency and political meaning. No longer was it exclusively popular for natural food consumers; purchasing locally grown food also became a form of resistance to the transnational corporations that were reaping the benefits of globalization. Yet, even though localism emerged as a powerful discourse to contest corporate consolidation and economic inequalities produced by neoliberal globalization, it also produced new inequalities. Like the organic movement before it, "local" food movements became a powerful site for experimentation with new forms of organization and alternative social values while simultaneously reproducing market exclusions. Middle- and upper-class residents celebrated local food as a reflection of their progressive politics and culinary distinction, but local food was inaccessible to working-class and low-income residents of the city's south side. In fact, for the poor the push for local food seemed a double act of dispossession, at once both a judgment of their bad diet choices and the creation of a new out-of-reach necessity.[15]

It was in opposition to the dominant consumerist understanding of localism that activists in Seattle first adopted the claim of food sovereignty. One of the first organizations to begin using the language of food sovereignty was the Community Alliance for Global Justice (CAGJ). CAGJ was founded shortly after the 1999 World Trade Organization protest with the goal of maintaining the momentum of the alter-globalization movement. In the early 2000s CAGJ focused primarily on mobilizing against free trade agreements such as the Central American Free Trade Agreement. In doing so, CAGJ often found itself working on issues of fair trade, particularly on coffee and other foodstuffs, but food was initially only a secondary concern. By the mid-2000s, however, co-founder Heather Day had grown unhappy with the way CAGJ was organizing. In focusing on global policy issues, CAGJ found itself working in coalitions with professionalized nongovernmental organizations (NGOs) that felt increasingly disconnected from social movements and activism on the ground in Seattle. During this period, while serving on the board of CAGJ, Day went to graduate school at the University of Washington and attended the World Social Forums in Brazil and Venezuela. These experiences deeply influenced her vision of social change. When she became the sole staff member of CAGJ, she and other member-volunteers of the organization sought to shift the organization from its work in policy coalitions to a movement-building organization dedicated to the solidarity economy and alternatives to capitalism.

As the alter-globalization movement began to dissipate,[16] CAGJ was left trying to figure out a new approach and focus for organizing. In 2007, in a bid to reinvigorate the organization, Day and her husband, Travis, decided to organize a fundraising dinner focused on food. Both of them had long worked in the food service industry and had built a large urban farm at their Seattle home. Drawing on relationships with local farms, fisherfolk, and other food producers, they were able to gather enough donations to host a large dinner in the basement of the Russian Community Center, which they called Strengthening Local Economies Everywhere. They framed the event as a challenge to the mainstream locavore movement in the Pacific Northwest, which they saw as an opportunity to continue their work on trade and global justice in a way that would be more meaningful for Seattleites' everyday lives. As the name of the event made clear, they sought to reframe the meaning of local food by emphasizing the structural conditions of neoliberalism that inhibited communities from democratically determining their food and agricultural systems. The enthusiasm for this new approach inspired the board of CAGJ to completely restructure the organization's programs. CAGJ started a food justice project to politicize the locavore movement through small campaigns and quickly began framing their work through the language of food sovereignty. In 2009, at the second annual Food Sovereignty Prize ceremony, the organization was awarded an honorable mention "for enabling people to (1) build connections with local farms, kitchens and community gardens; (2) better understand global justice and the corporate-driven economic model informing globalization; and (3) take part in collective action furthering sustainable agriculture, democracy and self-determination in the food system."[17]

In translating the claim of food sovereignty, CAGJ built on the strategies and visions of the alter-globalization movement by transforming the consumer-oriented locavore movement into a solidarity economy. Through the claim of food sovereignty, CAGJ began to construct a network of activists within communities and constituencies marginalized by the industrial food system. This included small-scale farmers in the Snoqualmie valley, low-income consumers in the historically African American Central District, unionized food chain workers at local grocery chains, and Native American tribes in the Puget Sound region. By bringing together these diverse groups, CAGJ aimed to construct long-term relations of mutual solidarity and build a network to challenge local and global inequalities in the food system.

THE CONSTRUCTION OF LOCAL FOOD GOVERNANCE NETWORKS

At the same time that CAGJ was organizing networks to support its vision of local food systems, so too were local policymakers. Before the 1980s and 1990s, food was not an issue that was addressed at the municipal level. Since the New Deal, when Congress took responsibility for managing the national agricultural economy and food system through the omnibus legislation known as the Farm Bill, food and agriculture had been seen largely as a state and federal issue. However, the withdrawal of welfare provisions combined with deindustrialization in the 1980s left municipalities responsible for a growing number of urban residents who were food insecure, leading cities and other regional authorities to take on food as an issue of local governance. In Seattle two policymakers—City Council member Richard Conlin and his senior adviser, Phyllis Shulman—led the effort to promote local food systems at the urban and regional levels.

Conlin and Shulman's approach to governing local food systems was shaped by the innovative ideas of governance they had begun to experiment with early on in Conlin's tenure on the City Council. One of the first major tasks Conlin and Shulman took on was developing a plan for emergency preparedness, a seemingly technocratic topic of interagency coordination. As they began to work on the issue, Shulman recounted to me their realization that emergency preparedness was framed too narrowly. To address disasters, they instead needed to be thinking about the broader issue of resiliency. The resiliency framework decentered top-down approaches to command-and-control regulation and focused Conlin and Shulman's attention instead on what they saw as the real challenge of emergencies: the existing social vulnerabilities in communities. Rather than focusing on interagency coordination, Conlin and Shulman looked for ways that government could help strengthen communities. "Strong communities are more resilient. The more connections between yourself and where you live, the stronger a community is, the more ability there is to adapt when something happens. It is more likely communities' needs will get met, not only through government, but through other elements as well," Shulman told me. This experience led Conlin and Shulman to become increasingly interested in the role that government could play in building community. "More and more," she told me, "we were seeing the connections, the whole systems element of governing." Through this project Conlin and Shulman began to re-envision government.[18]

Conlin and Shulman were not the first to develop these ideas or the first to seek to govern food at the local level. The first experiment with local food governance at the municipal level emerged in 1982, when the first "food policy council" began operating in Knoxville, Tennessee. Although it was originally developed as an advisory council to the mayor in anticipation of hosting the World's Fair, those who promoted the council were really concerned with addressing urban hunger, which was growing as a result of deindustrialization and the Reagan administration's cuts to the safety net. The council suggested that new approaches to urban-level coordination were needed to manage the emergency food system that religious groups and nonprofit organizations had developed overnight in response to the sharp rise in need. By inviting stakeholders from government, nonprofit organizations, and local businesses involved in the food system, the Knoxville Food Policy Council developed a collaborative approach to address the myriad challenges resulting from the withdrawal of the state from the social sector. Food policy councils are thus a case in point for the emergence of governance as a result of the vacuum left by neoliberal policies and the downward shift from the national government to *communities* to manage their own social reproduction. Almost immediately after it was developed, the food policy council model gained notoriety from the US Council of Mayors and other national and international bodies.[19] By the 1990s local food policy councils began to proliferate. Today, there are more than 300 food policy councils across North America.[20]

Conlin and Shulman got the idea to organize a local food policy council in 2001 after the Community Food Security Coalition (CFSC) held their annual meeting in Seattle. The CFSC had become a clearinghouse for new ideas related to food policy, particularly local food policy councils.

By then, food policy councils had been developed as a framework not just for dealing with urban food insecurity but also for supporting regional small-scale food producers whose livelihoods had also been undermined by neoliberal agricultural policies. Motivated by the meetings, a small group of local food advocates began discussing the possibility of developing a local food policy council for Seattle. The group, which ranged from progressive reformers to activists seeking broader political and legal transformation of the food system, worked together between 2001 and 2006 to publish a series of reports and white papers to raise awareness about the importance of local food as well as to identify and cultivate a local food network. During this period, the group formed the Seattle–King County Acting Food Policy Council "in response to an expressed community need for a comprehensive vision to address food security and farmer viability issues."[21] But promoters of the Seattle–King County council struggled to find the right institution and jurisdiction to which to attach the council. Conlin was clear that he did not want to create a Seattle food policy council, he told me, because the City Council was already doing a lot to promote the local food system.

One of the main challenges of finding an institutional home for a local food council was explaining to municipal and regional authorities why and how they should get involved in food production and provisioning. As Shulman, Conlin, and other members of the Seattle–King County Acting Food Policy Council searched for an institution that would support a local food policy council, they began to share their vision of governance through networks. They were not alone in promoting this approach. Just as the devolution to the local level was the product of neoliberalism, so too was the idea of governing through networks or communities. Peter Miller and Nikolas Rose describe how the idea of "government through community" arose as "a new territory for the administration of individual and collective existence, a new plan or surface upon which micro-moral relations among persons are conceptualized and administered."[22] Networks became the primary framework through which community was conceptualized. As Miller and Rose describe, communities are "nothing more—or less—than those networks of allegiance with which one identifies existentially, traditionally, emotionally or spontaneously, seemingly beyond and above any calculated assessment of self-interest."[23] In constituting a local food policy council in the Puget Sound, the Seattle–King County Acting Food Policy Council was actively disseminating this vision of governance through networks.

The Seattle–King County council was led by local elites, mostly elected officials and academics. These leaders were the ones deciding who to include and how to construct the network that would ultimately be institutionalized through this new arena of governance. Indeed, it is often elites and members of the middle class who have the social and cultural capital to develop new arenas of governance. As a result, Boaventura de Sousa Santos and Cesar Rodríguez-Garavito point out that "those at the bottom are either incorporated only once the institutional blueprint has been fully laid out or are not incorporated at all."[24] But the initial leadership of the Seattle–King County council was not necessarily determinative of the power relations produced by the council. The networked representation of community neither specified the kinds of relations nor the calculative logics that mediated social relations. Rather, it offered a set of symbols and an arena of struggle through which competing actors and groups struggled to *frame* social relations.

FRAMING THE LOCAL FOOD NETWORK

To understand how power operates through networked forms of governance, it is necessary to empirically attend to processes of framing. Framing is a symbolic and cultural process of representation through which collective action is motivated. The concept of framing has been mobilized to analyze the development of social movements,[25] the construction of markets,[26] and the governance of society.[27] Framing a sphere of social relations through a shared set of symbolic representations enables those relations to become objects of governance, or what Miller and Rose describe as "conscious political calculation."[28] Framing provides actors in networks with the evaluative and calculative criteria by which to assess their relationships.[29] It signifies the kinds of social bonds—whether those are relationships of solidarity or those mediated by the market—that are contained in networks. In the context of food systems, frames represent the agents of networks (individuals, consumers, citizens, or groups), the objects (food as a commodity or a public good), and the kinds of relations that connect them (exchange through capitalist markets or ties of social solidarity). Framing therefore determines how communities and markets are constituted by providing a cultural schema and set of values through which the meaning of *local* is constituted.

In the following subsections I describe two competing frames that were developed in relation to local food networks, what I call the market community and the political community. The market community was premised on capitalist markets as the basis for building community, whereas the political community was mobilized by food sovereignty activists to constitute social ties based on shared culture and opposition to industrial food systems as a platform for social mobilization. Examining how these two frames represented the relationship between community, markets, and authority and were mobilized by different actors reveals how local food governance provided an arena of struggle in which groups with competing values sought to contest the political rationalities of local food governance.

The Market Community

When the Seattle–King County Acting Food Policy Council was looking for an institutional home, the organization Sustainable Seattle (which Conlin co-founded in the 1990s) hired a local researcher to help define and conceptualize the meaning of the "local food economy." The researcher they hired, Viki Sonntag, was a local environmental and food activist who had recently received a PhD in evolutionary economics. Her report, *Why Local Linkages Matter: Findings from the Local Food Economy Study*, which was published in 2008, became a touchstone for local food advocates in conceptualizing the role of governance. It provided the frame through which advocates framed and promoted the Seattle–King County council.

Sonntag began her report by reframing the local food *economy* from its dominant ideology steeped in neoclassical economics—in which the economy is conceptualized through "undifferentiated price competition"[30]—to a sociological lens in which the economy is composed of a web of relationships.

> The value of relationships is that they are dynamic and unique to the local food economy. When people shop at farmers markets or eat out at neighborhood restaurants that feature sustainably grown food, they are participating in something much greater than product consumption. They are participating in community. The same goes for local food economy

businesses—they too experience community. Community is a resource that cannot be bought as a brand or copied through industrial production models. Communities are particular to the relationships involved.[31]

By situating markets within the web of relationships that constitute community, Sonntag described food not merely as an object of alienated exchange but rather as a common good.

Sonntag provided a framework for how to conceptualize the systems through which the common good was provisioned. In articulating the calculative logics through which food is exchanged, she argued that market exchange can facilitate relationships of common concern. She described weak ties as simple buy-sell relationships and strong ties as those in which individuals are motivated to spend locally because of their relationships with producers. She suggested that strong ties—such as when farmers and consumers get to know each other and even consider one another friends—encourage local consumption. Sonntag argued that strong ties should be promoted because they create a "multiplier effect" that drives economic growth and keeps money in the local economy.

> The pattern of network linkages bears a close relationship to dollar flows. In general, high local food dollar flows are associated with leveraging product variety through stronger, more highly developed relationships and a greater number of linkages, whereas low multipliers are associated with moving high volumes of commodified food.[32]

Sonntag avoided the language of ethical consumption, but her model of the local food economy was deeply shaped by the decisions of individuals to purchase locally based on their values. This was evident when she discussed the challenge of including low-income consumers in local food webs. She explained that the reason that low-income consumers do not purchase locally is that they perceive local food products as more expensive than commodity food and "expect a lot for their food dollars—in quantity, if not quality." To address this, Sonntag suggested a mix of education and cultural change to solve this problem. "The particular challenge is showing customers how offering the right products contributes to sustainability. In other words, consumer perceptions of value are critical to winning them over."[33]

This rendering of community diverges from the ways that anthropologists have understood the distinction between community and markets. Stephen Gudeman describes markets and communities as separate but mutually constitutive realms of the economy. Communities are defined by the strength of ties and the connection to what he calls the base or commons. He argues that commons can be a representation of a shared social identity, culture, social values, or a material base of sustenance. However, regardless of the form the commons take, community "has a superordinate value of the good of all taken as a whole over the good of an individual."[34] By contrast, markets are realms of impersonal exchange in which goods are exchanged through the price mechanism. Both markets and communities are different realms of economies; each produces its own inequalities, and they are premised on a critique of one another.[35] But fundamentally the community realm of the economy "is built on social values that are different from those of anonymous exchange."[36]

By contrast, the model of the community conceptualized in Sonntag's report remains premised on a liberal assumption of possessive individualism. In other words, community is constituted *through* exchange in capitalist markets. The report was packed with denunciations of the harmful effects of globalization and the commodification of food. Sonntag described how the expansion of global capitalism not only sucked money out of communities but also reduced the social life of communities to mere economics. Thus, I wondered, why had Sonntag chosen to conceptualize community through the mechanism of market exchange?

When I asked her over coffee at a local bookstore why she approached community from this vantage point, she elaborated on some of her assumptions. She told me that "the local economy is an alternative and it has the contradiction of operating within this larger system of markets that are traditionally capitalist. There are some things that it can escape from and some things it can't. In terms of market growth, I believe the relationship-based economy is different from the traditional economy, mainly because it builds social capital such as trust and relationships. Resources flow in ways that don't happen in the mainstream economy, where you have concentration and everyone is out for themselves." This theory of the local food economy contained an inherent tension. Although it sought to encourage the development of a local food economy based on social solidarity, it ultimately framed the relationships that constituted network ties through the mechanism of market exchange.[37] This assumption that market transactions formed the basis for relationships had important implications for governance. For example, when I probed more into what Sonntag thought the role of government was in shaping the local food network, she told me that the primary arena for change was ultimately in shaping consumer behavior: "I would say you could use the metaphor of organic and sustainable farming for what kind of marketplace you want to have, so there are ways that you could do that in the marketplace and, so far as I'm concerned, there are probably more opportunities there than there are in policy."

This framing of local food networks played a significant role in what would become the PSRFPC by representing the local food system in ways that rendered it governable. First, it defined localism not as a geographically bound entity but as a web of relationships or network that expanded beyond jurisdictions. In her report Sonntag described at length how any boundaries of "local" food are arbitrary and artificial, instead arguing that it is best to understand the local food system as a network rather than as a fixed geographic jurisdiction. This helped to allay concerns of policymakers who worried that governing food was beyond their jurisdiction of authority. Second, by conceptualizing local food exchange somewhat ambiguously as a network of relations, Sonntag offered a symbolic representation that provided future members of the PSRFPC with a set of political and calculative logics in which their responsibility was not "regulation" so much as facilitating the "web of relations" and educating each other about the value of localism to build strong communities.

Sonntag's report was presented to the Puget Sound Regional Council (PSRC), a metropolitan planning organization, which was considering hosting what had previously operated as the Seattle–King County council. Eventually, the PSRC agreed to host the council as an "independent forum."[38] Although the PSRC has little actual authority over food and agriculture, its eighty jurisdictions, including cities and Indigenous tribes across four counties, better reflected the spatial scale of local food networks. Modeled on the networked form, the PSRFPC was finally institutionalized as an arena of collaborative governance. It was premised on the belief that stakeholders of the food system could work together to solve problems and develop collaborative solutions to help build a fair "thriving, inclusive and just local and regional food system that enhances the health of people, diverse communities, economies, and environments."[39] Its founding document defines the "food system" as "the network of people and activities connecting growing and harvesting, processing, distribution, consumption, and residue utilization, as well as associated government and non-government institutions, regulations and programs." This vision was further elaborated in the PSRFPC's guiding principles, which state that the PSRFPC "envisions a thriving, inclusive and just local and regional food system that enhances the health of: people, diverse communities, economies, and environments."[40]

In 2010 the PSRFPC began operation. Membership in the council was formalized with about thirty members that spread across the four-county region of the PSRC. Members were solicited by the leaders of the PSRFPC, through individual connections and discussions about who was missing from the roster of members. Members then had to apply to participate. Between 2010 and 2014 the PSRFPC met monthly in a building overlooking Elliott Bay in downtown Seattle. Over the course of my two years of participant observation, a core group of members regularly attended these meetings. The group included officials from city and county agencies, city council members from towns and cities in the four-county region, and academics from Washington State University and the University of Washington. Several nonprofit organizations and tribal organizations attended the council less regularly but still took part occasionally.

As food sovereignty activists from CAGJ and other organizations began to participate in the PSRFPC, they offered an alternative framing of local food networks that contained different assumptions. It was soon clear that there were other framings of the local food network that conceptualized markets, communities, and authority quite differently.

Food Sovereignty and the Political Community

In the early 2000s, as Conlin was laying the groundwork for the formation of the PSRFPC, he told me that he had a hard time identifying stakeholders to participate in the council. At first, he could identify only two: emergency food providers and the community garden program that the city had administered since the 1970s. Beyond those stakeholders, "there was also sort of a general social movement perspective of food as an issue. There were a lot of people engaged in organic food and things of that nature, but they were amorphous." One of the goals of forming the food policy council was therefore to create a space in which social movements could actively represent their interests and values. By the time the PSRFPC began its operation, many social movements were advocating for different elements of local food—from farmland preservation, to healthy diets, to urban farming. Only one organization, CAGJ, was using the framework of food sovereignty, however. CAGJ was invited to be a member of the PSRFPC.

CAGJ offered a different framing of local food networks from the market community frame. By drawing on the claim of food sovereignty, CAGJ sought to politicize local food systems and highlight the asymmetries of power that shape both disparities in access to local food and benefits from local food markets. In their "cookbook," *Our Food, Our Right: Recipes for Food Justice*, which was published in 2012, CAGJ described their view of local food networks.

> Eating locally isn't just about the exponentially expanding network of farmers' markets, getting your CSA box, growing some kale, and buying Fair Trade and organic. Those are certainly part of it, but "voting with your dollar" can only go so far when pitted against the conventional, corporate, industrial food system. For example, consider the large number of people who cannot afford these normally expensive items or the plight of conventional food workers and producers who are exploited in the food chain. And this is exactly the point. Consumers cannot simply buy a better food system. Only systemic, political, and social change brought about by diverse groups of people can build real alternatives to the broken way we produce and eat our food. How we grow and eat our food is too important an issue to keep in the hands of a few profit-driven decision makers who have enforced policies and practices that turn food into a commodity rather than treating it as a basic human need and right with intimate ties to place and culture.[41]

Activists in CAGJ made clear their opposition to the individualist approach to social change by "voting with your fork," which had become the rallying cry for consumer-centered approaches to local food movements.[42] They argued that mainstream local food movements threatened to reproduce economic and racial inequalities by leaving markets as the unquestioned and natural relations among people. As food sovereignty activists Eric Holt-Giménez and Yi Wang explain, the consumer-driven approach to localization "not only takes the access and purchasing power of the predominantly white, middle-class consumer for granted, but also it assumes that our food system can be reformed through informed consumer choice, and ignores the ways working-class and people of color have historically brought about social change."[43]

This was certainly true in Seattle. Minority farmers were often excluded from the benefits of Seattle's thriving local farmers markets. One Hmong farmer that I spoke to made this disparity clear to me.[44] Although Hmong farmers grew excellent products, often without chemical inputs, he explained that they often had trouble selling at local farmers markets. "The Hmong farmers come from very different backgrounds, so the concept of selling yourself, selling your identity, selling your entity, building a brand or a name for yourself, is very foreign," he told me. "It's hard for Hmong farmers to grasp and then to implement this concept. They often cannot compete with traditional farmers who already have brands, who can talk to the customer, who can communicate and build better relationships with the customers. So Hmong farmers are at a disadvantage." By "traditional farmers" he meant white farmers. Down the street from where he farmed in the Snoqualmie Valley, a family from Capitol Hill had established one of the most successful farms in the region, largely because of their networks of friends and family in the region. They had become celebrated by local foodies and were a popular presence at the Capitol Hill farmers market. As the Hmong farmer told me, "It's more about relationships than the products themselves."

CAGJ and other food sovereignty activists therefore sought to denaturalize the network as a relationship based on market exchange. Instead, they wanted to reframe local food networks as a *political* community, a set of social bonds connected by social solidarity. They drew on practices of movement building and network formation with other food sovereignty activists that were rooted in opposition to the industrial food system, a commitment to egalitarian political and economic transformation, and their view of food not as a commodity but as a common good. At a local level CAGJ and other food sovereignty activists emphasized their shared social values to constitute networked social ties. This approach to cultivating community is more in line with what Gudeman describes as the realm of community constituted by a shared social base.

CAGJ tried to construct this political community by developing relationships with different constituencies and movements for food sovereignty across the Puget Sound. For example, it forged close ties with unionized workers at grocery retailers when it helped lead a campaign against building permits for a nonunion grocery store. It later deepened its ties with Indigenous communities by organizing against the introduction of genetically engineered salmon into Washington State. It supported small-scale family farmers in the Snoqualmie Valley who faced struggles from flooding. And it organized boycotts and raised funding for farmworkers as they went on strike and fought for a union. These ties of solidarity across different constituencies served to build a political community that could mobilize for more expansive political, social, and environmental transformation.

By the time I began my research, CAGJ had stopped regularly attending the PSRFPC meetings because of limited staffing resources. However, another food sovereignty organization, the Muckleshoot Food Sovereignty Project (MFSP), soon replaced it. The Muckleshoot are one of the traditional Coast Salish inhabitants of the Puget Sound. They are a federally recognized tribe that historically resided between the White and Green Rivers at the base of Mt. Rainier. Today, many tribal members reside in a reservation just 35 miles southeast of Seattle. Valerie Segrest, a nutrition educator, founded the MFSP in 2007 while working in the Muckleshoot community to address diet-related illnesses such as obesity and type 2 diabetes. She saw food sovereignty as a way not only to address these health disparities but also to build Indigenous sovereignty. As she told me, "Food sovereignty means the right to define our own diet. . . . Our food is our culture. For us, food sovereignty means the right to practice our culture."

Segrest was invited to be a stakeholder of the PSRFPC when I was observing the council between 2013 and 2014. During one of the first meetings that she attended, she was asked to give a presentation on the work of the MFSP. During her talk, she showed images of the traditional food map that she had developed with a local artist. The map located the traditional and accustomed hunting grounds on Mount Tahoma (Rainier), where the community could harvest clams, mussels, nettles, and horsetails, berries, and other traditional foods. As she showed images of these places on the map, she emphasized the importance of food for both the cultural identity of the Muckleshoot and their political sovereignty. She explained this through her own personal history, telling the PSRFPC,

> My ancestor Pat-ka-nam was one of the original signers of the Treaty of Point Elliott, and there's some ethnographic recordings of his speech given during that time, and the very first thing that he talked about was access to foods—that we were not even to be discussing land agreements without considering our access to all of the wild game and the roots and the fish and the berries and the cedar tree until time ceases to exist. And that to me is food sovereignty. It's in our oral traditions and our belief system that when we cease to exist, so do we as a people. That's why it's so important for us to be active citizens in our food system, and that's why this initiative is nothing new really. It's just about remembering what we know to be true and right and celebrating those traditions with one another. As you can tell, there are many opportunities for the food policy council to help support food sovereignty initiatives in Muckleshoot and many local tribes.[45]

In her framing, local food networks were about communal identity, common resources, and political control. However, they did not exclude market-based forms of exchange. After all, the Muckleshoot sold fish through an enterprise called Muckleshoot Seafood Products. For the Muckleshoot, however, their land, resources, and identity formed the base of the community from which the local food economy and food sovereignty were constructed.[46]

When I spoke to her about her vision of food sovereignty and the local food economy, Segrest also drew on language of the network. For her, the network was rooted in communal rather than market relationships: "Our food system precontact was a system of economics; it was based on social status. How well you were networked meant how much diversity there was in your diet. That might be why we only eat 13–20 foods in a year. We talk about increasing diversity in our diet, but we also need to expand the relationships between people." This framing of the network as a community based on shared knowledge, culture, identities, land, access to resources, and solidarity has been echoed by other Indigenous scholars to reconceptualize Indigenous sovereignty. Indigenous scholars have turned the metaphor of the relational network to escape from the Western emphasis on exclusive territorial control.[47] Mississauga Nishnaabeg scholar and activist Leanne Betasamosake Simpson explains,

> Nishnaabeg life didn't rely on institutionality to hold the structure of life. We relied upon process that created networked relationship. Our intelligence system is a series of interconnected and overlapping algorithms—stories, ceremonies, and the land itself are procedures for solving the problems of life. Networked because the modes of communication and interaction between beings occur in complex nonlinear forms, across time and space. Governance was *made* every day. Leadership was embodied and acted out every day.[48]

Simpson's description of Indigenous forms of networked governance as comprising everyday knowledges, affinities, and identities celebrates networked forms of sovereignty not as a product of neoliberal "responsibilization" but rather as a form of governance through community that is a product of ongoing creation and struggle. This model of sovereignty does not depend on institutions but rather on autonomous relationships of governance. It provides one model for noncapitalist, postliberal democratic politics.

Indigenous claims for political and food sovereignty are based on the identities, histories, relations to land, and epistemologies of Indigenous peoples. However, they have been deeply influential in shaping claims and practices to food sovereignty. CAGJ was a largely white organization on unceded land, but in translating food sovereignty and constructing networks, they too emphasized the importance of food as a cultural object, a set of relationships tied to place, and a set of oppositional social and political values to extractive economies. In challenging the commodification of food, they built communities that could act as political constituencies to mobilize for political and legal transformation, not just at the local level but at the national and global levels as well. They sought to subordinate market-based forms of exchange to community control.

THE STRUGGLE OVER FARMERS MARKETS

These two frames of the local food network were in constant tension throughout my observation of the PSRFPC. Although the market community frame suggested that the PSRFPC's primary responsibility was to support localization efforts through education and building connections between producers and consumers, the political community frame suggested that the PSRFPC's role was to build relationships and coalitions that could serve as a political constituency to challenge the industrial food system and demand regulation that would promote more equitable relationships in the food system. However, these two frames were rarely in direct conflict because the PSRFPC scarcely made decisions in which one frame had to be chosen over the other. The few moments that I observed in which these frames were in conflict therefore provide a window into the way that power was mediated and negotiated through the practice of governance on the PSRFPC.

One of the disputes in which this tension was made clear was during a process when the PSRFPC was commissioned to develop policy recommendations for Seattle's farmers markets in 2013 and 2014. Seattle's farmers markets were already a site of political contention on two fronts. First, in 2011 low-income consumers began to organize in South Seattle to push for more access to farmers markets. Although there were several markets throughout the affluent northern part of Seattle, there was only one stable farmers market on the south side of Seattle. Got Green, a people-of-color-led organization, led a campaign to extend Supplemental Nutrition Assistance Program (SNAP) benefits at Seattle farmers markets after they conducted a survey and found that food access was the number one issue that women of color faced in South Seattle. After one year of petitions, demonstrations, and lobbying, Seattle created the Fresh Bucks program. The program was initially funded by Chase Bank (the corporation that had been awarded the lucrative contract to administer electronic SNAP benefits), but after the grant ran out, Seattle was pressed to continue funding the program.

Farmers markets organizations were also pushing the city for funding. This funding was necessary, the director of one of the local farmers market associations told me, to ensure that the markets were profitable for farmers. As she explained to me, "It's not a real economy." She meant that farmers markets were not a "free market"; they were highly curated and managed. The association intentionally made stall fees low to ensure that farmers would be profitable. They also required a great deal of management to ensure that there would not be too many farmers selling the same products and thus facing too much competition. For example, they could not have too many people selling peaches, because then all the farms selling peaches would each make less money. The price of organizing the highly managed market meant that farmers market associations were not sustainable on their own. At least a quarter of their funding came from sponsorships and grants from the city, which supported the staff time and marketing necessary for farmers to be profitable. The director of the farmers market associations told me that farmers market organizations provide farmers with "a subsidized sales opportunity, which they may not totally understand."

The subsidies that both producers and consumers received from the city made farmers markets an ambiguous policy area. As one Seattle official told me, the City of Seattle saw farmers markets as a "private market activity." However, they also saw farmers markets as a public good; farmers markets provided neighborhoods with a sense of community, created opportunities for local farmers, artists, and entrepreneurs, and contributed to healthy diets. To manage this tension, the City of Seattle therefore provided a small grant to the PSRFPC to "study the obstacles to the stability of farmers' markets and develop potential solutions to these projects."[49] Although the contract was with the City of Seattle, members hoped to develop broad solutions that would work for other jurisdictions as well.

When discussion began in the PSRFPC about potential obstacles to farmers market viability, it was clear that members understood farmers markets in different ways. One member explained that local jurisdictions' policies depended on how they saw farmers markets, explaining that they could be seen as "a tool used to build equity, [an] opportunity for small business economically, or [a way of] educating our children and having a place for them to go gather." As PSRFPC members discussed it more, some argued that the issue was clearly related to the public good. The PSRFPC had, after all, convened to strengthen local food systems with the idea that access to local food had a number of benefits, from improving public health to mitigating urban food insecurity. "There is a public outcome and public commitment. . . . It is not simply a free market; this is very contrived and controlled," one PSRFPC member explained.

Others, however, struggled to reconcile the private market interests with the benefits to the community. During their open discussion, one member thought out loud as she explained to the PSRFPC, "You have this two-tier level organization; you end up having profit-making on one side and you have losses on the other, so it creates a difficulty in terms of figuring out how you are going to manage public policy because there are so many competing demands. The market organization needs the funds, the farmers are trying to maximize their profits, and it creates an enormous amount of complexity with the choices involved." These debates over the public or private nature of the farmers markets reflected the competing frames of the local food network. Was the PSRFPC's goal to simply promote the creation of local markets? Or should the PSRFPC take an active political role in promoting government intervention to create equitable markets?

This debate became more adversarial as specific issues of government regulation came up. When the PSRFPC began to discuss the contentious issue of the location of farmers markets, one member, an academic who was aligned with the food sovereignty/political community framing, suggested that the jurisdiction should develop a system of regulation to ensure that farmers markets were evenly spread across both wealthy and low-income neighborhoods. Given that farmers benefit from many other government regulations—including zoning regulation to allow farmers markets as well as grants to support the organizations that coordinate and manage the market—he suggested that farmers markets should also be equitably distributed. This drew a strong rebuke from several farmers on the PSRFPC. One rancher responded, "I'm the guy that represents or has to deal with some of the people that actually have the booths in those locations. . . . This is a market-driven thing, not a social-engineered thing." In counterposing the market versus social engineering, he disparaged state intervention into the market. Another rancher responded that her concern was that, when farmers go to the market, it was important to "make sure there's enough business to make it worth their while." In turn, the member who first proposed the idea, defended it, arguing that "unless we want a bunch of raging individualist farmers to go out of business because they're always on the edge . . . we may need to think differently." In his comments, he challenged the individualist framing of the local food network, emphasizing the importance of government intervention into the market to ensure equity in access to markets and to ensure that farmers were profitable. In doing so, he emphasized the constructed nature of markets and the underlying regulations and values that drive support for farmers markets.

As the debate became heated in the conference room, Conlin intervened: "The thing I want to take from that part of the discussion is that there's a really big difference between having a management [approach] and putting together a cooperative or collaborative approach that has central coordination." In this moment he aimed to diffuse tension, reminding PSRFPC members of the imperative of *collaboration*. At the time, however, it struck me as his effort to suppress this political conflict.

When I asked Conlin and Shulman about this intervention a few weeks later, their comments reflected a tension between encouraging collaboration and conflict. Conlin contrasted the politics of collaboration with what he called the Chicago model of acrimonious and adversarial politics, one in which there was intractable conflict. He presented collaboration as a morally superior mode of politics that relied on people to solve conflicts through dialogue. He acknowledged that the consensus model could "really be bad when it goes to the wrong place because sometimes it's a recipe for delay and cannot really tackle hard issues. If it's done right, though, it can be really, really good." Similarly, Shulman told me how she relished the "juicy conversations" when conflict came up, recalling another heated conversation about farmworker rights that I had observed. In her rendering, collaboration was a process that served to cultivate personal and social transformation.

> So much that gets done in the world is about relationships, and we have a political structure that gets structured in certain [negative] ways. If you look through that, however, it is all about relationships. . . . We have to be doing cross-disciplinary collaboration, different kinds of ways to think about things, different kinds of value frames in a conversation. I think we have to get really good at it, and we have to think about how to really nurture that process. I think there is a learning curve because people have to learn different ways of being and how to be in groups and how to get work done that is in some ways somewhat slower. . . . In many ways we are talking about culture change, and I guess system change, in that then you create the conditions that support the kind of world you want. And to be able to do that needs more than one person's ideology or one person's authority.

Shulman described collaboration as a process of trust building and mutual self-transformation rather than as a technology of depoliticization.

I understood Conlin and Shulman's approach to collaboration and their evasion of my questions to frame the network not as a form of depoliticization but rather as an effort to allow space for both of these frames. After all, Conlin and Shulman were deeply dedicated to local food systems. They had leveraged the authority of the Seattle City Council to support local food through the pathbreaking Local Food Action Initiative. By inviting food sovereignty organizations and activists from marginalized communities to participate in the PSRFPC, they sought to bring these voices into the policymaking process and potentially cultivate constituencies for more widespread political and economic transformation. At the same time, though, the market community frame also had appeal to participants in the network, who were more focused on creating economic growth and opportunities for entrepreneurship. Given the historical inequalities of land ownership, this tended to favor white farmers and ranchers. Collaboration for Conlin and Shulman was thus not an instrumental process or a language of forced consensus but rather a more ambiguous and potentially volatile process of conflict and transformation.

This approach engendered mixed responses from many of the participants I spoke to. One member of the PSRFPC who had served on the council for four years told me that she was still struggling to understand the purpose of the PSRFPC. When I asked her why it was important to have this forum, she explained that multistakeholder bodies "eliminate the silos. So, if you look at [the PSRFPC] as a place to share information and a place to gather information, then you're good." Similarly, another member who had served on the PSRFPC since it began said to me that it was a "slow-moving train." "I get really really frustrated more than any group I've been on. There's so many people on that . . . and still I've been on there four years. I don't know what our direction is." Meanwhile, the leaders of the PSRFPC, those on the Steering Committee, were certain that they were having an impact, even if they were having trouble articulating and demonstrating it to others. In one of the Steering Committee meetings, a participant explained that the council should find a way to present its accomplishments in the PSRFPC because they were "kinda squishy and not so hard." One attendee summarized the struggle to elaborate their impact by responding, "Everybody is asking what we have done, but when you're not a for-profit business, where you measure your impact by your profit, how do we measure it?"

This challenge of measurement ultimately reflected the PSRFPC's lack of consensus over its shared values. However, as anthropologist David Graeber reminds us, "The ultimate stakes of politics . . . is the struggle to establish what value *is*."[50] The struggle over the farmers market thus reflected the competing values and frames mobilized by different members of the PSRFPC. Thus, although the council may have potentially reinforced neoliberal subjectivities by embedding sociomoral concerns in the market, it also could serve to constitute political constituencies and build alliances for larger political and economic transformation. The PSRFPC thus provided an arena for this struggle. It offered food sovereignty activists a platform against which to further refine their autonomous practices beyond the governmental gaze, to articulate new understandings of the relationship between community and market, and to make visible the constitutive outsides of the capitalist food system.

CONCLUSIONS

During the first meeting I attended of the Puget Sound Regional Food Policy Council in 2012, I listened to a presentation by a local tech entrepreneur as he presented the "Food Web Food Policy Landscape Map." The speaker pulled up an image of an illustrated tree that he had projected onto a screen at the front of a large conference room. Across the roots, branches, and leaves of the tree, different actors in the local food system were displayed, including farmers, government agencies, nonprofits, and "food citizens." As he clicked around the tree, he described to the council members why he had created this virtual tool. By graphically depicting all the various nodes of the local food system, he hoped they would "design and implement a new form of network that will weave together efforts and steward integration and collaboration over time." Seamlessly blending technological and organic metaphors, the speaker suggested that cultivating a local food system simply required collaboration.

Throughout my time observing the PSRFPC, its promoters worked continuously to reaffirm this networked representation of the local food system to make the food system governable. For example, during one heated conversation, the co-chairs told the council, "There are lots of eaters in our communities, and when we talk about the food system, we need to expand our network of discussion. . . . That network will help provide a structure for collaborating more broadly." Through this continual reaffirmation of the network representation of social and economic relations, leaders of the PSRFPC sought to build relations between those involved in the food system, for they too were engaging in a practice of translation, but one that refused any allegiance to any substantive norms or specific social values.

The PSRFPC thus became an arena in which different actors engaged in struggles to frame the network. Framing, as I have described in this chapter, is a cultural and interpretive process that makes possible the calculative agencies that are involved in mediating social relations. Anthropologist Kregg Hetherington emphasizes that the purpose of framing is to determine the kinds of relations within networks. Using the language of Marilyn Strathern, he argues that framing serves to cut the network by ending the infinite interplay of interpretation.[51] His point is not that framing prevents the extension of networks but rather that dominant or accepted frames assert the primacy of particular social values and calculative logics, stabilizing and giving meaning to a set of relationships. In the PSRFPC the market community frame and the political community frame each asserted different values and calculative logics. The market community sought to construct community through individual decisions and consumption in capitalist markets. By contrast, the political community, which was promoted by food sovereignty activists, sought to create communal relations based on shared values, knowledge, and culture. By mobilizing this frame, activists formed a political constituency that could subordinate capitalist markets to the needs of the community and thereby mobilize communities for social and political change.[52] As they articulated this framing of food sovereignty in dialectical relation to competing representations of the network, they not only influenced the framing of the network within the PSRFPC but also cultivated a shared set of meanings and practices of "local" for themselves. In this chapter I have therefore emphasized that even the local is a site of translation through which rival actors seek to enroll others into networks shaped by particular social values, norms, and calculative logics.[53]

The conflict between the two frames in the PSRFPC serves as a microcosm of a larger dispute over the progressive possibilities of both local food movements and collaborative planning and governance. Many critics have illuminated how localization and local food governance can limit the horizons of political change and produce neoliberal subjectivities in which politics becomes limited to consumption and anemic forms of participation. Given that neoliberalism created the conditions for the devolution of governance, critical scholars suggest that arenas of networked governance operate in the shadow of neoliberal inequalities and embed social relations in the rationality of the market. However, these proliferating arenas of governance need not serve only to embed neoliberal subjectivity; they can also serve as spaces that illuminate alternative configurations of communities and markets.

Ultimately, for food sovereignty movements, the "local" is not a homogeneous, self-sufficient community that acts as a bulwark against the market. The "local" is just one geographic scale at which food sovereignty activists seek to construct relations of social solidarity and constitute political constituencies that can subordinate the market to social values. Arenas of collaborative local food governance thus serve as critical spaces of struggle for food sovereignty activists to dialectically develop practices of translation, articulate frames, and make visible the antagonisms and power inequalities that are necessary for political change. Although participation in these arenas comes with risks, they also serve as a critical space in which competing networks and values are exposed. By engaging in these arenas of food sovereignty, activists not only have the potential to shape the institutional practices of governance and norms produced through local food governance but can also constitute new relations among themselves and provide alternative imaginaries of social organization. In the next chapter I describe how another form of neoliberal governance, private governance through global value chains, is emerging as yet another arena of struggle through which food sovereignty activists are dialectically constituting alternative value practices across different constituencies.

3   Revaluing Agricultural Labor

IN 2011 THE FIRST US Food Sovereignty National Assembly began with farmworker leader Rosalinda Guillen reciting Cesar Chavez's "Prayer of the Farmworker's Struggle." "Show me the suffering of the most miserable; / so I will know my people's plight," the poem began. The prayer is a meditation on the strength and resilience of farmworkers who work in one of the most dangerous and low-paid occupations in the United States. It is also about the need to build collective relations of solidarity with other workers and with adversaries to improve these conditions. "Give me honesty and patience; / so that I can work with other workers . . . / Help us love even those who hate us; / so we can change the world," the prayer continues. Guillen's recitation of the prayer at the US Food Sovereignty National Assembly was a powerful reminder of the value that food sovereignty movements place on those most marginalized in the food and agricultural system. In the United States farmworkers have therefore emerged at the forefront of the food sovereignty movement.

The inclusion and leadership of farmworkers in the food sovereignty movement stands in stark contrast to most agrarian movements in US history. Past agrarian movements have drawn on the powerful symbol of the "idealized agrarian vision of soil-and-toil harmony on family farms," as Margaret Gray puts it, to assert political influence.[1] Farmworkers' exclusion from this imagery reflects the long history of settler colonial agriculture, which has relied on racial distinctions to devalue and exploit agricultural labor since the formation of the colonial plantation. Although small-scale family farmers and farmworkers have a shared interest in preventing the devaluation of farm labor by large-scale industrial agriculture, they have rarely worked together. In large part, this is because white small-scale farmers have been able to draw on the symbolic value of their labor stemming from romantic agrarian imaginaries to market their products in niche and "alternative" markets. Julie Guthman argues that the alternative agriculture movement's reliance on this exclusionary narrative is what led it to reproduce agrarian inequalities in the development of the organic sector.[2] Yet as a growing number of small-scale farmers recognize the limits of these markets in addressing the structural inequalities caused by the industrial food system, they too are turning to food sovereignty to challenge this imaginary and the conditions that lower the value of *all* labor in the food and agricultural system. As small-scale farmers and farmworkers attempt to translate food sovereignty across their differences, they are constructing new alliances and networks through which they are not just challenging *what* food systems value but also *how* they value.

In this chapter I examine how farmworkers and small-scale farmers are translating food sovereignty in the United States to transform the governance of agricultural labor. In contrast to the last chapter, which focused on the representational practices of translocal translation that food sovereignty movements have developed through their engagement with local food governance, here I analyze how farmworkers have cultivated networks in relation to the private forms of regulation that have proliferated with neoliberalism. In doing so, I focus on another key dimension of translation: commensuration. As I described in chapter 1, commensuration is the social and communicative practice through which objects, persons, and ideas that are understood as distinct in nature are made equivalent and comparable. Both capitalism and liberalism rely on social processes of commensuration to enable commodification and market exchange and to produce formal *individual* equality. Labor movements have consistently challenged processes of commensuration to resist the commodification of their labor. Counterhegemonic coalitions also often resist commensuration by developing alternative value practices that enable diverse groups to construct solidaristic ties while recognizing meaningful differences. Therefore

I examine the alternative value practices of translocal translation that have been key to cultivating relationships between diverse constituencies in food sovereignty movements.

Farmworkers and other constituencies of the food sovereignty movement have constituted these value practices in response to shifting forms of labor governance. For the past several decades, as states have rolled back labor protections to encourage private investment, private firms have grown powerful in setting the terms and conditions of labor and in exercising control over the entire production process across borders. As a result of market liberalization, production in both the agricultural and manufacturing sectors has been increasingly restructured through global value chains (GVCs)—networks of interfirm relations in which powerful firms exercise control or *governance* across the entire chain through formal and informal standards through which they create (or extract) value.[3] The rise of value chain governance has been criticized for privatizing labor regulation and enabling corporations to dictate the conditions of work in lieu of state regulation.[4] Although GVCs have certainly facilitated greater corporate control of food systems, my analysis suggests that by constituting their claims and cultivating alternative value practices in relation to GVCs, food sovereignty movements are also shaping private governance from below.

I focus on one struggle over farm labor that emerged during my fieldwork in Skagit County, Washington, an hour north of Seattle. There, a group of 500 workers worked with Guillen's organization, Community to Community Development (C2C), to organize an independent farmworker association and union, Familias Unidas por la Justicia (FUJ). In their four-year struggle to collectively bargain a contract in which they could codetermine their wages and working conditions, FUJ drew on a combination of legal mobilization and translocal translation of food sovereignty to develop a more expansive justice claim than they were able to do through litigation alone. In its first year of organizing, FUJ engaged in successful legal mobilization to protect its rights to organize, to win restitution for the most egregious harms of its employer, and to politicize private governance of the berry value chain. But it was ultimately by assembling a counternetwork of small-scale producers and other food sovereignty activists to challenge the informal governance standards of the value chain within which they worked that FUJ was able to improve both their own working conditions and those across the entire value chain. I argue that the value practices constituted in relation to GVCs prefigured new forms of food system governance that transcended both the industrial and the romantic agrarian ideal that has consistently reproduced racialized agrarian inequalities.

This chapter draws on ethnographic fieldwork I undertook between 2013 and 2015 with the workers and supporters of FUJ. Over that period I volunteered to document the conditions of farm labor, participated in boycott committees across the Puget Sound region, organized fundraisers, and wrote about the labor dispute for local publications. In the first part of this chapter I briefly trace how the doctrine of agricultural exceptionalism shaped the racialized regulation of farmworker labor and its impact on past generations of farmworker movements. I then discuss how neoliberalism has produced not only a new regulatory landscape but also a new racialized farm labor force. In the second part of this chapter, I describe how farmworkers in the Pacific Northwest responded by claiming food sovereignty and how they have cultivated creative practices of translocal translation alongside the fresh berry value chain to improve their working conditions.

FARMWORKERS AND US LABOR LAW

In the United States struggles over agricultural labor are as old as the nation itself. Although Thomas Jefferson waxed poetic about the small-scale yeoman farmer, he was himself a Southern planter and slave owner. In fact, by the time of his presidency, many farmers were integrated into commercial markets.[5] Yet Jefferson's agrarian ideal nonetheless served as a powerful cultural imaginary. It celebrated the masculine, white, small-scale farmer as the basis for an agrarian democracy, excluding the unfree labor on which the plantation system depended. Large-scale agricultural production in the United States has long relied on exploited labor. From the enslavement of Africans and their descendants on Southern plantations by rendering people as property, to the proscription of nonwhite immigrants of naturalization rights,[6] to the exclusion of agricultural labor from the workplace protections extended to workers in other sectors, public law has served primarily to facilitate a racialized and docile agricultural labor force. Guadalupe Luna describes this situation as "agricultural exceptionalism," the doctrine that has continuously provided farmers and the agricultural industry with exemptions to federal labor legislation.[7]

One of the clearest examples of the doctrine of agricultural exceptionalism is the National Labor Relations Act (NLRA). In 1935 farmworkers and domestic workers were excluded from both the NLRA and the Fair Labor Standards Act (1938), two pieces of New Deal legislation that institutionalized the relationship between the state, capital, and labor during the mid-twentieth century.[8] Soon after the NLRA was passed, Congress recognized the horrid conditions of farmworkers. A subcommittee in the US Senate led by Robert La Follette reported that California workers were "miserable beyond belief" and that the California Chamber of Commerce "could conceive but one objective: the suppression by all available means of the unrest among agricultural employees."[9] However, rather than addressing the racialized exclusion of farmworkers by providing them with collective bargaining rights, Congress instead passed piecemeal legislation that addressed only specific work practices.[10]

In their struggles to assert self-determination, agricultural workers have therefore been skeptical of law. The zenith of farmworker organizing is typically associated with the 1960s and 1970s, when the United Farm Workers (UFW) in California made significant advances in expanding their rights. Cesar Chavez and Dolores Huerta organized the National Farm Workers Association (which eventually became the UFW) in 1962 amid struggles by farmworkers against the Bracero Program.[11] Chavez and Huerta did not come from a traditional union-organizing background but rather from a community-organizing background. They approached the issue of farmworker exploitation from a social movement perspective, drawing on a shared Chicano/a identity as well as nonviolent tactics from the civil rights movement to build the power of farmworkers on large-scale commercial farms in California. In addition to traditional labor action such as strikes, the UFW allied with consumers to bring attention to the plight of farmworkers.[12]

Yet although the UFW drew on the civil rights movement's discourses, its members were skeptical of litigation and legal mobilization as the primary strategy of social change. Through her interviews with the legal staff of the UFW, labor law scholar Jennifer Gordon describes how litigation was always subordinated to the political aims and organizing tactics of the UFW. The goal of lawyers, Gordan writes, was "to open the field for organizing and to advance the union's ultimate goal of large-scale farmworker representation."[13] Attorneys would challenge injunctions, defend supporters and organizers who had been placed in detention, and litigate to protect workers' rights to organize.[14]

Chavez and Huerta were particularly attuned to the demobilizing effects of public law. Chavez opposed incorporating farmworkers into the NLRA, which by then had been significantly decapacitated by subsequent judicial and legislative modifications that limited the abilities of labor movements to strike.[15] Asked why he was opposed, Chavez told *The Nation* magazine in 1971 that it "would take away the only non-violent tools available to us."[16] Nonetheless, amid one of the largest strikes in farmworker history, the UFW took a $1.6 million contribution from the AFL-CIO on the condition that the union pursue an agricultural labor relations law.[17] When elected governor in 1974, Jerry Brown worked with the UFW to develop the California Agricultural Labor Relations Act. Although the law that was ultimately passed contained many of the provisions demanded by the UFW, it was not long before the premonitions of Chavez came true. Struggles in the Agricultural Labor Relations Board sucked the energy out of organizing and into the administrative process. Growers focused their energies on defunding and eventually taking control of the board altogether.

During the 1980s and 1990s, the farmworker movement declined. By the time of Chavez's death, the UFW had only a few contracts covering 5,000 workers, compared to the 60,000 workers covered under 120 contracts in the early 1980s.[18] The story of the UFW's decline is more complex than the juridification of farm labor in California; internal conflicts and problems within the UFW played a significant role.[19] However, farmworkers' experience with the California Agricultural Labor Relations Act offers important insights into the role of legalization. Jennifer Gordon argues that labor law may have a cyclical effect, at once opening up some opportunities while foreclosing others: "Seeking the aid of the state is always a double-edged sword, not only dangerous or only helpful but both simultaneously. The passage of a new law creates new obstacles and new opportunities for players already engaged in an ongoing game."[20] Although Chavez may have faltered in engaging with the California labor act, if the NLRA is any indication, it is unlikely that the California law would have continued to empower farmworkers; today, US labor law has actively impeded labor organization and has drawn it into a technocratic legal struggle.[21] Gordon therefore suggests that the lesson of the

UFW and the Agricultural Labor Relations Act is that law instead should be seen as creating windows of opportunity to build power. As neoliberalism took hold in the late 1980s and 1990s, these lessons would prove useful for food sovereignty movements.

NEOLIBERALISM AND THE PRIVATE
GOVERNANCE OF FARM LABOR

Neoliberalism transformed the rural landscape in innumerable ways. During the 1980s, rising global competition for agricultural goods led the farm sector in the United States, especially small-scale farmers, to face its worst crisis since the Great Depression.[22] Meanwhile, the US farmworker labor force was almost completely replaced as a result of two major political changes. First, neoliberal structural adjustment policies and free trade agreements forced peasant farmers in Mexico to migrate northward in search of work. In the 1980s the International Monetary Fund and the World Bank required the Mexican government to reduce its public expenditures, privatize state enterprises, and liberalize the economy in exchange for loans to service its foreign debt. As a result of these structural adjustment policies, many *campesinos* lost access to credit and technical assistance. Peasant farmers faced further pressure when Mexico agreed to the North American Free Trade Agreement (NAFTA) in 1994 and the price of maize dropped below the costs of production for Mexican farmers. As a result, migration surged. Second, in 1986 the United States passed the Immigration Reform and Control Act, which offered a generation of migrant farmworkers legal status. Many farmworkers took advantage of this new legal status to transition into other, higher paid sectors.[23] For the UFW and other established farmworker organizations, this loss of workers undermined years of organizing work in which they had raised the consciousness of farmworkers and built structures of solidarity and resistance. It also provided commercial producers with a new generation of undocumented workers who lacked the organization of previous workers.

Whereas *roll-back* neoliberalism in agriculture provided large-scale producers in the United States with a new agricultural workforce and forced many small-scale farmers out of farming, *roll-out* neoliberalism transformed the structure and governance of agriculture and farm labor.[24] As a result of the liberalization of agriculture through NAFTA and the World Trade Organization, transnational corporations—especially retailers, processors, and other firms not directly involved in agricultural production—grew immensely powerful. As states rolled back regulation of their agricultural sectors, transnational corporations became increasingly responsible for determining production standards across their production networks.

Although states continue to regulate their economic sectors, neoliberal regulatory restructuring has led state regulation to play a primarily facilitative function by setting the background conditions for the development of GVCs and the proliferation of private governance.[25] "Governance" in GVCs is constituted through the contingent structure of interfirm relations in production networks. Although each value chain is differently organized, "lead firms," which can be producers, processors, or distributors depending on the specific commodity being produced, often exercise informal control over product quality, prices, and labor. Governance can also be exercised more formally through corporate codes of conduct, multistakeholder standards, and voluntary certifications.[26] When more formal standards are developed by lead firms, their goal is often to differentiate their brands. But as private governance has proliferated in the global economy, civil society organizations have also influenced private governance and exercise governance from below by creating voluntary certifications and standards that compete with those created by multinational corporations. These forms of private value chain governance have proliferated in recent years to influence production standards related to environmental sustainability, labor conditions, and fair trade.[27] Through different modes of governance, rival actors struggle to create and extract value through value chains.

The rise of GVCs has transformed the governance of labor in the agricultural sector and beyond. Labor is, of course, critical for the extraction of value in production. In most value chains, lead firms seek out the lowest possible labor costs to capture the greatest value. In the global context this practice of global labor arbitrage is shaped by the fundamental inequality that, though capital is mobile, labor is not.[28] However, in the national context lead firms can also practice labor arbitrage by drawing on the labor of socially marginalized populations. Just as transnational apparel corporations moved factories to countries with minimal labor regulations and low standards of living, agricultural corporations and commercial farms in the United States exploit undocumented migrant laborers who have little recourse to domestic labor protections.

In response to these changing forms of labor governance, labor movements and civil society have sought to leverage private value chain governance. In the context of farm labor in the United States, these include voluntary certifications such as the "Food Justice Certified" label developed by the Agricultural Justice Project and administered by the Ohio Ecological Food and Farm Association and the "Responsibly Grown, Farmworker Assured" label developed by the Equitable Food Initiative, to name a few. In addition, in response to pressure from consumers, some retailers have developed their own certification programs, such as Whole Foods' "Whole Trade" program.

Scholars and activists debate whether this shift toward certifications and private governance merely reproduces neoliberal market rationalities or whether it has the potential to significantly transform market conditions. Many have been critical of the effects of value chain governance on farmworkers. In their analysis of certification programs related to farmworker justice in California, Sandy Brown and Christy Getz contend that the proliferation of farmworker certification effectively privatizes farmworker justice. They argue that certification "reflects a highly circumscribed realm of possibility, which is shaped by the consolidation of the agrifood system, the shift from government to governance."[29] They criticize the consumer-driven approach to governance and push for a rights-centered approach that calls on the coercive regulatory power of the state to ensure farmworker rights.

However, an emerging set of studies have suggested that private forms of governance can sometimes provide opportunities for workers that they may not have from state labor regulation alone. For example, César Rodríguez-Garavito describes how student movements against sweatshop labor drew on corporate codes of conduct to force their union-busting employers to recognize their union.[30] In this context private governance operates as another lever for social movements to challenge the alliances between capital and the state. In addition, workers themselves have developed new forms of worker-driven social responsibility that draw on similar codes of conduct developed through corporate social responsibility but are designed by workers. Worker-driven social responsibility has emerged in the agricultural sector through initiatives such as the Coalition of Immokalee Workers' "Fair

Food Contract" for tomato pickers in Florida and Migrant Justice's "Milk with Dignity" campaign for farmworkers in Vermont.[31]

These innovative uses of private governance suggest that workers may be able to use private governance to leverage interfirm governance relations within value chains not simply to challenge the distribution of rents along the value chain but also to challenge the *values* that underlie GVCs and thereby influence labor standards beyond single workplaces and farms. By allying with different constituencies, such as small-scale farmers, labor activists can make more expansive claims for representation across borders and sectors and thus also potentially transcend the limitations and obstacles inherent in many state labor law regimes. Therefore, although critical analyses of GVCs offer important critiques of the limitations of these certifications to provide a structural solution to farmworker exploitation, new studies also provide examples of how grassroots actors can use standards, certifications, and other forms of private governance to build power in struggles for food sovereignty and farmworker justice. Integrated into a bottom-up analysis, we can see how food sovereignty activists can leverage both state law and private governance not only to shape the conditions of farmworker labor but also to cultivate prefigurative value practices through which a new food system might one day be born.

FARMWORKERS AND THE FOOD SOVEREIGNTY MOVEMENT

I first met Rosalinda Guillen at the US Food Sovereignty National Assembly in 2011. Guillen's organization, Community to Community Development (C2C), was one of the founding members of the US Food Sovereignty Alliance and one of the reasons I decided to do my fieldwork in the Pacific Northwest. Guillen was a renowned farmworker organizer by the time I met her. Her approach was very much shaped by her own history and career trajectory. The child of farmworkers, Guillen grew up in Western Washington. It was not until she was an adult, however, that she became politically active, through the Rainbow Coalition during Jesse Jackson's bid for president in the 1980s. After Jackson's failed presidential campaign, she got involved in farmworker advocacy through a campaign by the UFW to organize the nationally known winery Chateau Ste. Michelle. Although she began as a volunteer in Western Washington, Guillen soon moved to Eastern Washington and was hired as the main organizer of the campaign. With the help of her organizing leadership, Chateau Ste. Michelle became the first winery and agricultural operation to sign a collectively bargained labor contract in Washington State history. Afterward, Guillen went on to work for the UFW in California.

In the late 1990s Guillen was working as a lobbyist for the UFW in Sacramento when she was asked to represent the UFW at the World Social Forum in Porto Alegre, Brazil. The forum transformed her perspective. "At the forum, I saw the solidarity economy after it was created. I saw the power of people engaged in economic self-sustainability in a diverse manner," she told me. There she observed people "wholly engaged" in the process of social and economic transformation. Soon after the World Social Forum, Guillen moved back to Western Washington and started C2C. When she did so, she "came with some really clear concepts of building power for farmworkers through a solidarity economy and participatory democracy." She saw C2C as building a movement of farmworkers and allies in Northwest Washington and beyond around shared values and principles of ecofeminism and food sovereignty.

Guillen's food-sovereignty-focused approach to farmworker rights made her a unique and creative leader. C2C did not just describe itself as a farmworkers' rights organization; instead Guillen told me that she saw C2C as a "movement-building [organization] that is specifically related to human rights linked to the food system." By framing farmworkers' rights through the language of food sovereignty, she linked farmworkers' liberation from exploitation to larger efforts to redefine how food and those who produce it are valued. She therefore built alliances with small-scale food producers to resist dominant forms of valuation in the industrial food system.

In translating the framework of food sovereignty to address the issue of farm labor, Guillen has sought to unify what have often been understood as competing interest groups as part of the same struggle. Activist-scholar Eric Holt-Giménez describes how these different constituencies—farmers and farmworkers—are linked to the same set of value relations.

> Much of the global food movement is concerned with the intrinsic use-fulness and importance of good, healthy food (its use value). The food justice movement fights for affordable healthy food (use value and ex-

change value). Farmworkers and food workers are on the other side of the equation; they want living wages and decent working conditions. These are aspects that are not recognized by a system designed for profit above all else and in which (a) labor time of the most labor-efficient operations governs the worth of labor in less efficient operations; and (b) labor is purchased as cheaply as possible and laborers work under conditions to increase their efficiency to the limit (socially necessary labor time).[32]

As Holt-Giménez points out, one of the challenges facing small-scale farmers is that their labor and the food they produce is measured against the industrial food system. As a result, they are often forced to sell at lower prices than they can economically sustain. For this reason, Holt-Giménez argues that allying with farmworkers is critical for small-scale farmers: "If all farmworkers received living wages and basic social benefits, it would help to level the playing field between large-scale industrial operations and small-scale production, ultimately benefiting family farms that use family labor."[33] Put another way, the problem for both farmworkers and small-scale farmers is the way that their labor is *commensurated*.

Scholars have pointed out that "those who see their identities jeopardized by the commodification of their work and quantification of their investments" often resist commensuration.[34] Commensuration is a process that "abstracts away the distinctiveness of the particular forms of work, objects of work, and practical uses of these objects" in order to render them quantifiable for exchange.[35] Movements that seek greater control over their labor resist commensuration by developing alternative value practices that seek to shape cultural expectations of what is socially necessary.[36] Rather than commensurate their labor, food sovereignty activists seek to recognize the cultural values of food and thereby honor food chain labor for its contribution to the common good.

In translating food sovereignty, activists challenge commensuration to cultivate new relations and articulate alternative values to those of the industrial food system. In other words, instead of seeing themselves in conflict, farmworkers and small-scale food producers work to imagine and build a food system in which they are compensated fairly. As they form new alliances, however, they also resist commensurating their struggles through a single demand or claim; doing so would fail to acknowledge the intersecting and differential experiences of oppression. One of the most pressing goals of this collaboration is opposing the racialized hierarchies that have been consistently reconstituted to legitimize farmworker exploitation. Through their practices of translocal translation, food sovereignty activists do not subsume difference but attempt to develop relations of solidarity and equivalence while also recognizing difference.

When I met with Guillen in the summer of 2012, she had developed a sophisticated framework for thinking about social change. She explained to me that she took a fundamentally different approach to labor activism than other labor organizations: "The movement building that we do is not about getting power. It's about transforming our consciousness about what power is and redefining power." Although she emphasized that collective bargaining is a useful tool, she also pointed out that the way it had been practiced often lacked a transformational component. Unions had declined, she contended, because the "self-governance process of unions had not developed so that it really is participatory democracy." Instead, many unions replicated the corporate structures of the entities that they were established to resist. She saw the work of C2C as transforming how farmworkers saw themselves through creating democratic practices and building strategic alliances premised on a shared commitment to undoing oppression and structural racism through movement building. "When we're talking about movement building, that's the core of where changing structures and transformations come out of. Food sovereignty and participatory democracy are the *hows*," she explained.

Guillen's comments suggest that organizing through the framework of food sovereignty is different from previous approaches to labor mobilization and social change. Although workers still fight to organize unions, food sovereignty provides a framework for building alliances and relationships with other sectors and movements based on common values. Rather than commensurating different struggles or labor, food sovereignty is centered on promoting democratic governance and self-representation. As Guillen explained, "Our movement begins with creating spaces where people from marginalized, underrepresented, and oppressed communities can begin to enter the majority or the broader community by building spaces of self-representation. That's the ultimate goal, to develop movements that create gateways into governance spaces."

When I first interviewed Guillen, it was eight years after she had founded C2C. During that time, Guillen had become a national food sovereignty leader, but C2C had not yet won any major campaigns in Western Washington. Instead, most of the successes of C2C were related to local policy or interpersonal; they were about building leaders in the community and slowly changing the consciousness of farmworkers. However, when she reflected on this, Guillen told me that Chavez had always said it took five to seven years to build the foundations for a movement. She was right. By the next summer, C2C was helping to organize one of the most successful farmworker mobilizations in Washington State's history.

LAW AND GOVERNANCE IN THE BERRY
FIELDS OF SKAGIT COUNTY

It took me half an hour to find Labor Camp #2 on my first visit, even with the address in my GPS device. I drove past it a handful of times, crisscrossing the country roads of a bucolic agricultural town in Skagit County. The "Magic Skagit," as it is known, is the river valley that runs from the snowy peaks of the North Cascades to the blue waters of the Puget Sound. An hour north of Seattle, the area has capitalized on the local food movement. Farm to Table Road, for example, winds along beautiful old wooden barns and agrarian-chic restaurants where you can dig your own clams, buy pastries from locally milled grains, and purchase produce from beginning farmers. As I passed quaint farmhouses and large fields filled with summer crops, I looked for the farmworker labor camp, not exactly knowing what to expect.

After driving down the same road three or four times, I noticed a break in some overgrown hedges and pulled over to investigate. Crossing an irrigation ditch, I finally found the labor camp. Spread over two acres were ramshackle cabins constructed from corrugated steel and plywood. A few cinderblock structures housing showers and bathrooms as well as a shelter with a few picnic tables under it filled the rest of the muddy area. I was shocked by the incongruity between the pastoral roads that lay on the other side of the hedges and the poor conditions in which the farmworkers were expected to live. Clearly the agrarian ideal celebrated in Skagit County concealed the racialized inequality of those who toiled over its rich soils.

I was visiting the camp because the workers living there were on strike and I had been asked to deliver some food and other basic needs from supporters in Seattle. A few days earlier, farmworker Federico Lopez had been fired from his job at Sakuma Brothers Farms when he complained to his supervisor about the piece rate set for that day: 30 cents per pound of berries. At that rate farmworkers would need to pick about 31 pounds of fruit just to make Washington State's minimum wage of $9.19 per hour. When Lopez was fired, he was given an eviction notice that he would need to vacate the housing provided by the farm. The next day, many of Lopez's colleagues refused to go back to work. They were angry that Lopez had been fired for raising concerns over how the farm's managers set the piece rate for the day, that he was called racial epithets by his supervisor, and that he was evicted from the terrible housing conditions that farmworkers were paying for. They compiled a list of demands, which included not only that their colleague be rehired but also that they be offered better housing, wage increases, overtime pay, and respect from the managers and that the farm not bring in guest workers through the H-2A program. What was at first a spontaneous protest to protect their colleague's job quickly turned into a longer-term mobilization to improve their conditions.

All the farmworkers at Labor Camp #2 worked for Sakuma Brothers Farms. The farm, which was first started in 1935 by Atsusa Sakuma and is still owned by the family, extends over 1,000 acres in Skagit County. It sells fresh and processed strawberries, blueberries, raspberries, and blackberries for local and national markets.[37] At peak harvest season, Sakuma Brothers employs over 500 farmworkers to harvest the berries. Picking berries is among the most difficult and dangerous forms of farm labor. It can cause musculoskeletal injuries that profoundly limit the lifespan of the harvesters.[38] Life expectancy for migrant and seasonal farmworkers is only 49 years, twenty-six years younger than the average life expectancy in the United States.[39] Because berry picking is so difficult, it has been traditionally occupied by shifting groups who have been placed on the lowest rung of the racial hierarchy of farm labor. Thirty years ago, Mexican laborers from Michoacán, Jalisco, Guanajuato, and Zacatecas made up this population of "traditional sending regions." However, beginning in the 1980s they began to be replaced by Indigenous Mexicans who were among the hardest hit in the 1980s crisis.[40] The seasonal migrant workers at the Sakuma farm reflect this shift. They are primarily Indigenous Mixtec and Triqui speakers from the state of Oaxaca. Most migrate with their families each year from the

Central Valley of California, where they work during the winter, to Western Washington for the summer harvesting season.

Part of what makes seasonal migrant farmworkers like those at Sakuma vulnerable is their immigration status. I never inquired about the immigration status of farmworkers at Sakuma Brothers Farm. But on one of my first trips to the labor camps, one worker asked me if I wanted a ride to Labor Camp #1. After all my trouble finding Labor Camp #2, I graciously took her offer. But as we drove down the empty county roads, I couldn't help but notice the glacial pace at which we were moving. Normally I zipped through those country roads, rarely worrying about my speed. When I impatiently asked why we were driving so slowly, she explained to me why we couldn't be pulled over. Skagit County is just 50 miles south of the Canadian border and police regularly cooperate with Immigration and Customs Enforcement. Nationally, as much as 70% of the seasonal migrant labor force is thought to be undocumented, with many in mixed-status households with citizen children and noncitizen parents.[41] This fear of deportation keeps workers in a structurally vulnerable position ripe for exploitation.

Despite whatever migration status they may hold, the farmworkers at Sakuma Brothers Farms have a history of collective action to challenge their working conditions. In the past the workers engaged in short strikes to address their wages. However, these disputes were usually resolved quickly, and farmworkers went back to work. This changed in 2013. Although Sakuma rehired Lopez, few of the farmworkers' other demands were met. Neither their wages nor their housing was improved. When the workers went on strike again, they contacted Rosalinda Guillen and asked for her guidance. Quickly, they established a committee to negotiate with Sakuma Brothers. They called themselves Familias Unidas por la Justicia.

During the first couple of weeks, Guillen and a handful of volunteers were still trying to assess the situation. In an effort to assist, I helped to survey the workers about their wages with a few other volunteers. One of the major grievances of the workers was the piece rate, a system of compensation in which managers set the price per pound of fruit picked. The piece rate is a system used across the large-scale commercial agricultural sector. Farmers claim that the piece rate allows farmworkers to earn more than the minimum wage. However, it is a system that also forces workers to pick as quickly as possible with few breaks. Farmworkers generally oppose the piece-rate system because it creates opportunities for employers to engage in wage theft, encourages worker self-exploitation to the point of bodily injury, and disadvantages older workers and those disabled from their injuries.

To get a better handle on this, I worked with a team to try to determine the average wages that farmworkers were making and whether they were making the minimum wage, as required by Washington State law. This turned out to be a monumental challenge. To keep track of their compensation, farmworkers must maintain meticulous records and, if possible, keep all the tickets that record the weight of the berries picked and the piece rate for that day's tickets (if they are provided). Between the constantly changing piece rate, the hot sun, and the unreliable availability of paper tickets for workers, it is almost impossible for farmworkers to know if they are being paid fairly. In attempting to reconstruct farmworker's wages, I found that some of them were making above the minimum wage, but many workers were also making below the minimum wage.

Beyond the actual wages that farmworkers were paid, it was clear that the piece rate also worked as a tool of systematic exploitation. Farmworkers never knew how many days they would work in a given week, for how many hours, or for how much money. This made it impossible for them to live any semblance of a normal life because they had to be constantly on call and ready for work. Moreover, given that there is no sick or overtime pay, they must also be willing to work no matter what condition they are in. Beyond the actual wages they are paid, the piece rate operates as a system to maintain a docile workforce.

As it became clear to the workers that their problems were not going to be addressed by Sakuma Brothers management anytime soon, they began to think about how to develop a more prolonged campaign. They faced several challenges in maintaining their momentum, however. First, although many of the workers at Sakuma returned yearly during harvest season, most traveled to the Central Valley of California during the winter to find work. This meant not only that they could possibly lose their jobs for the next season if they continued to strike but also that they would need to start organizing afresh the following year. Second, although volunteers were bringing supplies such as food and diapers to the labor camps while the workers were on strike, neither the workers nor C2C had the resources to support a longer-term strike. C2C had a skeletal staff and no money to provide workers with a strike fund. Third, no unions in the area had the capacity to support this campaign. The UFW had little presence in Western Washington, and few other unions had the experience supporting farmworkers.

However, as farmworkers began to develop their demands, including a call for $15 per hour minimum wage, they grew more emboldened. By August 2013 it became clear that they would need to form a union if it wished to substantially improve working conditions and also protect those who had been organizing from retaliation. One cold and wet evening in mid-August, the president-elect of FUJ held a barbeque with the help of C2C for at least 150 workers and their children. While carne asada was cooking on the grills, he told the workers that FUJ had negotiated with the farm and that no one would be retaliated against for participating in the strikes. He held up cards and told workers that FUJ wished to establish a union and that if they wished to join, they should sign the cards. Over the next hour almost all the workers present signed cards, which formally established their support for the union.

Legal Mobilization and Legitimating the Struggle

As FUJ formalized their union, Sakuma Brothers Farms became increasingly aggressive in its tactics to prevent unionization. Toward the end of the growing season, they hired private security guards to prevent supporters from entering the labor camps. Working with a nonprofit legal services firm, the vice president of FUJ, Felimon Piñeda, filed a complaint against Sakuma Brothers in Skagit Superior Court on the basis of Washington State's Little Norris LaGuardia Act, a law modeled on federal legislation passed by the Washington State legislature in 1933 to protect workers' freedom of association. The complaint claimed that Sakuma had violated their right to be "free from interference, restraint, or coercion of employers . . . in self-organization or in other concerted activities for the purpose of collective bargaining or other mutual aid or protections," as provided by the Little Norris LaGuardia Act. The following day, the local court found that FUJ enjoyed the right to freedom of association and that FUJ had a "well-grounded fear of continuing invasion of those rights" as a result of Sakuma's placement of security personnel in the labor camps. As a result, the judge issued a temporary restraining order.[42] The order provided FUJ with legal recognition and formal protection for the workers' organizing

FIGURE 5   FUJ president Ramon Torres helping his co-workers sign union cards in August 2013. Photo by author.

activities. FUJ returned to court several times over the next month to enforce the original court order.

As the summer season grew to a close, workers also filed a claim in federal courts to recover lost wages. Working with the same nonprofit law firm and with a Seattle-based law firm specializing in class actions, two farmworkers filed a class action lawsuit in the Western District of Washington on behalf of 400 farmworkers. The complaint alleged several violations of the Migrant and Seasonal Agricultural Worker Protection Act of 1983 and Washington State agricultural employment laws. These included "failure to provide rest breaks,[43] failure to keep accurate records of the actual hours worked, failure to provide pay statements with accurate statements of the actual hours worked, and failure to comply with agreed-upon working arrangements."[44] Eventually, the farm settled the federal wage and hour claim for $850,000, while denying any wrongdoing. It paid $500,000 toward damages incurred by the workers, the maximum sum allowed under the Migrant and Seasonal Agricultural Worker Protection Act. This amounted to $1,221.30 in back pay for each of the affected workers, and the remaining amount went toward legal fees. The question of rest breaks, however, was referred to the Washington State Supreme Court for separate judgment and was not addressed until the following year.

Over the winter months, however, Sakuma reneged on its promise not to retaliate against the workers and attempted to replace those who went on strike with guest workers through the H-2A program.[45] Sakuma filed an application with the Washington State Employment Security Department to hire 438 guest workers from Mexico for the 2014 harvest season. In response, FUJ collected letters from more than 460 workers and delivered them in three batches to the Department of Labor; the letters stated that the workers were willing and wanted to return to their jobs. On the same day that the Department of Labor received the letters, Ryan Sakuma sent a letter to workers explaining that there would be no housing for nonworkers (i.e., families), who had for years been provided with housing at Sakuma (rent for the housing was automatically deducted from workers' earnings). Two days later he sent a letter telling workers that if they had been absent for more than five days in the previous season, they had been reported as "abandoned" to the Department of Labor. On its website, Sakuma Brothers posted a statement making this clear.[46] Working with national farmworker advocacy organizations and public interest attorneys, FUJ sent letters to the Department of Labor with evidence that a willing domestic labor force already existed and that there was an ongoing labor dispute between Sakuma and FUJ. Under the controlling legislation of the H-2A program, this would disqualify Sakuma from being granted authorization to hire guest workers.[47] As a result, an administrative court rejected Sakuma's request for H-2A guest workers based on numerous problems related to housing, the hiring of minors, and rates of pay.[48]

In the first year of FUJ's struggle, the organization engaged in legal mobilization in state, federal, and administrative legal arenas. They did so to protect their right to organize, challenge their employer for wage theft violations, and protect their jobs. These forms of legal mobilization all played a critical role in recognizing their basic rights as workers. However, their strategy was ultimately not legal in focus. Guillen told me that even before FUJ had begun to organize, she had approached her relationship with lawyers carefully. She explained that she told lawyers working as allies with C2C that "you are not going to come in and tell us what we have to do because of what the law says. You are going to come in and the farmworkers are going to tell you what they need and you have to figure out how to use the law that exists to get us as close to what we want to do as we can." She approached lawyers and the law more generally, just as the UFW first had, as a means for empowering farmworkers, not as an end.

This approach worked in FUJ's favor. The litigation provided FUJ with the basic legal conditions necessary for organizing and for preventing wage theft and (as it would be later decided) providing paid rest breaks. However, litigation could not address issues such as the pay rate and benefits. Farmworkers therefore relied just as much on the symbolic effects of the cases. With each case they won, FUJ received media attention from the local press in the Puget Sound region and updates through the Washington State Labor Council and national food sovereignty networks. In October 2014, just a year and a half after FUJ began organizing, C2C won the Food Sovereignty Prize from the US Food Sovereignty Alliance and FUJ was recognized by the Washington State AFL-CIO as a member union. These legal cases therefore publicly legitimized FUJ's struggles and facilitated the formation of allies in the labor, faith, and social justice communities. Nevertheless, Sakuma Brothers refused to acknowledge FUJ. Without a formal legal framework requiring farmers to recognize farmworker unions, FUJ looked for other ways to build power and transform their working conditions.

Networking Along the Value Chain

In the summer of 2014, when it became clear that the courts could not compel Sakuma Brothers Farms to bargain a contract with FUJ or substantially improve their working conditions, FUJ decided to call a boycott of Sakuma Brothers berries. Over the summer, I frequently traveled back and forth between Skagit County and Seattle to assist with the boycott and to attend pickets outside grocery stores in the Seattle area to raise awareness about the labor dispute. Yet, even though the boycott was well publicized, it was hard to operationalize. Sakuma marketed few berries under its own name. Identifying which berries actually came from Sakuma Brothers Farms turned out to be difficult. The workers sent text messages to various boycott leaders with pictures of the labels on the crates into which they were packing berries, but it was almost impossible to communicate this constantly changing information to consumers. Each week, food and labor activists would show up outside various grocery stores that sourced local berries and pass out flyers, but it was not always clear which berries we were asking consumers to boycott. Even those who wanted to be supportive were unclear how to follow the boycott. As the summer progressed, FUJ leaders decided to switch tactics and focus instead on the largest buyer of Sakuma Brothers' berries: Driscoll's.

Since the 1980s, Driscoll's has grown immensely in order to compete with large competitors and retail chains. The privately held, family-owned company is a large multinational operation. It grows organic and conventional berries in twenty-one countries and sells them in forty-eight.[49] Driscoll's dominates one-third of berry sales in the United States, "including sixty percent of organic strawberries, forty-six percent of blackberries, fourteen percent of blueberries, and just about every raspberry you don't pick yourself."[50] However, the company grows only one-third of its fruit; the rest is purchased from nearly 750 "independent growers" in over twenty countries.[51] As a result of its dominant market share, Driscoll's has become what scholars of value chains call the "lead firm" in the global berry value chain and a recognizable brand name. It exercises governance over the berry value chain both formally and informally. More formally, Driscoll's has strict standards related to quality, such as their proprietary cultivars, the appearance and size of berries, branding, and packaging. Such standards often serve to differentiate brands to strengthen their competitive advantage.[52] By contrast, Driscoll's governance over labor was more informal. Through their independent growers' program, they were able to evade responsibility for the labor conditions of farmworkers.

Rather than merely calling for a boycott, FUJ allied with small-scale producers in the food sovereignty movement to develop alternative standards through which to value labor power in the food system. Before the boycott was even initiated, Guillen had cultivated alliances with small-scale producers to shape the standards in value chains. She was a founding member of the Domestic Fair-Trade Association (DFTA), which was established in 2008 "to unite the values of organic agriculture with the principles of fair trade for the Global North."[53] Although the concept of fair trade in the United States has typically referred to imports from other countries, the DFTA challenged this understanding and reconceptualized fair trade around domestic labor of both farmworkers and small-scale family farmers in the United States.

The DFTA does not operate as a purveyor of private standards but has nonetheless been formed in reaction to GVCs. It has developed a network of small-scale farmers, farmworker organizations, food retail co-ops, and fair-trade supporters that promote the concept and develop principles of domestic fair trade. As the former Seattle-based executive director of the DFTA explained to me, the association saw itself primarily as a movement-building organization committed to building constituencies for domestic fair trade. It was formed to facilitate cross-sector dialogue. Rather than certify agricultural goods, it has audited existing certifications to see how they stack up against the DFTA's values and principles. In doing so, it has sought to influence the public and private governance of labor not only by shaping the standards of GVCs but also by challenging the way labor is valued (or Marx's socially necessary labor time) in the food and agricultural sectors. Guillen's work in building a network to support domestic fair trade proved essential in the struggle against Sakuma Brothers.

With the help of Guillen and C2C, FUJ activated a counternetwork of small-scale farmers, food sovereignty organizations, and fair-trade advocates that resisted the commensuration of farm labor. The first phase of the boycott of Driscoll's stayed primarily local. Sympathetic food cooperatives in the Pacific Northwest wrote to Driscoll's to inquire about their labor standards and to voice their concerns about the labor dispute at Sakuma Brothers Farms. However, Driscoll's was largely unresponsive. This changed during the following growing season in 2015, when 30,000 farmworkers in the berry value chain went on strike in San Quintín, Mexico. Many of the workers were employed by BerryMex, part of Reiter Affiliated Companies, which is "the largest fresh, multi-berry producer in the world."[54] Driscoll's is Reiter's only customer and the CEOs of Reiter and Driscoll's are siblings. Some of the workers involved in the San Quintín strikes had also been involved in labor struggles with the United Farm Workers of Washington and the Coalition of Immokalee Workers.[55] Felimon Piñeda, the FUJ vice president, began communicating with the workers in San Quintín through the Frente Indígena de Organizaciones Binacionales (Binational Front of Indigenous Organizations), an organization established in 1991 to advocate for the rights of migrant and nonmigrant Indigenous peoples based in Oaxaca, Baja California, and the United States. Because many of the workers in Baja California were also Triqui

FIGURE 6 Boycott outside a local consumer cooperative in Seattle. Photo by author.

and Mixtec speakers, a close alliance soon formed. The two labor disputes created increasing pressure on Driscoll's to take stronger responsibility for the workers in its value chain.

The conflict between FUJ and Sakuma thus became a struggle between rival networks. On the one hand, FUJ was supported by a network of workers, fair-trade advocates, small-scale farmers, students, and food co-operatives. Their network was constructed through the food sovereignty movements' practices of translation, which challenged the commensu-ration of workers' labor by both organizing around alternative forms of value and promoting competing standards that demanded that workers have representation in determining their working conditions. On the other hand, Sakuma Brothers Farms was supported by the Driscoll's production network. This network, which included Driscoll's, Berry-Mex, and Sakuma, extracted value from farmers and farmworkers. To do so, Driscoll's evaded its responsibility for working conditions in its value chain by minimizing the conflicts and localizing them to specific independent growers.

Pressure built throughout 2015. In the spring, Fair World Project, a non-governmental organization (NGO) allied with FUJ, sent a letter to Driscoll's signed by 10,000 individuals pledging to boycott Driscoll's if the labor dispute was not resolved. The letter urged Driscoll's "to insist on a fair contract for farmworkers before you continue to purchase berries from [Sakuma Brothers]. Given your commitment to community and sustainability, this should be standard practice."[56] Soon after, the DFTA sent a letter to Driscoll's signed by many food and labor organizations across the country. Their letter highlighted the many legal victories of FUJ and expressed increasing concern about the working conditions across the berry value chain as a result of the labor dispute in San Quintín. As a result of these letters, Driscoll's agreed to meet with Fair World Project, the DFTA, and FUJ. During the meeting they agreed to send a third-party auditor to Sakuma Brothers. However, Driscoll's made no commitment to force Sakuma to bargain with FUJ. Sakuma began negotiating with FUJ but said that union recognition was off the table.[57] This refusal led pickets and pressure to grow. FUJ organized boycott committees throughout the West Coast, and food sovereignty activists were active on social media targeting Driscoll's. In addition, during the summer of 2015, the Washington State Supreme Court also issued a decision in *Lopez Demetrio v. Sakuma*, which had been filed in 2014. The court ruled that farmworkers were entitled to rest breaks. The decision applied to 180,000 farmworkers. Sakuma Brothers settled the suit by paying $87,160 in additional back wages.

Facing growing pressure, Driscoll's responded by introducing a corporate code of conduct to govern labor in its value chain, which it called the Worker Welfare Program. In addition, it agreed to pilot a small program with Fair Trade USA to certify fair-trade berries from Baja California. The Worker Welfare Program governs Driscoll's value chain across the twenty-one countries where it purchases berries. It draws on international standards set forth in International Labor Organization conventions, the Global Social Compliance Program standards, and Business Social Compliance Initiative standards.[58] By adopting global labor standards rather than US labor law, the program specifically recognizes worker's right to freedom of association. In addition, Driscoll's explicitly advocated that states lacking legal frameworks to address farmworker labor rights in the United States should follow California's approach and implement legislation such as the

Agricultural Labor Relations Act.[59] Although Driscoll's corporate code of conduct operated through voluntary self-regulation, it nonetheless provided an important tool for activists in holding Driscoll's accountable for the labor standards at Sakuma Brothers.

The next year, however, workers at Sakuma were still working without a contract. In May 2016 there was an international day of action against Driscoll's, which included forty picket lines. The day of action was covered by national media outlets, such as *Democracy Now!* and Public Radio International's *The World*. Fair World Project sent yet another letter to Driscoll's demanding that it make good on its promise to ensure freedom of association, which had been included as part of its Worker Welfare Program. As a result, the CEO of Sakuma Brothers Farms, Danny Weeden, signed a memorandum of understanding with Sakuma Brothers to establish a process for creating a secret election for the union. The process for establishing the terms of the memorandum was intense, with many work stoppages in August 2016. However, in September 2016 farmworkers voted in a secret election to have FUJ represent them with a 77% margin. The memorandum included a provision that the farm would bargain should FUJ win.

Finally, in July 2017 FUJ and Sakuma Brothers Farms signed a two-year contract. The contract not only guaranteed a $15 minimum wage but also set up a process for workers and management to calculate a fair piece rate, established a grievance procedure, and prevented arbitrary termination. In 2017 the Driscoll's website proudly announced the end to the labor dispute and the election of FUJ. By mobilizing the standards set forth in Driscoll's labor standards, FUJ was able to negotiate a legally binding contract.

Although FUJ claimed victory by bargaining a contract with Sakuma Brothers Farms, the contract was only a starting point in promoting farmworker autonomy. As Guillen told me, farmworkers' struggle for food sovereignty is not simply about collective bargaining; it is about farmworkers being able to assert greater control over their lives and labor and about working toward transformative change in which farm labor is valued in ways that allow farmworkers and others who work in the food system to live lives of dignity. To that end, FUJ leaders have begun to develop farming cooperatives and small-scale farms. In addition, they have begun to organize other farmworkers across the region—even H-2A guest workers—with the support of small-scale farmers in the region. In cultivating concepts of fair trade and food sovereignty, therefore, farmworkers have continued to challenge the agrarian ideal and reconstruct a food movement that respects the dignity of all those who toil in the food system.

CONCLUSIONS

Global value chains are a product of neoliberalism, but they also serve as an important form of governance in relation to which activists are assembling counternetworks and constituting practices of translocal translation. Although much of the conversation about the progressive possibility of value chains has been limited to questions of whether those lower down on the value chain are able to upgrade to capture greater value in the global economy, value chains also offer a framework that structures collective action. By mobilizing in relation to value chains, activists are organizing across borders and sectors in ways that were once limited by legal liberalism and are politicizing spaces of governance through which they seek to shape economic organization.

FUJ provides important insights into the opportunities and limitations of value chains. Through their struggle FUJ was able to organize a counternetwork to leverage interfirm relationships to shape the standards through which labor was governed across the berry value chain. Moreover, they also built relationships between small-scale food producers, consumers, food cooperatives, and other actors in the food system with the goal of challenging the cultural expectations of farm labor value or its socially necessary labor time. By placing struggles over labor at the center of the food sovereignty movement, farmworkers developed new relations with small-scale producers, overcoming a regulatory framework that had cast them as antagonists rather than as partners in a shared struggle. Through the relationships they cultivated, farmworkers and small-scale farmers in the food sovereignty movement contest the commensuration of their labor through capitalist forms of value and develop competing value practices that may one day abrogate the doctrine of agricultural exceptionalism. These value practices provide the foundation for constructing new value relations in the food system, which farmers, farmworkers, and other food sovereignty activists seek to institutionalize in the production of value chains from below.

However, there remain important reasons to be skeptical of private governance to transform market conditions. A number of scholars have argued that the promotion of private certification by food and agricultural activists reflects an uncritical adoption of neoliberal technologies of rule. Frederick Mayer and Nicola Phillips argue that the rise of GVCs promotes the "outsourcing" of state regulation to private actors, which has facilitated "the concentration of wealth in the hands of those with power in the chain."[60] More specifically, scholars have pointed out several limitations of GVC governance to address inequalities. First, there is a great deal of competition among different standards. These standards are often promoted by actors with differing interests, and the level of protection for workers varies widely.[61] The proliferation of standards can confuse consumers if they are seeking out goods that are fairly produced and exchanged. Second, even if corporations adopt codes of conduct or voluntary certifications, enforcement is difficult. Although some standards may require intermittent auditing, the rigor of these auditing practices varies widely, and in most cases corporations ultimately remain accountable only to themselves for compliance.[62] Third, studies suggest that in the best of circumstances private forms of governance may affect outcome standards (such as worker safety), but they rarely provide *process rights*, such as freedom of association and the right to collectively bargain.[63] Finally, critics have charged that the rise of corporate social responsibility expands inequality and narrows our horizons of social change. For example, Ronen Shamir argues that corporate social responsibility "entails the economization of morality; a process which is compatible with the general neo-liberal drive to ground social relations in the economic rationality of markets."[64]

These critiques point to the critical and enduring role of state law in shaping the opportunities available in value chains. Comparing the labor struggle of farmworkers in Baja California to those in Washington State reveals how access to the law is critical for movements seeking to shape value chain governance. FUJ was able to effectively leverage the Driscoll's corporate code of conduct, but workers in San Quintín were less successful. The two struggles had many differences that limited the workers' ability to leverage these codes, including the fact that workers in San Quintín were already unionized through a "yellow" union with close ties to the state.[65] Although a number of fair-trade pilot programs in Baja California were created as a result of workers' mobilization with FUJ, these programs do not require farmworkers to have a voice in their working conditions. The differences between the two cases therefore affirms sociologist Tim Bartley's conclusions that workers in states more constrained by global capital are less likely to be able to take advantage of corporate codes of conduct and other soft law standards.[66]

For FUJ, public law litigation combined with value chain mobilization worked together to fundamentally transform FUJ's working conditions. Through legal mobilization, FUJ was able to protect workers' right to assert their freedom of association and highlight the worst violations of basic employment standards, and it provided significant material victories in the way of back pay. It also legitimized FUJ's struggle by spotlighting the injustices farmworkers faced. This litigation enabled FUJ to politicize the value chain and form alliances with other constituencies in the food sovereignty movement to put pressure on the lead firm in the fresh berry value chain. By constituting their claims in relation to these broader forms of governance, FUJ cultivated networks through practices of translation that articulated alternative values to the dominant industrial food system. Ultimately, these values may play a key role in transforming food system governance.

4   Protecting People's Knowledge

IN 2014 I WANDERED through the public gallery of the Bill & Melinda Gates Foundation's Discovery Center with Mariann Bassey, a food sovereignty activist who was visiting Seattle from Nigeria. Bassey was in town for the Africa-US Food Sovereignty Strategy Summit, which I was helping to coordinate. After she arrived, I offered to show her around town. Of all the beautiful sights in the region, the first place she wanted to visit was the Gates Foundation's headquarters. The Discovery Center is the only part of the foundation's massive Seattle campus that is open to the general public. Located in a small building near the iconic Space Needle, it has the feel of both a museum and a monument to the Gates Foundation's good works. Arrayed across a large hall are interactive exhibits that describe the global issues that the Gates Foundation focuses on, from infectious diseases to global hunger. From its modern architecture to its digitized exhibits, the Discovery Center celebrates the foundation's technology-driven approach to global problems.

As we walked through the Discovery Center, we came across an exhibit that described some of the foundation's more contentious programs, from its support for the quantitative measurement of teacher effectiveness in the United States[1] to its vast funding for agricultural biotechnology on the African continent. These issues are controversial because they reflect the Gates Foundation's technology-focused approach. Critics charge that these silver bullet, market-based solutions overlook the larger structural inequalities that are at the root of the problems that the Gates Foundation seeks to address and that they end up benefiting corporations and wealthy countries in the global North. But what has drawn even more frustration is that the foundation pressures governments to reform regulations and spend public money to adopt the technologies that the foundation promotes. The exhibit acknowledged that "sometimes people disagree with our approach," and it invited visitors to "join these important discussions" by typing their comments into electronic kiosks organized around each of the controversial issues. Bassey sat down at the station allocated to agricultural biotechnology and composed a thoughtful response: "Farmers who know the land, pests, and weather patterns are the best agricultural innovators and as such they should handle our agriculture."

Bassey's comment reflected food sovereignty activists' opposition to the Gates Foundation's approach to agricultural development, which since 2006 has sought to overhaul African food systems by promoting a Green Revolution on the African continent. Building on the first Green Revolution, which introduced hybrid seeds and agrochemical inputs to farmers in Latin America and Asia, the Gates Foundation has spent billions of dollars on its campaign to encourage African agricultural commercialization, with particular fervor for biotechnology. Food sovereignty activists oppose the foundation's top-down philanthropic approach to agricultural development, which they contend threatens to dispossess small-scale farmers of the knowledge that they have cultivated over generations, replacing it with expensive inputs and proprietary technologies owned by corporations in the global North. As a result, the Gates Foundation has emerged as a key front of struggle for food sovereignty activists worldwide.

After our tour of the Gates Foundation, Bassey was joined by six other food sovereignty leaders from the African continent and thirteen US-based food sovereignty activists for a four-day-long set of meetings. The Africa-US Food Sovereignty Strategy Summit had been organized by the Community Alliance for Global Justice (CAGJ) to build solidarity between African and US food sovereignty movements and to develop a transnational movement to challenge the Gates Foundation. Over the next few days activists shared information about their struggles for food sovereignty, creatively attempting to translate food sovereignty across distinct political, economic, and agrarian conditions. As they searched for strategic opportunities to mobilize shared meanings of food sovereignty, activists converged on a curious project of the Gates Foundation that connected many of their concerns: the Super Banana.

The Super Banana was a signature project of the Gates Foundation. The genetically modified East African Highland Banana, a "biofortified staple crop," was funded with the goal of addressing vitamin A deficiency in Uganda. The Gates Foundation funded many genetically modified crops, but the Super Banana was developed to serve as an emissary for agricultural biotechnology, because genetically modified foods that offer benefits to consumers are thought to be more likely to win over skeptical publics.[2] To promote the Super Banana, the foundation assembled a transnational network of scientists, regulatory experts, and public relations specialists to convince Ugandans of the safety and necessity of GMOs (genetically modified organisms). In doing so, the foundation encouraged Uganda's lawmakers to develop a permissive regulatory framework for biotechnology.

Yet, even though the Gates Foundation presented the Super Banana as a philanthropic gift, activists saw it as a trojan horse that would open up the African continent to corporate agricultural biotechnology. Food sovereignty activists oppose genetic engineering not only because of concerns about the human safety of these crops but also because of the risks they pose to biodiversity and the ownership of plant genetic resources that technology developers demand. By reinterpreting and translating the Super Banana through the frame of food sovereignty, activists constructed a transnational counternetwork to challenge the foundation's interpretive authority. Through this network activists hoped not just to resist the incursion of agricultural biotechnology on the African continent but also to promote alternative knowledges of nature rooted in agroecology.

In this chapter I examine how food sovereignty movements mobilized to challenge the Gates Foundation–led transnational regulatory networks promoting the Super Banana. Whereas the last two chapters focused on particular forms and technologies of governance produced by neoliberalism (local collaborative governance and private governance stemming from global value chains), in this chapter I turn to the transnational regulatory networks constituted by struggles over new technologies. As explained in chapter 1, epistemic communities are a key mode through which governance networks are constructed.[3] By drawing on different knowledge practices and translating these practices in networks, actors in transnational governance seek to cultivate interpretive authority and thereby exercise power. In doing so, these epistemic networks often draw on supranational institutions to create laws and regulations that institutionalize their power, which they then export and translate to local contexts.[4]

The Super Banana, and agricultural biotechnology more broadly, is a salient example of the way that hegemonic actors seek to exercise power through epistemic networks. As Sheila Jasanoff notes, "For the products of GM [genetically modified] agriculture to locate themselves securely in global markets, there has to be broad agreement on what these entities actually *are*."[5] The Super Banana served as a proxy for this debate. As I describe in this chapter, the Gates Foundation labored to exert authority by interpreting biotechnology through the language of Northern agricultural science and assembled a transnational governance network of actors rooted in technical knowledge of biosafety. In doing so, it attempted to render the regulation of biotechnology as a technical issue of risk regulation. By contrast, food sovereignty activists mobilized to challenge the transnational regulatory networks promoting the Super Banana by engaging in translocal translation that emphasized agroecological knowledge practices over and above the proprietary forms of knowledge emanating from metropolitan centers of science and technology. By interpreting agricultural biotechnology as a threat to control over their Indigenous knowledge systems, they reframed biotechnology through global regulatory frameworks centered on biodiversity and on ownership of and control over plant genetic resources.

The struggle over the Super Banana illuminates how the changing relationships between power, authority, and knowledge in transnational governance threaten to deepen modes of global domination. As I recounted in the introduction, agricultural knowledge has long been an important site of knowledge production through which power has been exercised. English philosophers once premised their theories of private property and liberal state sovereignty on scientific forms of commercial agricultural production. Private ownership, they reasoned, was necessary to incentivize "improvement" of land.[6] English beliefs about the superiority of their agricultural practices, knowledge, and land use were mobilized to provide a justification for the dispossession of Indigenous peoples from their lands in the

New World.[7] Today, these same discourses of improvement and innovation are being deployed by states and powerful corporations. But in contrast to the past when agricultural knowledge was mobilized by colonial states to dispossess small-scale food producers from their *territories*, today it is increasingly being mobilized to enclose the *knowledge practices* of small-scale food producers by enrolling them into global markets for seeds and other agricultural inputs.

By analyzing how food sovereignty activists drew on their commitment to local and Indigenous forms of knowledge—or *people's knowledge*[8]—to construct a counternetwork to challenge the epistemic enclosure of knowledge of plant genetic resources, in this chapter I also reveal how these same conditions of transnational governance offer new conditions of possibility. Rooted in alternative epistemologies and cosmovisions of nature, food sovereignty activists seek to widen the commons over knowledge, seeds, and other productive resources. In doing so, transnational agroecological networks challenge the ideology of agricultural improvement and the modernist separation of human and nonhuman nature that continues to legitimate liberal state sovereignty and its regimes of private property. By drawing on alternative epistemologies of nature, I show how food sovereignty activists are reimagining the relationship between the state, society, and nature by constructing common property regimes to protect Indigenous knowledge and biodiversity.

This chapter draws on participant observation in the Africa-US Food Sovereignty Strategy Summit and the networks of transnational food sovereignty activism that developed in the years thereafter. I begin by recounting how African and American food sovereignty activists converged on the Super Banana as they translated food sovereignty across divergent contexts. Following that, I describe the global law and politics of agricultural biotechnology (or GMOs) and the role that transnational networks play in the regulation of GMOs. Based on this discussion, I analyze how the Super Banana was translated by the Gates Foundation and food sovereignty activists. Although the struggle over biosafety regulation in Uganda remains unresolved even at the time of writing, I explain how food sovereignty activists seem to have won a significant victory in the struggle over the Super Banana. Ultimately, this chapter illustrates how food sovereignty movements' commitment to agroecology and people's knowledge are being mobilized through social practices of translocal translation to shape the governance of agricultural biotechnology and global food governance more broadly.

CONTESTING THE GATES FOUNDATION'S GENE REVOLUTION

When I began my research, I did not intend to investigate struggles over African agriculture. I was interested in how food sovereignty was being translated in the United States. But as I was carrying out my research in Seattle, the Bill & Melinda Gates Foundation loomed large. The Gates Foundation, which is based in Seattle, is the world's largest philanthropic foundation, with more than $51 billion in assets as of 2019.[9] Since 2006 the Gates Foundation has become one of the most important players in agricultural development. Although it began by focusing on agricultural development on the African continent, it has become increasingly influential in the governance of global food security.[10] Therefore, when the executive director of CAGJ asked if I might consider getting involved with their program, AGRA Watch, I agreed. I was eager to learn about how they understood and mobilized for food sovereignty across the divergent contexts of Africa and the United States.

AGRA Watch was established by CAGJ in 2008 in response to the Gates Foundation's cofounding of the Alliance for a Green Revolution in Africa (AGRA) with the Rockefeller Foundation, which had been at the forefront of the first Green Revolution.[11] CAGJ leaders were well aware of critiques of the Green Revolution, which was premised on the supremacy of settler colonial forms of commercial agricultural production and scientific knowledge. During the first wave of the Green Revolution, the Rockefeller Foundation together with the US government funded the export of American agricultural science to Latin America and Asia and the import of indigenous seed varietals to American seed companies and international research institutions.[12] It encouraged farmers in these regions to adopt commercial agro-inputs, which facilitated farmer deskilling and conscription into debt.[13] Proponents of the Green Revolution celebrate it for ameliorating hunger in the developing world. But such claims have recently been challenged. Although the Green Revolution increased total grain yields, it did not end hunger. Rather, critics suggest that its greatest achievement was pacifying insurrectionary threats of rural classes and exacerbating rural inequalities.[14] Recent histories even question whether the technology package offered to farmers was the cause of grain yield increases or whether these increases were due to the widespread introduction of irrigation and state policies that offered credits and price supports.[15] These concerns led CAGJ to develop its AGRA Watch program with the goal of raising awareness in Seattle and beyond about the economic and ecological consequences of the Gates Foundation–led initiative to promote a new Green Revolution on the African continent.

Challenging the Gates Foundation is a Herculean task. The foundation provides more than $880 million per year to multilateral organizations, more than many countries.[16] Although he was once decried as a technology monopolist and intellectual property pariah,[17] Bill Gates is now described as "the most interesting man in the world." A *New York Times* op-ed penned in 2020 described Gates as a "lavender-sweatered Mister Rogers" and an "impatient optimist" poised to be a new global leader. "Gates is everywhere these days," columnist Timothy Egan wrote. "With the United States surrendering in the global war against a disease without borders, Gates has filled the void. The U.S. is isolated, pitied, scorned. Gates, by one measure, is the most admired man in the world."[18]

However, a growing number of observers are voicing concern about the influence of the Gates Foundation on global policymaking. Critics on the left have long been skeptical of the interest and capacity of charities to address the inequalities that lay at the roots of many social problems,[19] but the Gates Foundation has drawn especially sharp criticism because of its technology-driven and market-centered approach to philanthropy. Bill Gates is frank about his belief in capitalism. In 2008 he published an article in *Time Magazine* in which he explained that what is really needed to address global problems is "to bring far more people into the system—capitalism—that has done so much good in the world." To do so, Gates contends that "we need a system that draws in innovators and businesses in a far better way than we do today."[20] The Gates Foundation's philosophy of social change is driven by this theory and the belief that technological innovation by the private sector can address global problems ranging from the spread of infectious disease to global food security to climate change mitigation and adaptation. As he explains in his recent book, "The Gates Foundation's whole approach to saving lives is based on the idea that we need to be pushing innovation for the poor while also increasing demand for it."[21] This model has been termed philanthrocapitalism by Gates's supporters and critics alike.[22] Although Gates's supporters see his market-driven approach to social change as a pragmatic solution to addressing public goods, critics charge that the Gates Foundation has pioneered "a new model of charity in which the most direct beneficiaries are sometimes not the world's poor but the world's wealthiest, in which the goal is not to help the needy but to help the rich help the needy."[23]

The Gates Foundation's funding for African agricultural development exemplifies its philanthrocapitalist approach. As the former deputy director of agricultural development at the Bill & Melinda Gates Foundation explained, "Our approach to improving lives at scale embodies the concept of catalytic philanthropy, which seeks to identify market and government failures and address those gaps. Since our inception, we have focused on supporting the provision of international public goods and on catalyzing the invention of innovative, high-leverage solutions."[24] Through its Global Development Program, the Gates Foundation has disbursed over $5 billion. Although only a small portion of this funding has gone to AGRA, all of the foundation's funding is driven by a desire to promote a Green Revolution on the African continent.

Approximately 85% of the Gates Foundation's funding for agricultural development has been focused on industrial agriculture.[25] Given Bill Gates's deep-seated belief in technology, much of this funding has gone toward quick fixes, such as new plant varieties and agricultural mechanization. The Gates Foundation has focused on exporting American and European agricultural science and the collection of plant genetic resources in the biodiverse-rich global South, as was done in the first Green Revolution.[26] As a result, most of the research that has been allocated for African agricultural development has not, in fact, been directed to African organizations and institutions but rather to universities and research institutes in the United States and Europe that are developing these technologies.[27] In her interviews with employees of the Gates Foundation, Rachel Schurman reveals how the foundation has absorbed the corporate culture of Microsoft. As a result, she argues that the foundation has developed "a decontextualized program that abstracted away from farmers' real agricultural and sociocultural worlds and preferred a set of universal (and *universalizing*) solutions."[28]

Of all the foundation's projects in the sphere of agriculture, its continuing funding and advocacy for agricultural biotechnology is the most controversial.[29] Currently only seven countries in sub-Saharan Africa have approved GMOs for commercial production. Most of these approvals have been for fiber and feed crops, not food.[30] Nevertheless, the Gates Foundation has promoted them with zeal. It has funded the development of genetically modified crops, including cowpeas, pigeon peas, sweet potatoes, cassava, bananas, sorghum, maize, and rice. Moreover, it funds organizations on the African continent to lobby governments to adopt permissive biosafety standards to enable the commercial production and sale of agricultural biotechnology. Almost half of all the funding that the Gates Foundation has dispersed to individual African-based organizations has gone to the African Agricultural Technology Foundation based in Nairobi,[31] "the single most important, pan-African institution working to ensure that GM crops can and will be used on the continent."[32] Matthew Schnurr therefore suggests that the Gates Foundation–led Green Revolution can be more accurately described as a "Gene Revolution" because it "is underpinned by the involvement of the private sector, which owns and controls most of the genetic constructs that are being imported, developed, or refined."[33]

This aggressive support for biotechnology has motivated global resistance. One of the first findings of AGRA Watch was Gates's investment in the largest producer of agricultural biotechnology, Monsanto.[34] Through their research and awareness raising, AGRA Watch has helped to build a transnational network combining the anti-biotechnology movement and food sovereignty movement to challenge this gene revolution. Today, a growing number of groups are voicing concern about the influence of the Gates Foundation as it extends its influence in global governance.[35]

In 2013, when I was beginning my research, AGRA Watch was preparing to host the Africa-US Food Sovereignty Strategy Summit. The meeting had been in the works since AGRA Watch was first established.[36] However, the organization had only recently secured funding from small family foundations and other grassroots organizations to actually hold the summit. AGRA Watch leaders had originally hoped to hold the summit in an African country, but they decided that it would be best to host the summit in Seattle and challenge the Gates Foundation on its home turf. When the coordinator of the summit had to step down, AGRA Watch asked me to work as a part-time coordinator of the summit.

Over four days in October 2014, seven African food sovereignty leaders and thirteen US-based food sovereignty activists convened at the Washington State Labor Council's office in Seattle's Central District. During the first day and a half, activists participated in structured activities, such as "fishbowls," in which they took turns sitting in circles and responding to questions about the issues they faced at home. Although all the activists mobilized the claim of food sovereignty, there were massive inequalities and differences between them—not only between the two continents but also within them. After one of the fishbowl activities in which US activists presented their struggles for food sovereignty, some of the African participants voiced skepticism that they would be able to find common ground. One South African activist asked what kinds of solidarity the participants from the United States even imagined when they claimed sovereignty. Another South African activist asked whether there were any realistic ways that activists from the United States and Africa could work together, given their different situations and struggles.

By the second day, however, the general coordinator of La Vía Campesina, a small-scale farmer from Zimbabwe, found herself surprised to find that activists from both continents were facing some of the same threats, from corporate consolidation and control to declining government support. "Growing up, I thought that these are the richest people in the whole world and the challenges we're facing as Africans never happen in the US," she told the activists at the summit. "But after yesterday's exercise about what's happening in Africa and the US, I have the sense that we are one, in one world. The most important thing about these challenges is coming up with strategies and unity. . . . If we can maintain this network and if there are those who have resources to strengthen this network, let it be done."

A key commonality that activists identified across both continents was their concern over corporate control of seeds. While the group was brainstorming on how they could collaborate beyond the summit, one activist rhetorically asked, "What realistically can we work together on? Food sovereignty is seeds and land." For food sovereignty activists, seeds have become a material and symbolic locus to challenge corporate control over agriculture. As another activist explained, seeds are critical because they "are the frontier to get people in the market. . . . When you control the seed market, every single farmer will need seeds to produce, so that's how the market's going to function." Food sovereignty movements have opposed the commercialization of seeds, instead promoting farmer-managed seed systems and common property regimes. This is because seeds are not just a product of natural biodiversity; they reflect the development of human knowledge of nature and culture over generations.[37]

In their struggle to promote diverse farmer-managed seed systems, much of food sovereignty activists' focus has been trained on contesting agricultural biotechnology and GMOs. Food sovereignty activists oppose GMOs because of both the intellectual property rights attached to these microorganisms and the potential threats that these crops pose to human health and biodiversity.[38] In the United States biotechnology is widespread in feed and fiber crops; 90% of the corn, cotton, and soy planted is genetically modified.[39] However, opponents of GMOs in the United States have faced obstacles to challenging biotechnology both because of the power of the agribusiness lobby in the United States and because of the US's permissive regulatory framework that treats genetically modified crops as substantially equivalent to conventional ones. Moreover, although genetically modified crops draw on new forms of technology and are provided with strong intellectual property protections, proprietary commercial seeds have been promoted by the US government since the 1930s. The spread of these seeds, historian Deborah Fitzgerald recounts, led to the deskilling of farmers and rendered most farmers reliant on markets to procure the inputs for agricultural production.[40] Biotech companies, the US government, and global philanthropies now seek to expand the markets for agricultural biotechnology to the global South. Proponents of agricultural biotechnology market it as "pro-poor" technology[41] and argue that GMOs can provide significant environmental and social benefits, from the reduction of pesticide use to the mitigation of global hunger as a result of greater agricultural productivity.[42] In promoting biotechnology, they seek to replicate the US's regulatory framework around the world.

In response to the growing efforts by biotechnology promoters to introduce GMOs worldwide, La Vía Campesina has become increasingly active in opposing GMOs. In 2003 La Vía Campesina unveiled its first campaign for "seed sovereignty." A recent publication by La Vía Campesina explains why seeds are so important for food sovereignty: "Seeds hold a special place in the struggle for food sovereignty. These small grains are the basis for the future. They shape, at each life cycle, the type of food people eat, how it is grown, and who grows it. Seeds are also a vessel that carries the past, the accumulated vision, and knowledge and practices of peasant and farming communities worldwide that over thousands of years created the basis of all that sustains us today."[43] For food sovereignty activists, seeds represent the accumulation and sharing of knowledge across generations. They have therefore reframed seeds as a struggle over knowledge.[44]

Thus, when the Super Banana was first described by a Ugandan activist at the summit, it seemed to capture many of the problems with the Gates Foundation–led gene revolution: its disregard for local knowledge, its emphasis on commercialized seeds ("suckers" in the case of bananas) that would need to be purchased by small-scale farmers, and its promotion of monocrop commercial farming over diversified food systems. However, the scientific and policy network that developed the Super Banana also offered a set of linkages that connected activists on both continents. By forming a counternetwork, they sought to challenge the Gates Foundation's effort to exert interpretive authority over GMOs and thereby influence the transnational regulation of agricultural biotechnology.

THE LAW AND POLITICS OF GENETICALLY MODIFIED SEEDS

Scientific innovations in plant breeding alone have not enabled corporate control over seeds and plant genetic resources. Rather, social technologies of law and regulation—especially the extension of intellectual property rights over plant germplasm—have shaped the politics of biotechnology and its distributive impacts. Corporations first pushed for patent rights over asexually reproduced seeds with the development of hybrid seeds in the United States. In 1930 the United States passed the Plant Patent Act, which recognized a set of limited rights for plant breeders. These rights were progressively expanded in the United States. Similar protections were created in Europe with the International Convention for the Protection of New Varieties of Plants in 1961. When recombinant DNA, or gene splicing, was discovered in the 1970s, the US Supreme Court extended intellectual property rights over these creations as well.[45] The development of intellectual property rights over agricultural biotechnology and other legal changes that made it profitable for firms to develop and market genetically engineered seeds significantly expanded the biotechnology industry in the United States.[46] As the industry grew and looked for new markets, the United States worked to institutionalize intellectual property rights over agricultural biotechnology through global treaties.

Outside the United States the conflict over agricultural biotechnology has been shaped by competing regulatory regimes and legal arenas. In fact, the fragmentation of transnational regulation of plant genetic resources has led scholars to study the regulation of plant genetic resources as a key case of legal pluralism and "regime complexity."[47] In this regulatory landscape two fields of law have developed to regulate agricultural biotechnology. The first includes those agreements that establish intellectual property rights over plant genetic resources. These include plant breeder's rights through the International Convention for the Protection of New Varieties of Plants[48] and the Agreement on Trade-Related Aspects of Intellectual Property Rights (TRIPS Agreement), which is enforced by the World Trade Organization.[49] These two agreements are largely a product of legal export from the United States and Europe. Together, they create alienable and privately owned rights in intellectual property over novel plant breeds and human-modified microorganisms, thereby incentivizing commercial seed breeding and development.

The second field of law regulates the risks of biotechnology to biodiversity and human health and limits access and benefit sharing to plant genetic resources. It is within this regulatory field that states from the global South have had greater influence. In particular, governments across the world were successful in countering the US's argument that modified microorganisms are substantially equivalent to their unmodified counterparts. Both the Convention on Biological Diversity and its Cartagena Protocol on Biosafety reflect the precautionary principle, which require states to develop regulatory frameworks to "ensure that the development, handling, transport, use, transfer and release of any living modified organisms are undertaken in a manner that prevents or reduces the risks to biological diversity, taking also into account risks to human health" *before* introducing these new technologies.[50]

The Cartagena Protocol on Biosafety provides states with some agency in determining whether to permit the production and marketing of agricultural biotechnology in their territories based on their assessments of the risks of these technologies. However, it does not challenge the underlying ideology of neoliberalism. Rather, it seeks to restrict resistance to GMOs by requiring opposition to be framed within the language of scientifically based evidence and risk assessment. Insisting that science is "the only *legitimate* ground for criticism" has served to constrain resistance to biotechnology.[51] In part this is because neoliberalism has led to the privatization and rolling-back of state funding for basic science and agricultural research. Much of the science produced in regard to agricultural biotechnology is funded by the industry in the global North.[52] The commercialization of knowledge has allowed private actors to claim expertise and therefore assert interpretive authority over biotechnology. Some scholars have described this restriction of regulatory science to the technical framework of risk as a form of biohegemony, a term developed by Peter Newell to refer to the "alignment of material, institutional, and discursive power in a way which sustains a coalition of forces which benefit from the prevailing model of agricultural development."[53] Biohegemony is produced by assembling scientists, regulatory reformers, and even genes themselves into networks based on shared knowledge practices. Through these networks, a cadre of powerful states, corporations, and philanthropies have sought to render debates about agricultural biotechnology as technical and apolitical.

Networks formed to resist biotechnology have nonetheless consistently reframed biotechnology through other cultural frameworks. In their study of the conflict between the United States and Europe over agricultural biotechnology, Mark Pollack and Gregory Shaffer describe how opponents of biotechnology mobilized cultural differences of risk to oppose the US's insistence on the substantial equivalence of GMOs to genetically modified products.[54] In her analysis of this conflict, science studies scholar Sheila Jasanoff similarly suggests that the conflict between the United States and Europe illustrates how "vast disagreements persist about the epistemological status of risk assessment."[55] She argues that by mobilizing competing cultural frameworks to interpret objects of biotechnology, opponents of GMOs challenge the interpretive authority of biotechnology promoters and illuminate the politics by which these products reconfigure nature and society.

How governments ultimately decide to regulate agricultural biotechnology is highly contingent on the actors, institutions, and crops involved.[56] However, across the global South, governments are facing strong pressure from transnational corporations, the United States, and philanthropies such as the Gates Foundation to permit the commercial production and marketing of agricultural biotechnology. Many of these countries have been slow to develop regulatory frameworks because of both skepticism of agricultural biotechnology and lack of capacity in managing risk. Signature genetically modified crops, such as the Super Banana, therefore serve as assemblages around which powerful actors seek to translate agricultural biotechnology and assert epistemological dominance. However, they also become a focal point for competing networks that seek to translate different forms of knowledge.

THE STRUGGLE OVER THE SUPER BANANA

The Gates Foundation began providing funding for the research and development of the Super Banana in 2005. Like Golden Rice in the Philippines (a project also funded by the Gates Foundation), the Super Banana is a beta-carotene-enhanced crop developed with the intention of preventing vitamin A deficiency, a problem linked to childhood blindness and even premature death. Vitamin A deficiency is a common form of micronutrient malnutrition, or "hidden hunger," that affects 2 billion people worldwide.[57] Beyond promoting more diverse diets, many effective interventions have been designed to target vitamin A deficiency, including pill-based supplements, enriched cooking oils, and traditionally bred seeds with high vitamin A content. However, the Gates Foundation has promoted biofortification of staple crops through genetic modification because it argues that they are more likely to reach rural populations who cannot access other types of interventions.

The Gates Foundation's decision to focus on a banana in Uganda to promote biotechnology in sub-Saharan Africa was a shrewd choice. Banana, or *matooke* as it is referred to locally, is a staple food in Uganda. The country is the world's largest consumer of bananas and is one of the largest producers. Seventy-five percent of small-scale farmers produce bananas for both subsistence consumption and markets, most of which are different cultivars of the East African Highland Banana.[58] Because bananas are sterile and difficult to breed conventionally, genetically modified bananas offer a potentially attractive solution to a range of widely recognized problems, including micronutrient deficiency and such plant diseases as Black Sigatoka and fusarium wilt. Moreover, whereas other East African countries have taken highly restrictive approaches to GMOs, Uganda has remained a lingering prospect for introducing agricultural biotechnology into African agricultural markets. Uganda has embraced a market-led approach since the 1990s, particularly in the agricultural sector; more than 80% of citizens depend on agriculture for their livelihoods.[59] The Gates Foundation and other promoters of agricultural biotechnology therefore saw the banana and its target country of Uganda as a new potential market for agricultural biotechnology. Eight different GM crops were being developed in Uganda at the time of the Africa-US Food Sovereignty Strategy Summit,[60] but the Gates Foundation selected the Super Banana as the primary emissary and face of biotechnology. The Super Banana thus emerged as a contentious object that competing networks sought to interpret, translating different forms of knowledge to influence Uganda's regulation of biotechnology.

The Super Banana Network
The Bill & Melinda Gates Foundation served as the primary translator of the Super Banana, beginning with the funding of its research and development. The Super Banana was developed at the Center for Tropical Crops and Biocommodities at the Queensland University of Technology in Australia by James Dale through support from the Gates Foundation's Grand Challenges in Global Health initiative. In 2003 the Gates Foundation issued a call for projects that "apply innovation in science and technology to the greatest health problems of the developing world." One of the grand challenges was to "create a full range of optimal, bioavailable nutrients in a single staple plant species." The Gates Foundation funded four projects—BioCassava Plus, Golden Rice, Africa Biofortified Sorghum, and Banana 21—each of which drew on technologies of genetic modification.[61] Banana 21 was a collaboration between the Queensland University of Technology and the National Banana Research Program of the National Agricultural Research Organization (NARO) of Uganda. Before he received funding, Dale had been working on the genetic modification of bananas

for several years. However, with the support of the Gates Foundation, Dale became an evangelist for biofortification. He starred in TED Talks and *New Yorker* articles arguing that genetic modification, or biofortification, of staple crops could be the solution to malnutrition for the poor.

Banana 21 was premised on the principle of technology transfer. Dale worked with and trained scientists at NARO to select cultivars of the East African Highland Banana that were good candidates for genetic modification. The first act of translation was a sociotechnical process in which Dale extracted a gene from the Asupina banana from Papua New Guinea and placed it first in a Cavendish cultivar to test it for increased levels of vitamin A. Dale used the gene from the Queensland Department of Primary Industries collection, an action that garnered some accusations of biopiracy.[62] This concern with biopiracy stems from the fact that, although seeds and plant genetic resources have been recognized as the common heritage of mankind, a controversial legal doctrine,[63] technology developers draw on these resources and then claim intellectual property rights over these genes when they are manipulated and inserted into the germplasm of another plant without providing compensation to the communities that developed and managed these resources. Nevertheless, the Queensland University of Technology planted field trials of the first genetically modified bananas in Australia in 2009. At the same time NARO scientists identified three cultivars that would be suitable for genetic modification: the Nakitembe, M9, and Sukali Ndiizi. In 2010 NARO launched the first trial in Uganda, which they hailed as the first confined field trial led by local scientists in sub-Saharan Africa.[64]

The next step in translation focused on convincing the Ugandan public and policymakers of the urgent need to develop permissive biosafety regulation so that these crops, once developed, could be commercially produced. As one of the original signatories of the Cartagena Protocol on Biosafety, Uganda was obliged to develop a set of regulatory guidelines for agricultural biotechnology before it could be commercially introduced. Although the Uganda National Council for Science and Technology had developed guidelines regarding confined field trials in 2006 and the containment of GMOs the following year, there was no national regulation to enable the commercial production of genetically modified crops. In 2012 the National Biotechnology and Biosafety Bill laid out objectives for the development of comprehensive regulation and identified relevant stakeholders, providing the framework for potential regulation.

A key challenge in developing a biosafety framework was the lack of regulatory capacity. Matthew Schnurr and Christopher Gore describe how the key agencies that were responsible for regulating biotechnology were highly donor dependent. Instead of receiving general funding from external donors, regulatory agencies in Uganda were shaped by specific projects. For example, NARO's institutional capacity was shaped by Banana 21 and another Gates-funded agricultural biotechnology project, Water Efficient Maize for Africa. The other regulatory agency responsible for biotechnology, the Uganda National Council for Science and Technology, relied on funding from the World Bank, the US Agency for International Development, and the African Biosafety Network of Expertise (which is also funded by Gates). Schnurr and Gore argue that "the regulatory system anchored by NARO and [the Uganda National Council for Science and Technology] has evolved such that those invested in the technology's success are also the ones evaluating its risks. The result is a system that is self-affirming and technology-affirming."[65] For this reason, Schnurr has described the regulatory networks produced by the Gates Foundation and its allies in Uganda as an example of biohegemony.[66]

In seeking to allay concerns about the potential risks to human health of the Super Banana, the Gates Foundation enrolled another set of actors: US-based food scientists. Some scientists have questioned whether beta-carotene-enriched bananas will have trouble being absorbed by the body or whether they may even be toxic.[67] The Gates Foundation therefore funded a human-feeding trial to test the uptake of the banana's beta-carotene in undergraduate students at Iowa State University. The study was conducted by Wendy White, a professor of food science and nutrition and an expert on vitamin A absorption. Her study on the Super Banana tested the absorption of vitamin A in twelve female undergraduates over four, three-day periods of banana consumption. The study aimed to dispel concerns about the health and safety of the Super Banana while demonstrating its efficacy.

Despite the seeming simplicity of the study, the Gates Foundation also developed yet another layer of actors to translate between the technical language of food science and vernacular understandings of safety. In 2014 the Gates Foundation gave a $5.6 million grant to Cornell University to create the Cornell Alliance for Science. The alliance is "an initiative for science-based agricultural communications that is focused on the global public good." Among the many goals in its mission statement, one is "reclaiming the conversation around agricultural biotechnology so that science- and evidence-based perspectives drive decision-making."[68] The Cornell Alliance for Science serves to equip local communications specialists with the knowledge and strategies to diffuse opposition to biotechnology. It funds a class of fellows each year to attend a twelve-week program in Ithaca, New York, to strengthen their strategic communication skills and to participate in regional leadership courses. Five of twenty-five inaugural Global Leadership Fellows came from Uganda. Among them was Consolata Acayo, the principal information scientist of the Ugandan Ministry of Agriculture, Animal Industry, and Fisheries, who in her web profile claims a "passion for biotechnology and GMOs." The other four Ugandan fellows all worked in communications for science and biotechnology related nongovernmental organizations, including one who worked specifically for Banana 21. These fellows published opinion pieces in local newspapers and engaged in policy advocacy in Uganda to promote agricultural biotechnology.

Together, this network of scientists, regulators, and journalists sought to shape the meaning of the Super Banana across divergent social contexts. Drawing on its vast financial resources, the Gates Foundation relied on the power of modernist, scientific epistemologies that seek to commensurate social, cultural, and ecological difference. As Sheila Jasanoff notes, the proliferation of biotechnology relies on "the assumption that socio-ecologies are as standard as the crops grown within them—put differently, that social and ecological circumstances at the periphery are not so radically different from those at the metropolitan center as to defeat the project of global technology transfer."[69] By framing the Super Banana through the technical language of risk and knowledge produced in Northern universities, the Gates Foundation and its allies sought to assure the Ugandan public and lawmakers that the banana would be assessed only through its biosafety rather than through other political, cultural, or economic calculi.

Yet, although the Gates Foundation aggressively promoted the Super Banana, it was met with intense resistance. In constructing a counternetwork to oppose the Gates Foundation and the Super Banana, activists drew on a competing set of epistemologies and knowledge practices.

Food Sovereignty Networks and
Resistance to the Super Banana

The Super Banana first came up at the Africa-US Food Sovereignty Strategy Summit during a public event at Seattle's Town Hall. The Super Banana seemed to be a perfect example not only of the Gates Foundation's hubris but also of how the foundation influences countries with its technology-driven vision of agricultural development. The following day, the Ugandan activist at the summit elaborated the problems with the Super Banana. First, she explained, the type of banana that the Gates Foundation sought to introduce was rarely fed to young children. Given that both James Dale and Bill Gates claimed that the Super Banana would save "millions of children," it was doubtful that it would even address the problem that it was developed to solve. Second, she pointed out, bananas are a key component of Ugandan culture and are a staple food. In fact, at least twenty-three different varieties of bananas are commonly grown by the many farmers who raise this crop in Uganda.[70] Many of these bananas are landraces, meaning that they are endemic to the region and have been developed over generations based on local knowledge and breeding practices. The speaker and other Ugandan activists worried that genetically modifying the matooke could erase the centuries of cultural and ecological heritage that the matooke represented. Finally, she pointed out that the Gates Foundation used the Super Banana to create a sense of greater urgency for introducing GMOs, even though Uganda had been purposely slow in regulating agricultural biotechnology. Indeed, Uganda has been developing regulation for more than twenty-two years, since a model piece of legislation was first developed by the Global Environment Facility.[71]

While activists in Uganda were quietly working to challenge the Super Banana through national political channels, they called on transnational solidarity to share information about the banana's development and challenge the Gates Foundation's legitimacy. In contrast to the limitless material resources of the Gates Foundation, CAGJ drew on its symbolic resources as a grassroots organization to coordinate a transnational counternetwork. Initially, the coalition included only a handful of participants from the summit. However, it soon grew to include organizations that mirrored the Gates Foundation's Super Banana network. CAGJ served as the main point

FIGURE 7 Panelists at the Africa-US Food Sovereignty Strategy Summit at Seattle's Town Hall, 2014. Photo by Alex Garland. Reprinted with permission.

of connection for activist groups based in Uganda, South Africa, Australia, and Iowa. Each group engaged in their own struggles and concerns, but they all participated (albeit to different extents) in the anti–Super Banana coalition. In Uganda and South Africa two continent-wide-focused networks and organizations—the Alliance for Food Sovereignty in Africa and the African Center for Biodiversity—participated in information sharing and provided connections to Kampala-based civil society activists who were directly lobbying members of Parliament.

Each of the participants in the network opposed the Super Banana and framed their arguments differently. In Australia and Iowa, where the research and testing of the Super Banana was carried out, activists focused on biosafety and the potential health risks of GMOs. In Australia activists in the anti-biotechnology movement focused their energy on directly confronting James Dale. In turn, a group of students at Iowa State University, one of whom had previously lived in Seattle and worked with CAGJ, challenged the human-feeding tests of the banana on undergraduate students. The university students were focused primarily on promoting sustainable agricultural research and practices at one of the US's preeminent land grant universities. They argued not only that the design of the study was arbitrary but also that it would fail to replicate the diets of rural Ugandans who were the target population for this intervention. In 2015 the internationally renowned activist Vandana Shiva visited the campus and spoke at Iowa State, where she specifically brought up the testing of the Super Banana. Students put together a petition and collected over 1,000 signatures to urge the university administration to stop the tests. Soon after, AGRA Watch worked with CREDO Mobile, a progressive cellular phone company, to gather over 57,000 names in an additional petition to the administration of Iowa State. When the petition was delivered on February 15, 2015, university students and AGRA Watch held simultaneous demonstrations outside the Iowa State campus and the Gates Foundation.

AGRA Watch and the Alliance for Food Sovereignty in Africa framed their challenge to the Super Banana around arguments of local control. In 2015 they sent a letter to the Gates Foundation signed by more than 125 organizations that raised concerns about the larger problem of philanthrocapitalism and foreign intervention in African agriculture.

FIGURE 8   AGRA Watch members, wearing banana costumes, protesting outside the Gates Foundation headquarters in Seattle. Photo by Jonathan Lee. Reprinted with permission.

These crops divert resources away from more locally appropriate and controlled agricultural solutions to nutritional concerns. If indeed the aim of those involved in the promotion of the project is truly to combat Vitamin A deficiency then surely they should be advocating for the consumption of more diverse fruits and foods, such as sweet potatoes that are rich in Vitamin A and that are in abundance in Africa. Ironically, the promotion of a GM food staple high in Vitamin A, risks perpetuating monolithic diets, the very causes of Vitamin A deficiency in the first place.[72]

AGRA Watch estimated that the Gates Foundation spent $30,385,393 on funding research and development of the Super Banana between 2005 and 2015. They challenged the use of these funds to promote a quick fix to a problem for which there were already well-proven solutions and argued that the research ultimately served to encourage agro-industrialization. Rather than embracing the technical framing of the Super Banana, they instead emphasized the structural inequalities that the Gates Foundation–led approach to industrializing agriculture would exacerbate.

In Uganda activists framed their concerns somewhat differently. In 2018 I met with several activists in Kampala who described the challenges they faced in opposing the Gates Foundation–led network. One challenge was the regulatory capture of scientific agencies by the Gates Foundation. As described earlier, the shift from general aid from donor countries to funding for specific projects has shaped the regulatory capacity and the knowledge practices of the two scientific agencies responsible for regulating biotechnology. However, another important challenge was the political environment of Uganda, which has remained under the rule of Yoweri Museveni for over thirty-five years. Although Museveni has pursued neoliberal reforms, Uganda remains a semi-authoritarian state in which the space for civil society has become increasingly limited.[73] This has constrained how aggressive civil society activists can be in challenging state institutions, especially because Museveni has in the past voiced support for agricultural biotechnology. Yet given that small-scale farmers remain a major part of the electorate and that Museveni has also supported efforts to protect Indigenous knowledge, civil society activists framed their challenges to the Super Banana through the language of culture. Over 100 indigenous cultivars of bananas are grown in East Africa, and bananas have many important cultural uses.[74]

For example, one of the cultivars that the Gates Foundation had targeted for biofortification, the Nakitembe, is often given as a gift during marriage ceremonies.[75] Ugandan activists thus framed their opposition to the Super Banana, and agricultural biotechnology more broadly, by asserting control over local and indigenous plant genetic resources.

Initially, the Gates Foundation's strategy of framing the debate in terms of safety and risk was successful in the Ugandan Parliament. In 2017 the Parliament finally passed the National Biosafety Act. Most observers expected that President Museveni would sign the bill into law. GMO supporters were therefore surprised when in December 2017 Museveni returned the bill to Parliament with a letter raising concerns. The president's letter is illuminating because it reflects the quiet work of a handful of local civil society organizations in Uganda that had been working through informal connections to translate the claim of food sovereignty into terms that resonated with the president. In his letter to Parliament Museveni challenged the technocratic language of the law: "I am writing in connection with the 'Bio-Safety Law' which, in fact, means 'genetic engineering.'" After unsettling the technocratic framing, he went on to address the question of property: "There are ancient crops and livestock with unique genetic configuration," and he named several examples, including Ankole cattle, the long-horned cattle from President Museveni's home region of which he was especially protective. He continued, "This law, apparently talks of giving monopoly of patent rights to this adder (*omwongyerezi*) and forgets about the communities that developed original material. This is wrong. Yes, we appreciate the adder. However, we cannot forget the original preservers, developers and multipliers of the original materials. This must be clarified."

Although the Gates Foundation and other actors had been careful to avoid questions of property, Museveni's response nevertheless went straight to this issue. The Gates Foundation framed biotechnology as a technical issue of risk and safety, but the issue of property rights loomed in the background. According to the TRIPS Agreement, countries that permit the commercial production of biotechnology must provide patent protections for genetically modified microorganisms. Museveni therefore moved to assert *communal* property rights over indigenous genetic resources. The framework of cultural property is closely aligned with food sovereignty. Both cultural property rights and food sovereignty have been used by postcolonial states as a framework to claim control over knowledge and practices that neoliberal actors seek to expropriate. Indeed, the recent proliferation of cultural property claims reflects the deepening ways in which countries and actors in the global North have appropriated greater control over subaltern resources, first through direct control over land and then through control over proprietary rights over knowledge and plant genetic resources. By declaring Ugandan sovereign control over indigenous knowledge practices and genetic resources, Museveni's claim reflects a new articulation of sovereignty premised on claims to common property over knowledge of plant genetic resources.

In 2018 the Ugandan Parliament passed the Genetic Engineering Regulatory Act. The act allows for genetic modification but contains several provisions that civil society advocated for, including a clause about benefit sharing, traceability, strict liability for resulting harms to human and environmental health, mandatory labeling, and a provision prohibiting the commingling of indigenous crops with GMOs.[76] Civil society publicly praised the national biosafety bill. However, the passage of the act generated criticism from GMO promoters and those within the Gates Foundation network, prompting renewed attacks on the "anti-GMO lobby."[77] Yet on July 22, 2019, President Museveni once again declined to sign the bill. "The issue of GMOs and genetic modification of our seeds and livestock . . . touches not only on science, but agriculture, ecology, and national security and, indeed, the sovereignty of our nation," he wrote to the Speaker of Parliament, Rebecca Kadaga.

In his letter to Parliament, President Museveni raised several concerns about the bill. He suggested that the benefits-sharing arrangements needed to be clarified, that additional regulations were needed to prevent the commingling of GMO materials with non-GMO materials, and that the scope of coverage of the law should be limited to genetic modification technologies that were well known and previously studied, such as crops developed for pest resistance. The president also reaffirmed the importance of the strict liability cause, which would make it the responsibility of technology developers to prove that their products would not harm human or ecological health. He concluded his letter by reminding Members of Parliament about the thalidomide controversy; thalidomide was marketed as a drug to treat nausea in pregnant women but ended up causing severe birth defects in thousands of children in the 1950s. He used this drug as a warning about the potential harm of new technologies. Ultimately, Museveni argued for a precautionary approach that balanced the ecological and human health of Uganda with economic goals. "I do understand that there are large commercial interests behind the promotion of this technology," he wrote. "These commercial interests, however, need to be balanced against the needs to protect the ordinary Ugandan citizens from real or potential harm. Health and well-being rather than profits must be our primary concern."

CONCLUSIONS

At the public event held during the Africa-US Food Sovereignty Strategy Summit in Seattle, one South African activist summarized her critique of the Gates Foundation to an audience of over 250 people: "We see the Green Revolution as another form, another phase of colonialism that's coming to take over the last parts of what is really African—our food, our land, and our sovereignty. We need people-to-people solidarity, not corporate takeover." She was not alone in depicting the Gates Foundation as a new wave of colonialism; scholars have identified many continuities between the "new" Green Revolution and earlier colonial ventures in which North Atlantic states took direct control over African territory and natural resources. During that era, science and biology were mobilized in the service of empire to catalogue and command the natural world. Colonialism was rationalized through what historian Peder Anker terms imperial ecologies: "an order of knowledge [developed] for managerial overview" that served to "naturalize imperialism."[78] Today, science is once again being deployed at the behest of power and control. But now, given that subaltern states have formal sovereignty over their territories, powerful actors seek to exercise power through transnational governance networks.

By drawing on the decontextualized knowledge of plant genetic resources developed by universities and corporations in the global North, powerful actors assemble networks of genes, scientists, and regulatory reformers who seek to claim a monopoly of knowledge over the natural world. In doing so, contemporary biotechnology networks attempt to naturalize and depoliticize agricultural biotechnology, just as former imperial ecologies did. They also marginalize other forms of knowledge to promote these highly profitable technologies. Thus, although actors in the global North may no longer have direct control over land and natural resources in the global South, corporations seek to maintain control through proprietary knowledge embedded in agricultural biotechnology.

In the struggle over agricultural biotechnology, corporations not only exert power *through* knowledge but also seek control *over* knowledge through intellectual property rights. The TRIPS Agreement specifically requires that governments protect intellectual property rights over genetically modified microorganisms. This is why GMOs are an object of neoliberal contention par excellence; they represent the confluence of market-driven state agriculture policy, the commercialization of scientific knowledge, and the expansion of property rights to life itself. Thus, even in states and regions that have embraced neoliberalism, such as Uganda, introducing GMOs into food systems represents a moral threshold that many states refuse to cross. Although some countries have been willing to adopt GMOs into feed and fiber crops, others have mounted powerful resistance to the introduction of biotechnology into food crops.

Transnational corporations have often been seen as the drivers of agricultural biotechnologies, but philanthropies are playing a growing role in promoting these technologies in the global South. With no declared financial interests in biotechnology, the Gates Foundation claims legitimacy to promote particular models of development based on its philanthropic goodwill and expertise. Through "gifts" like the Super Banana and other signature products, such as Golden Rice in the Philippines and Water Efficient Maize for Africa, the Gates Foundation enrolls scientists, regulators, and selective civil society actors into networks that seek to translate these objects transnationally. These networks seek to delegitimize critics of biotechnology by labeling them as antiscience and, in so doing, endeavor to shape a facilitative regulatory environment for its technology-driven approach to agricultural development.

Food sovereignty activists around the world have therefore converged to oppose the Green Revolution and agricultural biotechnology in an effort to protect local and Indigenous forms of knowledge that are embedded in plant genetic resources and food systems. Activists resist the Gates-funded networks' representation of its knowledge as universal and uncontroversial and instead seek to reveal it as an expression of power. Moreover, critics point out that the Gates-funded Green Revolution has failed even on its own terms. Since the Gates Foundation began its funding in 2006, hunger has increased by 30% in the thirteen sub-Saharan countries that the foundation targeted. Moreover, the small gains in production have been largely in expanding monocrop maize production, which in addition to being ecologically unsustainable has contributed to making diets less diverse.[79]

As food sovereignty movements challenge epistemological enclosure through the Green Revolution, they promote the transdisciplinary science of agroecology as an alternative to "innovations" premised on proprietary knowledge. Agroecology's commitment to people's knowledge, the free sharing of information through farmer-to-farmer exchange, and the emphasis on working *with* nature rather than against it serves as a competing epistemology through which food sovereignty activists construct counternetworks. As Eric Holt-Giménez and Miguel Altieri explain in their analysis of the Green Revolution for Africa, "The need for structural support for smallholders in locally based agroecology networks, and the globalized agrarian demands of food sovereignty movements are complementary areas of strategic synergy."[80] By promoting agroecology, food sovereignty activists seek to cultivate alternative ways of knowing and working with nature.

Following the Africa-US Food Sovereignty Strategy Summit, activists organized several agroecology exchanges. Initially, a small group of South African farmers and farmworkers visited the United States and toured farms on the East Coast, West Coast, and in the Midwest. Afterward, a group of US-based farmers and farmworkers from the US Food Sovereignty Alliance traveled to South Africa for another agroecology exchange. In contrast to the downward transmission of proprietary technologies promoted by neoliberal networks, these cross-continental knowledge exchanges offer a prefigurative model of horizontal knowledge exchange. They focus not just on the science of production but on agriculture in its total social, political, and ecological context.

By approaching agricultural knowledge holistically, agroecological food sovereignty networks stand in stark contrast to biotechnology networks. Whereas the biotechnology networks continue to draw on the colonial ideology of improvement and modernization to promote a vision of the liberal state whose authority is rooted in private property relations, food sovereignty movements draw on agroecology to imagine new relations between nature, property, and sovereignty rooted in common property regimes and communal governance. As food sovereignty activists form transnational networks, they are developing new visions of state authority. Yet it is in arenas of global governance where this can be seen most clearly. I explore this global context in the next chapter.

5   Democratizing Global Food Governance

I WAS FIRST INTRODUCED to the Committee on World Food Security (CFS) in autumn 2013 during a North American consultation on the Principles for Responsible Agricultural Investment (PRAI). Over thirty-five activists gathered in Washington, DC, to strategize on how to influence the process. There was a lot to learn; the PRAI reflected the complex political and legal field of global food governance, which is composed of competing international institutions and actors, all seeking to frame issues and establish regulatory control over food and agriculture. The PRAI had first been developed by the World Bank and several UN organizations to address the growing issue of "land grabs"—large-scale land acquisitions by foreign investors for food, fuel, and speculation.[1] But as soon as they were introduced in 2010, La Vía Campesina and its allies roundly rejected them. Activists described the PRAI as "window dressing" for the "corporate takeover of rural people's farmlands."[2] Food sovereignty activists called on the CFS to rewrite the PRAI through an inclusive process.

By 2013 the CFS had become the epicenter of struggles over global food governance. Once a relatively sleepy committee of the UN Food and Agriculture Organization (FAO) in Rome, the CFS underwent a reform in 2009 in response to the 2007–2008 food crisis that made it the "foremost international and intergovernmental platform for all stakeholders to work together to ensure food security and nutrition for all."[3] As a result of the reform, the CFS is now one of the only arenas in the United Nations where people's movements and civil society organizations have a direct voice in shaping global policy. Food sovereignty activists have therefore invested significant amounts of energy into the CFS, holding it up as an example of what democratic food governance might look like.

The importance of the CFS for the global food sovereignty movement is what initially led me to follow US-based food sovereignty activists as they participated in the PRAI process alongside global food sovereignty leaders. Over the next eight years, as I engaged in fieldwork with the networks of food sovereignty and civil society activists engaged in the CFS, I sought to understand how their participation in this global arena of governance shaped their practices of mobilization and translation at the regional and local levels. The CFS and, in particular, the Civil Society and Indigenous Peoples' Mechanism (CSM) of the CFS, I would learn, is a critical space where food sovereignty activists engage in translocal translation, bringing local knowledge and experiences to the global level and creating new understandings and strategies for engaging in governance back home. By participating in the CFS, a space where the stakes are high and the world is watching, food sovereignty activists constitute new political constituencies and dialectically articulate a new vision of global political and legal organization.

In this chapter I depart from the Pacific Northwest to examine how food sovereignty activists have cultivated new practices of representation in the CFS, focusing specifically on the transformation of the PRAI. In moving up to this global scale, I analyze how food sovereignty activists mobilize the language of human rights. The turn to human rights at the end of this book may strike the reader as surprising. As I argued earlier, human rights do not serve as the primary collective action frame of the food sovereignty movement. In fact, food sovereignty activists developed their claim to transcend the limits they saw in human rights. But in the context of international institutions, human rights play a critical role. As food sovereignty activists face a global order in which states are increasingly reduced to facilitators for neoliberal capitalism, human rights serve as a normative framework that food sovereignty activists mobilize to ground global governance in the obligations that states have to *people* rather than corporations. As frontline food sovereignty activists engage in the CFS, they demand that their voices be heard by emphasizing their role not as *stake*holders but as *rights* holders.

In analyzing how food sovereignty activists mobilize the right to food in the CFS, I argue that human rights operate as more than just a legal claim to hold states accountable for their obligations under international law. Activists mobilize human rights as a "representative claim," a political and symbolic claim through which food sovereignty activists constitute new political constituencies of those most affected by food insecurity and stake the legitimacy of the CFS in accountability to those constituencies.[4] By importing the antagonistic framework of liberal legalism back into what has been critiqued as postpolitical or neoliberal forms of governance, food sovereignty movements selectively draw on the logics of rights to create a political space through which to translate their own prefigurative practices of self-representation and to democratize global governance. Therefore in this chapter I illustrate how food sovereignty activists mobilize the right to food in the CFS as a representative claim to (1) demand inclusion of those most affected by food insecurity into arenas of governance through processes of self-organization and self-representation and (2) challenge the neoliberal rationalities produced by hegemonic forms of multistakeholder governance by politicizing global food and agricultural governance as a space of inequality.

The transformation of the PRAI offers a particularly productive example of how rights are mobilized to democratize global food security governance. During the negotiations over the principles, private sector participants in the CFS continually represented food and agricultural systems as markets that needed regulatory standards to facilitate corporate investment in land and resources. In opposing this narrative, food sovereignty activists mobilized the right to food. As one of the leaders of the negotiations for civil society explained to me, "Our argument was that, sure, investment is fine and important, but investment cannot trump rights. The role of the CFS is to protect and uphold the right to food, not to create apologies for rights in the name of food security or economic imperatives." By emphasizing rights as the primary framework through which food and agricultural governance must be guided, food sovereignty activists challenged the neoliberal representation of global food and agricultural governance while also demanding that food and agricultural governance be accountable to people facing food insecurity. Rights therefore served as a powerful legal and political resource in international institutions for activists pursuing food sovereignty.

This chapter is based on ethnographic fieldwork that I began in the CFS in 2013. Since then, I have attended six of the annual week-long meetings of the CFS and participated in the virtual networks of social movements and civil society organizations that participate in the CFS. In addition, I participated in many policymaking processes of the CFS and conducted both formal and informal interviews of civil society activists who participate in the CFS. Like all of my fieldwork, my participation in these networks was both as a scholar and as an activist. I often assisted in meetings by providing technical assistance to participants, whether that was note taking, advocacy, or coordinating communication among activists. Engaging in these struggles alongside activists allowed me to understand the profound challenges and often subtle victories of food sovereignty activists as they engaged in profoundly asymmetric power relations.

I begin by tracing the rise of the field of global food security governance that produced the CFS, locating contemporary struggles over the form and function of the CFS within broader debates over the democratic prospects of networked forms of governance. I then consider how the right to food has been elaborated by legal experts and mobilized by food sovereignty activists in the CFS. I illustrate how food sovereignty activists have drawn on legal and political meanings of the right to food to construct political spaces through which to cultivate their own representative practices and challenge hegemonic representations of global food and agricultural governance. Ultimately, I reveal how food sovereignty activists mobilize the right to food to cultivate new forms of representation and thereby democratize global food security governance.

CONSTRUCTING GLOBAL FOOD SECURITY GOVERNANCE

The field of what is often referred to as global food security governance is a contested regulatory space composed of competing institutions, actors, and bodies that have been layered on top of one another over time to advance various ideologies and agendas.[5] For years, de facto food security governance was asserted by hegemonic actors through colonial and capitalist forms of control.[6] However, in the 1940s, as the world responded to

President Franklin Roosevelt's call for "four essential freedoms," countries agreed to develop a permanent organization dedicated to ending global hunger. In fact, the establishment of the FAO preceded the UN General Assembly.[7] Although the FAO's first director, John Boyd Orr, sought to establish an organization with significant power and authority to influence national food production policies, his proposal was dismissed by the United States and other powerful countries.[8] Almost as soon as the FAO was founded, Orr's vision of public global food governance was undermined by the United States in an effort to maintain its political and economic dominance over the global food trade.

During the 1970s, when the world experienced a food price crisis, the architecture of global food governance was once again the subject of debate. During the crisis, it became apparent that the United States could no longer exercise political control over global trade and fossil fuel resources.[9] In response, countries convened in Rome for the World Food Conference in November 1974. Over ten days, governments participating in the conference struggled to address the problem of global hunger—or "food insecurity," as it was termed—then conservatively estimated to be 460 million people.[10] Western countries framed the crisis as a technical problem, offering to increase food aid and provide more technical assistance to developing states. By contrast, countries in the global South wished to address the problems of overconsumption by the industrialized global North and colonial underdevelopment by constructing a new international economic order based on more equitable relations of trade.

During the conference, a new global architecture to govern global food security was established. In a set of compromises the FAO's authority was diluted, and different functions were farmed out to a set of new organizations, including a new World Food Council and the International Fund for Agricultural Development.[11] In addition, the CFS was founded as a standing committee of the FAO. However, throughout the 1980s and 1990s a number of forces colluded to undermine the ability of any of these institutions to effectively govern global food. The World Food Council, which was always a creature of compromise, became mired in conflict. As a commodity crisis weakened the global South and demand for a new economic international order waned, traditional and new agricultural exporting countries began to compete over global markets. Neoliberalism emerged as the dominant ideology as powerful Northern states sought to assert control over former colonies through the market.[12] During this period, international finance institutions and even the FAO reinterpreted "food security" through a market-based framework of individual purchasing power.[13] In successive rounds of talks on the Global Agreement on Trade and Tariffs, countries began to negotiate the liberalization of global food and agricultural markets, a sector that had previously been understood as a realm of national value. Soon enough, the political will of countries in the global North to create a political institution dedicated to the global food system withered. By 1993 the World Food Council was disbanded. Two years later, the signing of the Agreement on Agriculture effectively made the World Trade Organization the dominant institution of global food security governance.

At the same time that free trade was ascending as the dominant principle of global food security, however, transnational food sovereignty networks were emerging. Although food sovereignty networks demanded that agriculture be removed from the free trade agreements of the World Trade Organization, they found a foothold in the FAO. The FAO's role as the only international institution dedicated to ending hunger and its structure as a multilateral organization premised on a one-country, one-vote system made the FAO more sympathetic to the demands of small-scale food producers. In 1996, just after states agreed to liberalize food and agricultural markets, food sovereignty activists organized one of the largest gatherings of small-scale producers, food chain workers, fisherfolk, NGOs (nongovernmental organizations), and youth in an attempt to influence the World Food Summit, which was hosted by the FAO. It was there, at a parallel summit, that NGOs and social movements demanded food sovereignty in front of the rest of the world in their statement at the plenary session of the summit. Yet as described in chapter 1, even though the statement was framed in the language of food sovereignty, La Vía Campesina did not participate in the statement. They demanded to represent themselves, establishing a new context of advocacy and activism in which questions of representation would be pivotal.

Five years after the 1996 summit, the FAO organized a follow-up World Food Summit. In preparation for the 2002 summit, La Vía Campesina, together with allied movements, international NGOs, and regional networks, formed what would later be named the International Planning Committee for Food Sovereignty (IPC). The IPC was a novel platform that organized itself as a facilitation mechanism, not a centralized structure of representation. It privileged the voices of social movements and frontline actors in food systems, notably small-scale and Indigenous food producers and workers. After facilitating participation in the 2002 summit, the IPC signed a formal letter of understanding with the FAO. Self-representation was a guiding principle of the IPC-FAO agreement from the start. The IPC set a precedent for a social movement–international organization interface by creating an autonomous space through which food sovereignty activists could translate their own representational practices.

One of the few outcomes of the 2002 World Food Summit was the formation of the Intergovernmental Working Group to elaborate a set of voluntary guidelines on the right to food. Over the next two years the IPC participated in negotiating the "Voluntary Guidelines to Support the Progressive Realization of the Right to Adequate Food in the Context of National Food Security," which were adopted by member states of the FAO in November 2004. Although academics and activists were critical of the final document, the guidelines were important because they gave significant weight to human rights as a normative framework for food security governance.[14] They also set a precedent for civil society engagement in policymaking processes through a set of principles to guide human-rights-based decision making: participation, accountability, nondiscrimination, transparency, human dignity, empowerment, and rule of law, collectively known as the PANTHER framework.

When the world experienced yet another global food price crisis in 2007 and it became clear that the market-based approach to regulating the global food system failed to ensure global food security, the lack of an institution with the ability to coordinate a global policy response was widely perceived as a problem. During the crisis, countries in the global South, transnational food sovereignty movements, and UN leaders all called for an international body that would be responsible for governing the global food system. Many institutions began to vie for authority, including the G8, international finance institutions, and other bodies in the UN system, but transnational movements and developing countries objected that these institutions neither had the expertise of the FAO nor included the voices of those whom these initiatives were designed to assist. La Vía Campesina and the IPC lobbied for the CFS to serve as the primary arena of global food governance, because it was the only international arena specifically dedicated to the issue of food security. Member states of the CFS eventually agreed to begin a reform process that would renew its importance in global food politics.

The reform of the CFS was based on two principles: evidence-based decision making and inclusivity. In terms of decision making, the CFS created the High Level Panel of Experts, a science-policy interface that develops reports on the topics and themes that the CFS seeks to address through policy guidelines.[15] In terms of inclusivity, there was significantly more contestation. During the reform process, many actors debated how inclusive to make the CFS. The US government consistently argued to "keep governance and CFS bureaucracy 'light.'" The United States was happy to use the language of inclusivity, but it was nervous about the involvement of "groups like Vía Campesino [sic] and others critical of US policies."[16] The United States used the language of inclusivity to argue for private sector involvement. On the other hand, civil society organizations, including La Vía Campesina, the IPC, and allied international NGOs, argued that those who were most affected by the global food system needed to be included in the decision-making processes of this new regulatory body. In this struggle over the structure of the CFS, different parties imbued inclusivity with distinct meanings that reflected different interests.

As a result of these debates, the CFS was redesigned with a unique structure. The CFS remains an intergovernmental body; states are the core members and the only actors with voting rights. However, in accordance with the PANTHER framework, the CFS includes a wide range of other participants, including other UN bodies, international agricultural research institutes, international financial and trade institutions, and two "autonomous" self-organized platforms: the CSM[17] and the Private Sector Mechanism, which were developed to facilitate participation from these groups. The construction of these two mechanisms was a major victory for food sovereignty movements. On the one hand, as a key organizer of IPC explained to me, the construction of the Private Sector Mechanism required the private sector to be transparently involved in the policymaking process rather than influencing it through back-channel lobbying. On the other hand, food sovereignty activists were able to autonomously determine their own structure of representation.

The Committee on World Food Security

Structure and Process

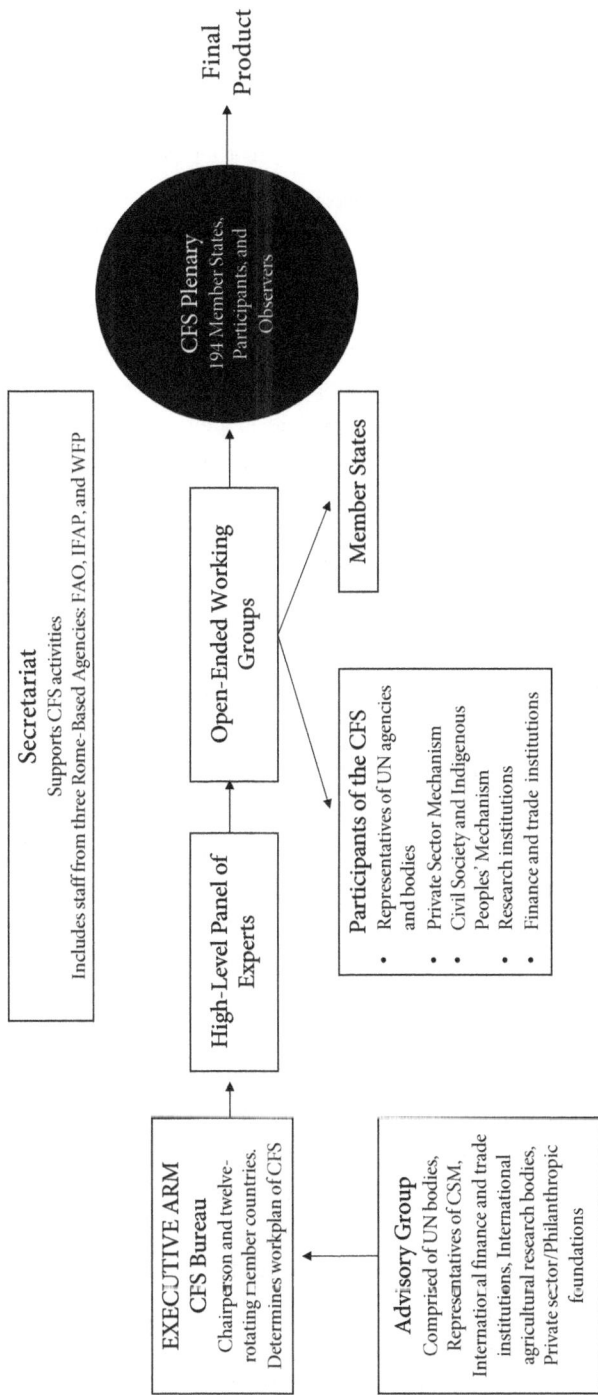

FIGURE 9 The process by which decisions are made in the CFS. Diagram by author.

By adopting this structure, a renewed and reformed CFS emerged. Its vision in its 2009 reform document describes the CFS as "the foremost inclusive international and intergovernmental platform for a broad range of committed stakeholders to work together in a coordinated manner and in support of country-led processes towards the elimination of hunger and ensuring food security and nutrition for all human beings. The CFS will strive for a world free from hunger where countries implement the voluntary guidelines for the progressive realization of the right to adequate food in the context of national food security."[18] This description carries an inherent tension. Although there is widespread consensus that states remain the only voting members of the CFS, there nevertheless remains a debate over how to characterize the CFS. Many of the chairs of the CFS—delegates from member states elected by member states for two-year terms—have described the CFS as a multistakeholder platform to give the CFS greater legitimacy among its participants. For example, in 2019 the chair of the CFS opened up the annual meetings by describing the CFS as a multistakeholder platform. Describing the reform of the CFS, he told the plenary session that "when, in 2007/2008, another global food crisis necessitated a fundamentally different approach, CFS was transformed into a multistakeholder platform which is a revolutionary advancement in United Nations architecture where governments, civil society, the private sector, scientists, and others now sit together as partners and we are, for the first time ever, sitting together here in this room today."

Food sovereignty activists, however, reject this characterization. In explaining to me the problem with the term *stakeholders*, one staff member of the CSM secretariat joked that "not everyone has a steak to eat." He told me that "the basic assumption is that [corporations] are actually on the same footing as we are. And this is absolutely a misconception. They do not represent small-scale food producers. They do not represent those that have been excluded traditionally at the national, regional, or global level." Food sovereignty activists prefer to describe the CFS as a "multi-actor" body or as an example of "inclusive multilateralism" in an effort to reaffirm that states are the main decision makers and that not every actor has an equal stake in the process.

These persisting conflicts over the structure of the CFS have significant stakes. Contests over how to represent actors in the CFS play a constitutive role in its decision-making processes. Powerful actors have leveraged the language of stakeholders in an attempt to change the composition of the CFS Advisory Group to minimize the voice of frontline food producers and workers organized in the CSM, a bid that powerful Northern states have promoted to suppress debates over their human rights obligations. Moreover, as the foremost international arena dedicated to food security, debates over the structure of the CFS reverberate across the world as other local, national, and international arenas look to the CFS as a best practice for participatory transnational governance.

CONTESTED FORMS OF PARTICIPATORY GOVERNANCE

The debate over how to characterize the inclusive structure of the CFS reflects larger debates over the democratic prospects of participatory global governance. Although the United Nations has granted consultative status to NGOs since the 1940s, pressure to expand participation grew in the 1990s from both above and below. On the one hand, transnational social movements sought to leverage international institutions to challenge neoliberalism, just as anticolonial movements had once drawn on the human rights ideals of the United Nations to oppose imperialism.[19] On the other hand, as global capitalism spread with the end of the cold war, multinational corporations sought to set the standards for growing global markets. Participatory approaches to governance began to be adopted by the United Nations, most famously with the 1992 Earth Summit held in Rio de Janeiro. Over the next several years a series of influential reports and UN summits across the entire United Nations continued to expand participation in UN processes as countries grappled with the structural transformation of the global order away from the Westphalian ideal.[20] Yet, although today support for inclusivity and participation is widespread, debates over how to recognize distinctions among nonstate actors and how to design participatory processes that account for uneven relations of power have been a significant source of friction.

In this debate multistakeholderism has emerged as a key framework through which participation has been framed. The term *multistakeholder*, which refers to all affected actors of a given issue, was originally developed in the scholarly field of business management. In the 1980s the concept of stakeholder management was promoted as an approach to deal with both

internal changes resulting from the expansion of global production networks and external changes related to growing environmental movements
and the looming threat of government regulation. The stakeholder model
of management was explicitly designed to reframe the relations between
corporations, society, and the state, moving away from the model of antagonistic, competing interest groups toward a more consensual framework in
which interdependent actors all contribute to "value creation."[21] During the
1990s, this model migrated from corporate boardrooms to public administration. Governments at local and regional levels adopted multistakeholder
models of governance as neoliberalism led them to adopt a more facilitative
regulatory posture. In the follow-up to the Earth Summit, at the 2002 World
Summit for Sustainable Development in Johannesburg, multistakeholder
and hybrid approaches to governance were explicitly endorsed.[22]

Given the origins of stakeholder theory, it is no surprise that corporations have been some of the strongest supporters of multistakeholder
governance. The World Economic Forum, the Davos-based organization
that represents the world's largest corporations, has been at the helm of
the effort to redesign global governance through the multistakeholder format. After the 2007–2008 food and financial crisis, the World Economic
Forum launched the Global Redesign Initiative through which it sought
to "redefine the international system as constituting a wider, multifaceted
system of global cooperation in which intergovernmental legal frameworks
and institutions are embedded as a core, but not the sole and sometimes
not the most crucial, component."[23] Amid the global pandemic the forum
renewed these calls to redesign international institutions in the model of
stakeholder capitalism. The executive chairman of the World Economic
Forum, Klaus Schwab, has called for a "Great Reset." He contends that
"COVID-19 is likely to sound the death knell of neoliberalism" and that
without reframing their contribution to economic and social governance,
the corporate sector is likely to experience serious threats to their bottom
line.[24] As part of this effort to engage more closely in global governance,
the World Economic Forum signed a "Strategic Partnership Framework"
with the United Nations in 2019.

Food sovereignty movements have increasingly organized against multistakeholderism. Activists argue that it creates a fiction of formal equality
among stakeholders and diminishes states' responsibilities for respecting,

protecting, and fulfilling human rights. Critical scholars further argue that multistakeholder models of governance operate as a form of neoliberal reason that displaces democratic norms. For example, Wendy Brown argues that "governance fundamentally reconceptualized democracy as distinct or divorced from politics and economics: democracy becomes purely procedural and is detached from the power that would give it substance and meaning as a form of rule."[25] Another similar strand of critique has argued that the absence of any substantive or symbolic public has depoliticized and technicalized participation, narrowing the scope of political change—what some analysts describe as the postpolitics of multistakeholder governance.[26]

Empirical findings of multistakeholder governance in the context of food and agriculture have supported these critical assessments. The CFS's High Level Panel of Experts urges great caution when considering multistakeholder approaches to address food security and nutrition. In a recent report the panel noted that "there is a risk for [multistakeholder platforms] to reproduce existing *power asymmetries* and to strengthen the position of more powerful actors."[27] Similarly, the Institute for Multi-Stakeholder Initiative Integrity, which was established at Harvard University in 2013 to study the potential of multistakeholder initiatives concluded that "[multistakeholder initiatives] are not effective tools for holding corporations accountable for abuses, protecting rights holders against rights violations, or providing survivors and victims' with access to remedy."[28] Research consistently demonstrates that multistakeholder forms of governance enable powerful voices to dominate decision-making processes and promote interpretive policy frames that privilege market-based forms of governance.[29]

Yet, even though food sovereignty activists oppose multistakeholder models of global governance, they nonetheless support participatory institutions that incorporate the voices of those most marginalized—small-scale food producers, rural workers, Indigenous peoples, and poor urban consumers—into policymaking. Increasingly disenchanted with the disciplining of existing forms of representation in nation-states by neoliberal forces, food sovereignty activists have sought to leverage arenas of global governance to hold corporations and states accountable for human rights violations and to promote new forms of global *democracy*.[30]

Whether any form of network governance can operate as a format of democratic decision making has generated significant debates. Even though it is widely acknowledged that contemporary economic structures and social relations have exceeded the confines of nation-state control, some scholars have argued that only the nation-state can provide adequate structures of representation.[31] In state-centered frameworks of democracy, consent, legitimacy, and ultimately accountability are secured through electoral systems in which "the people" can be represented. Networked arenas of governance suffer from a democratic deficit because they lack any direct connection to an authorizing public and thus adequate forms of representation. In fact, networked forms of organization challenge dominant models of democracy because they disaggregate the principal (the people) and the agent (the state) on which democratic theory has long rested.[32]

Those concerned with democratizing global governance have therefore tended to either advocate for a strictly statist model of global governance, where representation and accountability can be provided through liberal democratic structures of the nation-state, or, alternatively, to construct a global polity that transposes the structure of liberal democracy onto the global scale. However, more radical democratic theorists suggest that the postliberal politics of network governance can, in fact, *enhance* representation and deepen democracy. Eva Sørensen argues that network governance may be able to overcome the problem of liberal democracy, namely, the strict separation of the sphere of political equality and the sphere of liberty. In dominant models of liberal democracy, political equality has been premised on a system of political representation in which citizens have an equal opportunity to shape the political system. Although this has rarely been fully realized in practice, Sørensen, like many activists, argues that in the face of neoliberal globalization, "institutions of liberal democracy can no longer content themselves with aiming for liberty in the market and in civil society, and equality in the state. A democratic society must also pursue liberty in the state and equality in market and civil society."[33] By blurring liberal democracy's walls of separation, transnational governance may therefore provide a framework to deepen democratic claims beyond the formal sphere of political equality to the market.[34]

However, democratizing network governance requires reconfiguring processes of political representation both theoretically and practically. One of the advantages of the networked forms of governance is that political representation is never settled. Sørensen argues that network governance engenders political struggles in which actors compete for the "legitimate right to construct the identity of the represented, and make political decisions with reference to this identity."[35] This *constitutive* approach to representation emphasizes the symbolic and cultural aspects of representation over formalistic understandings in which delegates or representatives act for others in liberal democracy.[36] In other words, given that there is no pre-given public or "people" outside the nation-state framework, processes of network governance enable rival actors to compete to articulate representative claims that construct constituencies for social transformation.[37] This allows actors to form new identities and political subjectivities that cut across geographic and liberal boundaries between state, society, and markets. Arenas of network governance therefore provide opportunities for social movements to constitute constituencies to whom they may demand that the legitimacy and accountability of institutions be assessed.

The CFS is a powerful example of this. In demanding that international institutions, states, and the private sector respond to the needs of those most affected by food security, they mobilize the right to food as a representative claim.

THE RIGHT TO FOOD AND THE CFS

When I began my fieldwork among the civil society networks that participate in the CFS, I was initially surprised that activists were so focused on mobilizing the human right to food. After all, food sovereignty initially developed their novel social justice claim because the right to food was considered insufficiently radical—too individualistic and state centered—to be the main claim mobilized by global movements.[38] So I wondered how activists understood the right to food—how it interacted with their visions and practices of food sovereignty. In the context of the CFS, I soon learned that food sovereignty activists mobilize the right to food and food sovereignty as complementary and mutually reinforcing claims.

The right to food was formally articulated in the Universal Declaration of Human Rights and in Article 11 of the International Covenant on Economic, Social, and Cultural Rights. During the 1970s it was mobilized in conflicts over global food security governance, but it was not formally elaborated until the 1980s and 1990s. In the 1980s the general framework of the right to food was elaborated by Asbjørn Eide in his report to the United Nations

Sub-Commission on the Prevention of Discrimination and Protection of Minorities. Eide adopted Henry Shue's now well-known "respect-protect-fulfil" framework to describe states' obligations in relation to the right to food.[39] The significance of this framework was that it recognized states' responsibility not only for ensuring that citizens had enough food to eat through welfare policies but also for respecting and protecting the capacity of individuals "to provide for themselves." Eide argued that human rights require states to guard against powerful economic interests and unfair trade regulations that would undermine people's ability to be self-sufficient. Eide's framework was institutionalized in 1999 by the Committee on Economic, Social, and Cultural Right in their General Comment 12 on the Right to Food. Yet, although the right to food has been officially defined through many UN instruments and even recognized in many domestic constitutions and pieces of legislation, it has not been fully instituted in national contexts or international institutions.[40]

As global governance grows increasingly fragmented, human rights experts have elaborated several dimensions of the right to food. Olivier de Schutter, the former UN Special Rapporteur on the right to food, describes a "substantive component" of the right to food, which requires that human rights be the "reference through which progress is measured at national and international levels."[41] This component emphasizes that states are not the only actors that are legally bound to make substantive progress toward the realization of the right to food; international organizations are too. The substantive dimension of the right to food asserts the primacy of public international law across competing regimes of global governance, including the World Trade Organization, international finance institutions, UN human rights bodies, and other international institutions.

De Schutter also identifies an "institutional component" that demands "the establishment of fora where all relevant actors could strengthen coordination in order to ensure that the policies they adopt converge towards the full realization of human rights."[42] The institutional component expands on the PANTHER framework in the Voluntary Guidelines on the right to food, which require the participation of all actors affected by and involved in food systems. Since then, the FAO and other human rights actors have further elaborated the meaning of participation in a rights-based approach. The FAO emphasizes that those *most affected* by food insecurity should be able to not only meaningfully participate but also self-organize their participation. As the FAO explains in one of its policy briefs,

> Participation is the direct control, ownership and management by the people of public decision-making. Participation is inclusive; it actively encourages people to organize themselves and to genuinely, freely, actively participate in decision-making. Participation requires efforts to reach out to those most affected by public decisions and the inclusion of the less privileged, vulnerable and affected population in decision-making. It mandates the incorporation of people's views in all public decisions and actions and it must be voluntary, recognized by law, free or not subject to sanction or threat, and active.[43]

The institutional component of the right to food therefore not only demands participation by affected actors but also prescribes particular values that must guide the design of decision-making structures. Instead of cherry-picking individual nongovernmental and civil society organizations to participate in governance, the institutional component of the right to food requires that institutions allow civil society activists to organize their own representation.

Both of these components have been critical for food sovereignty activists as they engage in global governance. Indeed, the utility of human rights is that they confer "the element of legality, without being reducible to that element."[44] This is particularly significant in the context of the right to food, which does not dictate the exact conditions under which food must be produced and provisioned. Rights instead open a political space where these debates can take place.[45]

The right to food therefore operates as both a legal claim and a symbolic resource for food sovereignty movements engaged in transnational governance.[46] In the context of the CFS, food sovereignty activists draw on the substantive dimension of the right to food not just as a legal claim to assert the primacy of the CFS (as the institution dedicated to elaborating food security policy through a rights-based framework); they also mobilize it as a symbolic claim to represent food and agricultural systems as political systems that involve significant distributive consequences. The institutional dimension is similarly mobilized as a legal claim to ensure meaningful participation in governance and as a symbolic claim through which food sovereignty activists seek to assert their own forms of representation. Both substantive and institutional components therefore have crucial legal and symbolic effects on democratizing global food and agricultural governance.

RIGHTS AS REPRESENTATIVE CLAIMS

During the reform of the CFS, food sovereignty activists successfully built on their participation in the "Voluntary Guidelines to Support the Progressive Realization of the Right to Adequate Food" to advocate for their inclusion into the institutional redesign of the CFS. In line with the human-rights-based approach to policymaking elaborated in the guidelines, the CFS agreed to allow civil society to self-organize their participation in the CFS through the CSM. The CSM's design was based on a proposal initially developed by the IPC and the international NGOs Action Aid and Oxfam.[47] Like the IPC, the CSM's key principle is that it neither *represents* any particular movement nor provides a single voice of civil society. Rather, it serves as a facilitative mechanism. The CSM's founding document explains that the CSM will "respect pluralism, autonomy, and self-organization" and that "participation within the CSM should aim to preserve unity and solidarity amongst CSOs [civil society organizations], but should not imply a flattening of the diversity that exists between civil society in terms of objectives, strategies, and content."[48] At the same time, however, the CSM's documents and structure make it clear that it privileges particular constituencies—peasant and Indigenous food producers and workers who bear the brunt of food security—because it recognizes that "that victims of hunger are also the bearers of solutions."[49]

The CSM's approach to representation builds on the networking strategies of the IPC, La Vía Campesina, and alter-globalization movements, which promote direct self-representation of those most affected.[50] These movements reject the model of representation dominant in most liberal democracies where representatives act for their constituencies and instead construct constituencies that represent their own voices. This not only endows movements with legitimacy but also serves as a prefigurative process through which social movements reclaim control through horizontal decision-making processes.[51] Nora McKeon thus describes how during the development of the CSM, "the logic of representation was studiously

Constituency	Organizations	Country in which focal point is based
Smallholders Farmers (4)	La Via Campesina, Confederación de Organizaciones de Productores Familiares del Mercosur, International Federation of Rural Adults Catholic Movements	Romania, India (2), Brazil
Pastoralists/herders (2)	World Alliance of Mobile Indigenous Peoples	Italy, Jordan
Fisherfolks (2)	World Forum of Fisher Peoples, World Forum of Fish Harvesters and Fish Workers	Kenya, Nicaragua
Indigenous Peoples (2)	The Indigenous Peoples of Africa Co-ordinating Committee, International Indian Treaty Council	Cameroon, Mexico
Consumers (2)	Urgenci, Consumers International	USA, Ecuador
Agricultural and Food Workers (2)	International Union of Food, Agricultural, Hotel, Restaurant, Catering, Tobacco and Allied Workers' Association	Guyana, Kyrgyzstan
Urban food insecure (2)	Habitat International Coalition	Brazil, Iraq
Landless (2)	Asian Rural Women Coalition, La Via Campesina	India, Palestine
Youth (2)	La Via Campesina, World March of Women	Argentina, Mozambique
Women (2)	La Via Campesina, International Women's Alliance	Brazil, Pakistan
NGOs (2)	Rede da Sociedade Civil para a Segurança Alimentar e Nutricional na Comunidade de Países da Língua Portuguesa, Friends of the Earth	Portugal, Uruguay

FIGURE 10 Composition of the Coordination Committee of the CSM, 2019–2021.

avoided, since people's organizations cannot and will not delegate their self-representation."[52]

The CSM's structures and processes were designed to institutionalize the principle of self-representation. Food governance scholars Jessica Duncan and Priscilla Claeys argue that food sovereignty movements have developed their practices of direct representation by relying on two strategies: constituencies and quotas. Constituencies are "categories to identify, protect, foster, and guarantee the autonomy of different groups of people with distinct identities and lived realities."[53] Quotas include guidelines to distribute participants by "gender, age, constituency, and/or geography to protect diversity and the consolidation of power, and ensure the prioritized participation of affected marginalized groups."[54] The CSM uses both constituencies and quotas. It is organized through eleven constituencies and seventeen subregions. Constituencies in the CSM are global in scope; those that occupy the constituency groups are the main global movements of each constituency. Each constituency group is given two seats on the Coordination Committee, which is the main governance body of the CSM. Smallholder farmers, however, are allocated four seats in recognition that they not only bear the brunt of food insecurity and malnutrition but are also the primary food producers across the world.

Notably, NGOs operate as just one constituency of the CSM. The founding document of the CSM explains that recognizing NGOs as a distinct constituency is important because "while NGOs are organizations that represent the interests of a particular theme or support the interests of certain social groups, the other constituencies are self-organized social actors who share a common identity and have come together to represent their *own* interests. In this sense, an organization that represents the concerns of children, for example, but is not composed of and governed by children, would be classified as an NGO."[55] As explained in chapter 1, tensions over representation have animated the relationships between NGOs and social movements. Although social movements often depend on NGOs for technical support, the CSM has designed elaborate processes to make sure that they do not dominate the CSM.

In addition to the eleven constituencies, there are seventeen subregions: five in Africa, four in the Americas, six in Asia, and two in Europe. Each subregion selects one "focal point" and one alternate to sit on the Coordination

Committee. These seats are occupied by local and regional movements. The United States and Canada form one of the subregions. Together, the eleven constituencies and seventeen subregions make up the forty-one members of the Coordination Committee. The Coordination Committee makes decisions by consensus. If consensus cannot be reached, the committee has provisions for mediation and for voting. However, the decisions made in the CFS tend to focus on the governance of the CSM, not policy positions. In fact, the CSM itself does not take policy positions. As a draft set of guidelines for facilitating common policy positions made clear, "The CSM does not itself take positions and it does not represent CSOs [civil society organizations]. There is no such thing as a CSM statement, position, etc."[56] Rather, as a facilitative mechanism, the CSM aims to ensure that civil society is able to participate in the CFS and it helps the CFS move toward common policy positions when possible.

In this sense, the CSM approaches facilitation in a political rather than a technical sense. According to the CSM, facilitation "seeks to transform power relations and overcome historical patterns of asymmetry, marginalization and exclusion by privileging and supporting the participation and political protagonism of non-elite, rights-holding, affected constituencies committed to food sovereignty and agroecological approaches in the work of the CFS."[57] The main role of the CSM is to facilitate the exchange of information, knowledge, analysis, and strategy. Facilitation is not merely about bringing in the voices of those who are often excluded; it is a process of building trust and political solidarity.[58]

In addition to the Coordination Committee, a smaller Advisory Group is elected every two years by the Coordination Committee. The Advisory Group is made up of ten members who engage in the more day-to-day, intersessional work of the CFS. These members sit on a rotating basis on the CFS's Advisory Group (on which the CSM has four seats) and advise the CFS Bureau, which is the executive arm of the CFS that is composed of a rotating group of states. In the CFS Advisory Group, the CSM's Advisory Group advocates for the shared positions of the Coordination Committee. According to the terms of reference for the Advisory Group, three of the four members who attend must come from social movements. Members of the Advisory Group typically fly to Rome several times a year for face-to-face meetings. Finally, a small secretariat—just three full-time staff—help to

Civil Society and Indigenous Peoples' Mechanism of the CFS

Structure and Process

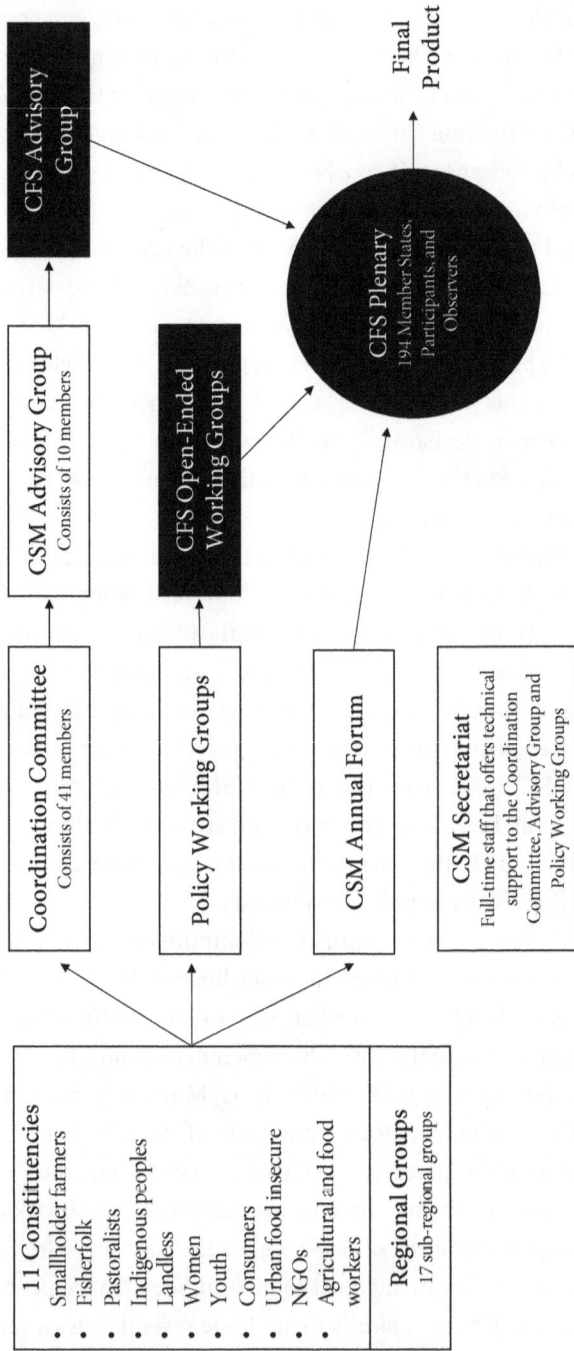

11 Constituencies
- Smallholder farmers
- Fisherfolk
- Pastoralists
- Indigenous peoples
- Landless
- Women
- Youth
- Consumers
- Urban food insecure
- NGOs
- Agricultural and food workers

Regional Groups
17 sub-regional groups

Coordination Committee
Consists of 41 members

CSM Advisory Group
Consists of 10 members

CFS Advisory Group

Policy Working Groups

CFS Open-Ended Working Groups

CSM Annual Forum

CSM Secretariat
Full-time staff that offers technical support to the Coordination Committee, Advisory Group and Policy Working Groups

CFS Plenary
194 Member States, Participants, and Observers

Final Product

FIGURE 11 Diagram illustrating how participation is organized by the CSM. Diagram by author.

coordinate the work of the CFS. The secretariat is "deliberately 'lightweight'" to ensure that ownership of the process is taken up by the Coordination Committee and social movements.[59]

Although the Advisory Group and the Coordination Committee play a critical role in governing the CSM and communicating the CSM agenda in the intersessional work of the CFS, the policy work of the CSM takes place through working groups that are consolidated around the various policy work streams of the CSM. These working groups are open to all members of the CSM. However, one member from the Coordination Committee and a technical facilitator (often from an NGO) serve to guide this process. In the working groups the constituencies of the Coordination Committee provide a set of guidelines to help the facilitators ensure meaningful participation across the constituencies and subregions.[60]

Through these structures of constituencies and quotas, the CSM seeks to facilitate the self-representation of those most affected by food insecurity. But this process has not been without its own challenges. Evaluations of the CSM completed in 2014 and 2018 pointed to a number of tensions. Most recently, challenges related to the underrepresentation of women and youth and the "guardianship of particular organizations" in specific constituencies have been raised as issues that need to be addressed by the CSM.[61] These are particularly difficult issues because the policymaking process of the CFS is incredibly complicated. For those who have never participated, it can take one to two years to understand how the CFS works. Even the architecture of the FAO, which occupies four buildings connected by a complicated array of staircases and hallways, is difficult to navigate. It took me two years of going to the CFS simply to remember how to reach the rooms where the policy recommendations were being negotiated. Understanding how the CFS and CSM function took several more years. As a result, it is a difficult task to engage new participants and build new leaders in the CSM.

In the eight years during which I have observed the CSM, I found that another ongoing challenge is to ensure that professionalized NGOs do not assert more weight than designated through the CSM's structure. This is difficult because the work streams of the CFS often entail many small decision-making processes, which can be difficult for people's movements (especially for those engaged in agricultural labor) to be consistently involved in. Tracking any single policymaking process of the CSM can be a part-time job. Each work stream includes a laborious process, from the definition of the scope of the topic to the negotiation over minutiae across multiple versions of policy recommendations. Some of the topics are also more technical than others, which also contributes to greater NGO participation. Even the annual CFS meetings, which take place in October, mean that food producers must leave their farms when many people are engaged in annual harvests. Nevertheless, through processes of ongoing evaluation and a secretariat that is deeply committed to ensuring the representation of people's movements, leaders in the CSM have worked diligently to facilitate the substantive participation of social movements. There is also an incentive for the CFS to ensure meaningful participation of social movements, because they rely on them to take the policies developed by the CFS back into local contexts.

Since its establishment in 2010, the CSM has therefore become more than simply a facilitative mechanism for the CFS. As Claeys and Duncan argue, "It would be inadequate to say that the Mechanism facilitates the participation of grassroots communities. The Mechanism is more adequately described as a 'political' space that brings together social movement leaders and organizations representing the affected."[62] Indeed, the CSM is a space where constituencies are not only labeled but also constituted. By protecting the diversity of different identities and movements, the CSM offers a space through which social movements can develop prefigurative forms of representation. Through these practices the CSM does not construct a singular "people"; rather, it is engaged in the ongoing process of construction and reconstruction of *peoples* to whom governance processes must be accountable.

By mobilizing the right to food as a representative claim, activists have not just successfully shaped the conditions of their own participation in the CFS; they have also challenged neoliberal representations of food and agricultural governance. This aspect of rights claiming is no less critical than asserting their own practices of representation. This became apparent to me through ethnographic observation and participation in the negotiation of the PRAI in 2013–2014.

RIGHTS AS SYMBOLIC FRAMES

When I began my fieldwork in 2013, the CFS was in the midst of negotiating the PRAI. The principles were among the most contentious debates since the CFS reform because they were developed to address land grabs, which were a key driver of the 2007–2008 global food crisis. Over several previous years, activists had voiced growing alarm over the rapid expansion of land grabs, especially in sub-Saharan Africa, as corporations and national governments (in both the global North and the global South) invested in land to produce food and fuel.[63] The extent of foreign direct investment was breathtaking; by 2013 foreign investors controlled 32.8 million hectares of land globally.[64] Although investment may have provided money to the governments of developing states, its consequences—environmental degradation, human rights violations, and vulnerability resulting from food price volatility—were profound, especially for small-scale food producers.

The World Bank, together with several other institutions, unilaterally developed the PRAI, but civil society's rejection of these principles successfully led to the CFS taking up the issue. The CFS first developed a set of terms of reference in 2012 to rewrite the PRAI. This was a major success for the CSM, in both getting the CFS to take up the issue and asserting the CFS's dominance as the foremost global arena of food security governance.

After an initial "Zero Draft" of the PRAI was released, activists in the CSM developed a sophisticated and wide-ranging critique. They argued that the principles were not grounded firmly enough in a rights-based framework; that it did not clearly identify stakeholder roles and responsibilities; that it had no tools for monitoring or evaluation; that it did not contain strong enough protections for Indigenous people; and that it failed to address food price volatility, among many other issues. Yet at the center of their concern was something far deeper: that in creating an undifferentiated set of standards for investment, the PRAI collapsed distinct social and economic values, integrating diverse communities and agricultural practices into the global market.

The conflict over the principles thus reflected a struggle between two competing framings of land grabs: one that framed them primarily around the issue of *investment* and another that framed them around *human rights*.[65] As Philip McMichael describes, the investment approach is "concerned with governing the rights of capital [and] projects a new concern with food security based on restructuring 'underutilized' land in the global South to expand yields via global value chains organized by agribusiness." On the other hand, the human rights approach is "concerned with protecting the material rights of rural inhabitants, [and] expresses an ontology centered on the sustainability of agroecological methods used by farmers who know and value their landscapes"[66]

The meeting in Washington, DC, described earlier was my introduction to a process that would take place over the next two years at the CFS's annual meetings every October, intersessional negotiation sessions, and consultations in the various subregions. Each draft of the principles—which in the CFS began to be described as the RAI rather than the PRAI, to distinguish it from the World Bank's initial set of principles—required negotiations. Over both the 2013 and 2014 annual meetings of the CFS, the RAI were a key work stream and a constant source of angst and concern for participants of the CSM. Through two years of phone calls, e-mails, and trips to Rome, CSM participants developed a shared critique of the RAI and struggled to imbue their rights-based perspective in the document.[67]

During the process of negotiation, food sovereignty activists and participants of the CSM drew on the human rights frame in their struggle to distinguish between the roles and responsibilities of states, the rights of smallholder producers versus larger transnational entities, and to politicize markets as creations of public policy. The human rights frame thus served to symbolically constitute the global food system as a field of power guided by many functions and values. How they mobilized rights can be seen in three key terms that engendered significant social struggle: *investment, farmers,* and *markets.*

Investment

The first goal of the CSM was to challenge the imperative of private investment. In the World Bank's PRAI, the term *investment* was used primarily to refer to large-scale foreign investment in land and natural resources. Although the PRAI sought to make these investments more responsible, they nonetheless viewed large-scale foreign direct investment and liberalized global markets for land and resources as key drivers for development and growth. Participants in the CSM challenged this view of investment and its implicit assumption that *all* investments come from foreign actors. In reinterpreting investment through the right to food, CSM participants not only sought to ensure that these transactions were governed through

FIGURE 12   The Committee on World Food Security at the UN Food and Agriculture Organization in Rome. Photo by author.

democratic mechanisms but also demanded that states recognize that small-scale food producers are the *primary* investors in the global food and agricultural system. Given that the right to food prioritizes states' obligation to *respect* and *protect* the ability of citizens to feed themselves, the CSM used the rights-based approach to expand the meaning of investment beyond global capital. In its first comments to the Open-Ended Working Group of the RAI process in the CFS, the CSM noted, "When we speak about investment, it must be understood in a broader context than just capital investment. Other forms of investment include labour, knowledge and ecosystem regeneration and community development."[68] This expansion of the term *investment* also enabled the CSM to demand protection for other actors without financial resources. As one La Vía Campesina organizer noted in the plenary session, "The document leaves out the millions of people who are landless but deeply involved in agricultural investment." Moreover, by mobilizing rights language, the CSM sought to shift the emphasis to the relationship between citizens and the state. They emphasized the importance of *public* investment in facilitating small-scale producers' ability to feed their communities. Thus the rights-based language enabled activists to politicize the meaning of investment, disrupt the representation of all food production dominated by a market calculus, and distinguish between the roles and responsibilities of different actors.

Farmers

The CSM also mobilized the right to food to emphasize the duties of the state to respect and protect small-scale producers as *rights holders*. Throughout the negotiation process, members of the CSM introduced the language of "small-scale producers and workers," specifically, to emphasize the obligations of states to those most marginalized and affected by food insecurity. However, members of the Private Sector Mechanism continually deployed the language of "farmers" in an effort to efface the distinction between large-scale commercial farmers and peasants and small-scale producers. In the end, the Private Sector Mechanism rejected this rights-based framework. A Wisconsin-based commercial farmer speaking on behalf of the private sector argued that the human rights framing constructed "an unhelpful and unrealistic dichotomy between being a small-holder and being a business." She told the CFS plenary session, "Farms are a business, even when small. . . . All farm to support their livelihoods. Establishing this division between farmers is not helping us support food and nutritional security." The language of farmers enabled the Private Sector Mechanism to collapse this distinction and represent all production and provisioning choices as guided by the calculative logics of capitalist market exchange.

The CSM responded with repeated explanations that smallholders were primarily subsistence producers and produced for local markets only secondarily. The distinction they attempted to make was focused not only on the scale of accumulation but also on the social values and choices that smallholders make in their decisions about how much to produce, which crops, and by which methods. Organizers of the CSM pointed out the long-term value of small-scale producers in terms of sustainability and social values.

> Small-scale food producers invest in their production. They maintain and build soil fertility, select and reproduce seeds, nurture their lands

and water sources, build production and storage infrastructure often in a multi-generational context. These are, and will continue to be, the most important investments in agriculture carried out on a day-to-day basis and need to be recognized as such. The recognition of such an assertion will be a very critical starting point of our consultation since it will bring other perspectives in the debates.[69]

Members of the CSM repeatedly stressed that the RAI should distinguish between the responsibilities and roles of small local producers and larger external investors.

By using rights language, food sovereignty activists sought to demarcate a clear separation between *stakeholders* (large-scale farmers and multinational corporations), *rights holders* (small-scale food producers and workers), and *duty bearers* (governments). This distinction was crucial, particularly in the context of multistakeholder negotiations, which by its nature collapses the walls of separation between society and economy in liberal legalism. As one of the leaders of the CSM negotiation team explained to me,

> In a multistakeholder process, everyone is supposed to find consensus to move forward, but the truth is that all stakes are not similar, and they come on quite different premises. The stake of a peasant who might lose their land, which is their resource and livelihood, or the community forest of Indigenous people who might lose their entire area, or fisherfolk who might lose access to beach-based fishing—the so-called stakes of these kind of participants are quite different from those who view this as a business enterprise, from the point of view of money, of profit, of revenue, of being able to maximize competitiveness in the market. But they also have a lot more capital to play with, a lot more cushion to fall back on, so the stakes are quite different. The issue of equity is hugely different, and the power asymmetries are significant.

Thus, in an effort to challenge the representation of all actors as formally equal, the CSM continually stressed the *rights* of small-scale producers and workers compared with large-scale enterprises.

This jockeying over the meaning of *farmers* has not been confined to the RAI process; it has been an ongoing struggle between the Private Sector Mechanism and the CSM. For example, in 2014 I attended an event during the weekly annual meeting of the CFS titled "Natural Resource Management for Food Security in the Context of the Post-2015 Development Agenda: Empowering Small-Scale Food Producers and Food Insecure Communities to Be Agents of Change." The panel discussion included a range of participants, including a Kenyan UN ambassador working on the sustainable development goals, the director of the UN Environment Program in Ethiopia, a member of the International Fertilizer Industry Association, and the leader from La Vía Campesina Niger. At one point, the moderator, a BBC news anchor, asked whether smallholder farmers were part of the private sector. The representative from the fertilizer association explained that smallholder farmers are entrepreneurial and wish to grow. Similarly, the former chair of the CFS, a Nigerian diplomat, elided the distinction between smallholders and corporations. "Whether smallholder, medium size, or giant corporation, the goal is to make money and make good livelihoods," he proclaimed. But the leader from La Vía Campesina disagreed. She explained that peasants produce primarily to feed themselves and then sell the rest. As the discussion continued among members of the audience, civil society leaders grew increasingly uneasy. Eventually, one civil society activist, a longtime leader of a Canadian NGO, exclaimed, "If farmers are the private sector, then we need to create another sector called the predatory or monopoly sector!" The private sector representative got the last word, saying, "Labels are not important."

Markets

Finally, the CSM mobilized the right to food to distinguish between "markets" and "the market." The CSM has continually distinguished between "territorial markets" (the "local, national and regional markets and food systems" that support small-scale producers) and global value chains.[70] During the plenary session, for example, one Uruguayan activist reiterated that smallholders produce for local markets after they have met their subsistence needs. These markets, she explained, differ from global or even national markets and are central to rural livelihoods. In constructing a rights-based framework for markets, food sovereignty activists thus seek to *denaturalize* markets and emphasize their political construction. "One of the problems that we have with the market now is that it is completely disembedded from social control," the technical facilitator of the CSM's

RAI negotiation team explained to me. Building from scholar-activist Peter Rosset's argument about food and the World Trade Organization, she said, "There are some things that should not even be on the market. Food is different, which is not to say that you don't buy food. Of course, you do buy food. But to put something as important as food and water, to put these, which are the basic conditions for life to exist, in the market and reduce them and expose them to the dangers of market reductionism, that is very dangerous." Using the language of rights thus not only politicizes the market but also serves as a language through which activists can distinguish between the types of markets that can serve to support small-scale producers and enable more local resilience to food price swings and the types of markets that are dominated by large-scale capital.

By the time the RAI negotiations neared completion, one Spanish leader from La Vía Campesina emphasized that a major problem was that the principles reduced rights related to economic activity to market-transactions.

> The Principles do not prioritize public policy at all. They prioritize an enabling environment for market-based solutions without any recognition of power imbalances. Markets do not work for the vulnerable and there is thus a strong need for market regulation to address problems that occur, for instance, in public-private partnerships, contract farming and abuse of concentrated market power.

On the one hand, the distinction between "markets" and "the market" was about the scale of economic organization, but his point was ultimately about power. He advocated for a set of standards anchored in a human rights framework and one that recognized small-scale producers and workers as the main investors in agriculture. Hence he sought to ground both the process of negotiation and the substantive document in a set of normative values oriented primarily around the needs of those less powerful.

Throughout the negotiations, rights thus served as a crucial language to challenge the symbolic representation of food and agricultural exchange as a market transaction and instead sought to politicize both the construction of markets and the power asymmetries between different actors. Rights serve to undermine the horizontal representation of equal actors, distinguishing the responsibilities of duty bearers from rights holders and thereby disrupting the depoliticizing subjectivity of stakeholders. Mobilized in the CFS, the right to food serves to reestablish the frontiers between actors and to reanimate the antagonisms that powerful actors seek to vanquish through the win-win façade of governance.

Ultimately, members of the CSM were dissatisfied with the outcome of the RAI negotiation. The document failed to adopt as strong a rights-based framework as civil society had advocated for. As the facilitator for civil society explained to me, "We got an outcome that we weren't happy with at all." During the plenary session, CSM members read a strong statement explaining that the document "was not useful." Afterward, the US representative also made a speech that the United States was not pleased with the outcome either. As the facilitator explained, "They saw it as a big loss because they didn't get what they wanted for the private sector. And they thought we lost because we didn't get what we wanted in terms of rights protection and the recognition of small-scale food providers. So I guess this is one of those classic cases where a multistakeholder process ends up being a zero sum game." When I asked what she meant by this, she explained that it is really civil society that gives the various policy instruments their legitimacy. "Governments negotiate with us because they know that if they don't get our buy-in, a document is a dead document," she said.

The RAI process thus reveals how food sovereignty activists seek to democratize the CFS, and global food governance more broadly, by engaging in a representational struggle in two ways. First, by mobilizing the right to food, food sovereignty activists seek to stake the democratic legitimacy of the CFS in its responsiveness to those most affected by food insecurity and malnutrition.[71] In doing so, they seek to ensure that people's movements can participate directly in the CFS without delegating their representation to states or international NGOs. However, it is not rights language alone that helps to constitute a shared set of claims or identities but rather the solidaristic ties and constituencies built into the CSM through self-representation. Second, the language of rights politicizes global food governance by challenging the representation of the global food system as governed by market calculi. Rights mobilization thus serves to open up political space to constitute new constituencies to whom global governance must be accountable and to make visible the entrenched asymmetries of power and the policies that facilitate existing inequalities.

CONCLUSIONS

In 2018 civil society organizations released a powerful statement to the CFS imploring governments to recommit to the committee's mandate of realizing the human right to food. In their 2018 statement to the CFS plenary session, titled "It's Time to Recommit," civil society members called on members of the CFS not only to defend and support the human rights mandate of the UN but also to recognize civil society as "the most critical agent for change." "We are the organizations of the rights-holders, while governments and intergovernmental institutions are duty-bearers," the statement read. "We are the most important producers, processors, and providers of food and nutrition world-wide." This recognition, they argued, "necessarily implies the inclusion, participation, and special attention to the rights-holders who suffer from violations or are most at risk." Moreover, in the statement the CSM demanded that "governments must not challenge but defend and support the human rights mandate of the United Nations. Governments and the UN need to implement their duties to promote and protect human rights of all people, including in those policies directly or indirectly affecting food security and nutrition. This approach necessarily implies the inclusion, participation and special attention to the rights-holders who suffer from violations or are most at risk."[72] The CSM's call to recommit to the human rights mandate of the CFS was a response to a perceived drift away from the rights focus of the CFS.

The CSM is not the only actor to observe this change. In 2018 a number of states led by the Brazilian government formed the Friends of the Right to Food to support the rights-centered approach of the CFS. Yet, aside from a handful of governments, ultimately it has been the CSM that has been the main voice demanding that the CFS maintain its commitment to a rights-based approach. This has led some actors, particularly in the private sector, to criticize the CSM. A self-evaluation commissioned by the CFS revealed that there are "CFS Members and stakeholders who were critical of the manner in which the CSM functions. The mechanism is seen to dominate discussions and overshadow the contributions of others. They were also critical of the CSM's use of language that appears confrontational to others and felt that the CSM pushed the 'rights agenda' too aggressively." In many ways, this critique can be read as evidence of the effectiveness of food sovereignty activists in politicizing this space.

Critics of the CSM have also been frustrated by its success in shaping the CFS agenda. In 2017, after years of advocacy by the CSM, the CFS embarked on a policymaking process on agroecology. The resulting workstream, *Agroecological and Other Innovative Approaches for Sustainable Agriculture and Food Systems That Enhance Food Security and Nutrition*, was a product of the sustained efforts to legitimize agroecology as the primary pathway in the transition toward a sustainable global food system. The process in the CFS began with a report by the High Level Panel of Experts, followed by the development of a set of policy recommendations that were completed in 2021. However, these negotiations were immensely difficult, in large part because powerful exporting agricultural states sought to reduce agroecology to one form of production among many, rather than recognize it as a comprehensive political, social, and ecological approach to transforming food systems. Donald Trump's ambassador to the Rome-based agencies, a commercial farmer from Indiana who owned 20,000 acres, led a crusade against the FAO and the CFS for even considering agroecology as a potential solution to the problems of contemporary food systems.[73]

Today, the successes of the CSM have led some activists to fear that powerful actors are attempting to engage in a regime shift to render the CFS powerless and create a new architecture for food security governance, much like what happened in the 1970s in response to the global South's resistance to powerful states. In 2019 the UN secretary-general announced a global Food Systems Summit for 2021 in partnership with the World Economic Forum. Soon after, he appointed Agnes Kalibata, the president of the Alliance for a Green Revolution in Africa (discussed in chapter 4), as his special envoy for this process. After her appointment, the CSM's fears only deepened as a result of the Food Systems Summit's nontransparent, top-down organization, which is guided not by human rights but by the logic of multistakeholderism. Rather than allowing civil society to self-organize or help shape the agenda, the Food Systems Summit cherry-picked organizations to engage.[74]

The CSM's letter to the secretary-general is worth reproducing at length, because it reflects the way that the CSM has opposed the multistakeholder model of the 2021 Food System Summit through the framework of human rights.

> Instead of drawing from the innovative governance experiences that the UN system has to offer, the UN-WEF [World Economic Forum] partnership is helping to establishing [*sic*] "stakeholder capitalism" as a governance model for the entire planet. The WEF's multi-stakeholder platforms lack democratic legitimacy and focus instead on harnessing the opportunities of the Fourth Industrial Revolution for the benefit of TNCs [transnational corporations] and global financial capital. In contrast, the UN Committee on World Food Security (CFS) and the FAO, with mandates for ending hunger and malnutrition, offer a different model. The CFS is widely recognized as the most inclusive and participatory UN Committee, where the constituencies most affected by hunger and malnutrition—indigenous peoples, landless people, women, rural workers, peasants, fisherfolk, pastoralists, consumers, urban food insecure people and youth—can meaningfully and actively participate in shaping intergovernmental decisions about the best policies to ensure the realization of the human right to adequate food for all.[75]

Food sovereignty activists in the CSM challenged the Food Systems Summit and defended the CFS as a more democratic arena of global food security governance grounded in a clear commitment to human rights.

Rights have thus served as an important claim for food sovereignty movements as they attempt to democratize global governance. By mobilizing the legal obligations of food sovereignty, in both its substantive and institutional dimensions, activists demand accountability in governance structures and also make representative claims through which they seek to translate their own practices of representation. This relationship between legal mobilization and representation points to the shifting role of rights in the postliberal framework of transnational governance. Building on Roberto Unger's notion of destabilization rights, Charles Sabel and William Simon argue that rights claims can "unsettle and open up public institutions that have chronically failed to meet their obligations and that are substantially insulated from the normal process of political accountability."[76] Similarly, Bronwen Morgan describes how rights can "open political space" in market-based forms of regulation.[77]

In the CFS, rights not only create political space through the CFS's insistence on social movement participation in decision-making processes but also politicize the neoliberal representation of global food and agricultural systems, making space for the needs and solutions of those most affected. Rights thus politicize transnational governance and raise critical questions about democratic representation and participation. Given that no pre-given political entity or "people" exist in these contexts, rights are vehicles for representative claims through which activists constitute constituencies to whom arenas of transnational network governance must be accountable.

In describing the importance of the CFS to me, a former leader of the IPC pointed to the immense power of enabling small-scale food producers and the food insecure to directly confront powerful governments and corporations. Peasants and small-scale producers from social movements often sit on the dais at the plenary session of the CFS in front of corporations and member states and insist on being at the center of decision-making processes. Although the standards produced by the CFS may not reflect all their demands—and sometimes none of them—these activists nonetheless have been successful in inserting the voices of the most marginalized in the governance process. This has powerful effects for social movements beyond the institutional outcomes of the CFS. As grassroots activists and small-scale food producers attend these global forums, they also constitute new solidaristic ties, identities, and strategies to persist in their movements for food sovereignty. "You don't consider what it means for the dignity" of fisherfolk, peasants, and small-scale producers who can look governments in the eye and challenge the governments that are attacking their livelihoods, the former leader of the IPC told me. "For me, this is enough," he said.

CONCLUSIONS
Cultivating Justice in an Age of Transnational Governance

FOOD HAS EMERGED as a critical battleground over growing global in-equalities. Despite decades of pledges by powerful countries to end hunger, food insecurity has been on the rise since 2014. In 2021 the UN Food and Agriculture Organization found that the rise of moderate and severe food insecurity "was equal to that of the five previous years combined" because of the COVID-19 pandemic.[1] Hunger is not the only sign that something is seriously wrong with global food systems. The impacts of food systems on human and planetary health—from the growing prevalence of malnutrition to the contribution of food systems to climate change and biodiversity loss—indicate that food systems are badly in need of transformation. Yet debates over what kind of transformation food systems need have generated a growing global struggle.

Powerful agricultural exporting states and transnational corporations have framed the issue of transforming global food systems around the threats of climate change and the lack of agricultural productivity in the regions most deeply affected by food insecurity. They promote technological innovations such as digitalization and genetically modified crops as solutions to contemporary problems. But such an approach evades the truth that the world is already producing enough food to feed the world. Focusing on food scarcity and production shifts our attention away from the fact that struggles over food systems are ultimately about power and control. They are about regulation and governance.

Powerful actors have long sought to subvert attention from the politics of food production and provisioning. Economist Amartya Sen demonstrated this in his historical study of famines, the most extreme form of food deprivation. Famines have typically been framed as natural disasters, but in his study Sen ultimately concluded that even during famines, hunger is "a characteristic of *some* people not having enough food to eat . . . not a characteristic of there not being enough food to eat."[2] In other words, hunger and malnutrition are not consequences of inadequate production but rather a product of the rules that govern access to food—the legal and regulatory arrangements that organize exchange, trade, and markets. As Sen famously proclaimed, "*Law* stands between food availability and food entitlement."[3]

Today, as movements of small-scale food producers, food-chain workers, and urban consumers confront rising global hunger and malnutrition, they face a global political and legal landscape that is fundamentally in flux. Neoliberalism reordered law and politics from local to global levels. Attempts to install the market as "the principle, form, and model for the state"[4] inadvertently upended liberalism's walls of separation and created new geographies of power no longer dominated by the nation-state. Although supporters of neoliberalism continue to evangelize about the necessity of "free" markets and deregulation, it is clear that markets are not free, nor can they exist without regulation. Markets require rules to function, from legal infrastructures that protect private property, manage disputes, and guarantee contracts to standards and rules that can facilitate the social coordination necessary for markets to work. New forms of transnational governance have thus emerged both to extend markets into new frontiers of accumulation and to manage the conflicts engendered by neoliberalism.

In their struggle to reclaim control over food systems, food sovereignty activists have constituted their claims in response to this emerging order. Indeed, throughout this book I have analyzed how food sovereignty activists are engaging in different forms and arenas of governance—from local food policy councils to global value chains to transnational networks—through which they are articulating holistic social justice claims that are no longer constrained by liberal legalism. Yet, although emerging forms of transnational governance may contain the seeds of an alternative political and economic order, arenas of governance are often constructed by hegemonic actors who seek to deepen their control over food systems, especially when anthropogenic climate change and global pandemics are generating greater uncertainty and global interdependence. For powerful states, transnational governance offers a framework to facilitate global markets and devolve responsibility for global problems to private actors. For transnational corporations, transnational governance offers an opportunity to enhance their role in global rule setting. Thus, whereas food sovereignty activists draw on the networked forms of transnational governance to construct new ways of organizing the social, economic, and ecological web of life, corporations and their powerful governmental allies have leveraged networked forms of governance in an attempt to deepen their power and regulatory control.

Examining how food sovereignty activists are responding to changing structures of law and regulation by developing new claims and practices of mobilization therefore offers an important window into the ways that power is constructed and contested in this emerging political and legal order. Sociolegal scholars who have examined other arenas of social movement struggle—from work to water—have also observed the increasingly important role of transnational governance for social movements' claims and strategies.[5] But new forms of governance are not just political and legal opportunities that social movements are exploiting; they are political and symbolic orders in relation to which social movements are dialectically developing new horizons of social justice. Thus, just as sociolegal scholars have long documented how social movements use the discursive and symbolic resources embedded in legal systems to culturally constitute change from below, so too can we see how food sovereignty activists are drawing on the symbols and arenas of transnational governance to cultivate new relations between communities, markets, and nature through democratically decentralized food systems.

In this conclusion, therefore, I reflect on the enduring significance of food activism as a constitutive site of political and legal struggle as well as on the possibility of justice in the era of postliberal legality. Food sovereignty activism, I suggest, has not only produced new forms of mobilization that are essential for understanding the paradoxes of power relations in the contemporary legal landscape but also offered new ways of seeing and analyzing transnational law and governance. As scholars, we must remember that we too are embedded in the legal systems we seek to analyze. We help to construct these systems through the knowledge we produce. Thus I argue that we must reimagine governance and justice not through the modernist and mechanistic lens that has dominated both jurisprudence and science but rather through an ecological lens that is grounded in the landscapes we inhabit. In doing so, we may be able to nourish more equitable and sustainable social relations between human and more-than-human nature growing in the shadows of hegemonic legality.

AGRARIAN QUESTIONS, OLD AND NEW

Agrarian movements have long posed a problem for capital's expansionary endeavors. Throughout the nineteenth and twentieth centuries, agrarian social movements mounted the strongest challenges to states seeking to incorporate them into capitalist markets. This resistance to capitalism preoccupied Marx and other critical theorists who saw capitalism as a progressive social force that would eventually lead to socialist development. Karl Kautsky, Marx, Lenin, and other revolutionary theorists all spent a great deal of time pondering the "agrarian question"—whether capitalism would be able to transform the countryside or whether it would pose obstacles to capitalist accumulation.[6] Barrington Moore convincingly argued that the process by which the agrarian question was addressed by nation-states shaped their political development. He illustrated how the efforts by national elites to incorporate rural classes into capitalist markets laid the pathway for the rise of liberal democracy, fascism, and communism.[7]

During the twentieth century, agrarian movements focused their resistance on the national scale. During the "peasant wars" that proliferated around the world, small-scale food producers and landless workers mobilized in opposition to state policies that sought to dispossess them of their land and livelihoods.[8] These struggles were reignited by the proliferation of neoliberal policies, which continue to integrate small-scale producers into capitalist value chains by dispossessing them of their territories and knowledge through epistemic enclosures of intellectual property regimes. Although many of the world's most oppressed—peasants, Indigenous peoples, landless workers, and the urban poor—experience market fundamentalism as part of the same inequalities perpetuated by colonialism and racial capitalism, a new generation of small-scale food producers and food-chain workers across the global North and South have now joined the ranks of those dispossessed by the ravenous demands of extractive neoliberal capitalism. As these movements join together, agrarian struggles have reemerged at the center of global political and economic transformations.

Today, however, agrarian struggles have changed in two major respects. First, the state is no longer the sole object of the movements' claims. The liberalization of global food and agricultural markets through the World Trade Organization has fundamentally transformed the global legal landscape. Although proponents of liberalizing global trade promised that it would lower prices and create new economic opportunities for farmers in the global South, it has exacerbated food insecurity by creating incentives for specialization and market dependence, aggravating the volatility of food prices, and encouraging unhealthy diets. As the UN special rapporteur on the right to food Michael Fakhri explained in his 2020 report to the United Nations General Assembly, "Existing WTO [World Trade Organization] disciplines lock in a profoundly unequal set of outcomes. They continue centuries of patterns of trade in which formerly colonized States, indigenous peoples, agricultural workers and peasants are denigrated by the trade system."[9] Although governments in the global South have sought to dismantle or reform the World Trade Organization for years, these efforts have failed.

As a result, contemporary agrarian movements are transnational in scope. By claiming food sovereignty, they reflect the shifting ways in which sovereignty effectively operates. Although states remain formally sovereign over their territories, today sovereignty is conditioned by transnational networks and institutions. As Saskia Sassen describes, "Sovereignty remains a systemic property but its institutional insertion and its capacity to legitimate and absorb all legitimating power, to be the source of law, have become unstable."[10] Thus, by claiming food sovereignty across these different sociopolitical scales, food sovereignty activists are politicizing neoliberal governance and challenging its authority. Whereas some agrarian movements have embraced regressive nationalism in response to neoliberalism, food sovereignty movements promote a progressive vision of grassroots globalization and decentralized democracy. Thus, even though the state remains a critical site of contestation, food sovereignty movements also seek to reclaim control at the sub- and supranational levels.

Second, the agrarian question that once motivated widespread revolutions is no longer just about rural producers; it has been reconfigured around *food*.[11] Whereas peasants were once the primary protagonists in challenging the underlying moral economy of capitalism, urban and rural movements are cultivating new visions of a moral economy as they oppose the subordination of food systems to global markets. As Marc Edelman puts it, "In recent years, urban and rural culture have converged in so many ways that it is necessary to consider the possibility of a new, contemporary rural moral economy, informed by an urban imaginary and urban consumption expectations."[12] The concept of the moral economy, first developed by E. P. Thompson to describe "confrontations in the marketplace," is useful because it highlights popular understandings that markets are products of political struggle.[13] Scholars have drawn on this concept specifically in the context of food because it is when people lack access to basic necessities that we see collective claims for moral economies emerge.

However, today the demands for moral economies that we see emerging are not just about subsistence; they are also about food quality and production practices. The consequences of the industrialization of food systems are a powerful reminder that diverse farming systems and diets are critical for human and environmental well-being. Vast swaths of monocropped land have transformed human diets, encouraging the mass consumption of cheap and often highly processed foods. These unhealthy diets have caused a surge in the incidence of noncommunicable diseases, including diabetes, cardiovascular disease, and some cancers. As diet-related diseases and malnutrition have spread, they have led to a critical reckoning with food systems. If current trends continue, experts estimate that over half the world will be overweight or obese.[14] Moreover, industrialized food systems are not just a key contributor to climate change; they are also being upended by it. As communities face drought, floods, desertification, and other effects of climate change, we are seeing a new generation of climate change refugees. The UN Food and Agriculture Organization reports that in developing countries the agriculture sectors sustained more than a quarter of the damage from climate change. It estimates that by 2050, 400 million people will be displaced by climate change.[15] Urban and rural movements are thus emerging to reimagine a new moral and *ecological* economy through food. This entails fundamentally transforming the systems of food production, provisioning, and consumption.

In mobilizing for social change, food sovereignty movements also draw on the symbolic meanings of food as a powerful cultural resource. Beyond the political-economic dimensions of food production and provisioning, food systems and quotidian acts of eating are shaped by a variety of social relations, values, and meanings that have deep resonance for people's ways of life. Food sits at the center of the ways that we express our relations to each other and the natural world—our identities, religions, and values. Acts of commensality are the cornerstone of many communities.[16] The effects of the dominant industrial food system on the cultures of people across the world have therefore been a major source of grievance. After all, it was the reminder of the cultural significance of food during the first world food crisis in the 1970s that inspired activists in the Puget Sound to turn to food politics. During his speech at Expo '74 in Spokane, Washington—the event that motivated Mark Musick and his colleagues to organize the first "alternative agriculture" conference in the Pacific Northwest—Wendell Berry sought to reenchant food for his audience: "Food is a cultural, not a technological, product. . . . A culture is not a collection of relics or ornaments, but a practical necessity, and its destruction invokes calamity."[17] For the alternative agriculture movement that eventually took up Berry's vision, food politics was not only about resisting the US's food and agricultural policies but also about rebuilding the social, economic, and ecological relations that had been eroded by the capitalist food system.

Given that industrial food systems are a nexus for so many of the global challenges we face today—including zoonotic spillover and disease spread as a result of deforestation, hunger and malnutrition in all its forms, economic inequality, and the existential threat of climate change—it is no wonder that political and legal analysts are paying closer attention to struggles over food. Scholars of agrarian studies are pointing to the vast inequalities between urban and rural residents as a key culprit in the global rise of right-wing populism.[18] Meanwhile, sociolegal scholars are also increasingly turning to food as a critical site through which to examine changing forms of law and regulation. As Christine Parker and Hope Johnson put it, "Because food is so central to everyday life, it also sits at the intersection of the most pressing regulatory governance challenges for capitalism: human rights to adequate food and a healthy environment, rights to meaningful work and labor justice, the responsibilities to care for animals and ecologies, and the need for meaning and social identity."[19] Agrarian struggles are thus once again emerging at the center of resistance to the dominant political and legal order and auger the possibilities of significant sociolegal transformations.

RIGHTS, REGULATION, AND THE PRACTICE OF FOOD SOVEREIGNTY MOBILIZATION

By analyzing how food sovereignty movements mobilize claims, I have proposed a new approach to understanding how power is constructed and contested in transnational governance. Through their claims of food sovereignty, activists have produced a new grammar of justice claims that directly confront the neoliberal mutations of transnational law and governance. In doing so, activists do not nostalgically seek to return to previous political and legal arrangements. Instead, they are appropriating the tools of transnational governance to build an alternative political and legal formation that transcends liberal legalism's boundaries. In an era when scholars are recognizing that human rights alone are not enough to challenge neoliberalism,[20] food sovereignty activists have developed creative practices of mobilization that combine both rights and regulation in one of the most expansive claims for social, economic, and environmental justice.

Rights remain critical for food sovereignty activists. Rights serve as a tool to politicize regulatory arenas, illuminate power asymmetries, and build on existing norms that require states to ensure the basic needs of their citizens. However, even when approached as discursive resources rather than instrumental claims, rights have limited efficacy in socioeconomic struggles. They remain decontextualized from existing relations and are not flexible enough to address the practical reality of distribution. Moreover, they are too individualistic and state focused to address the complex social relations through which food is produced and provisioned in the global political economy.

By combining rights with regulation, however, food sovereignty activists ground their demands in existing normative human rights commitments while also developing claims and practices to influence the regulatory processes through which markets are constituted. Throughout this book I have demonstrated how food sovereignty activists rely on liberal forms of legality and rights claims to politicize and open up spaces of governance in order to engage in more nuanced relational and distributive struggles. In chapter 3, for example, I described how farmworkers mobilized state and federal law to protect their rights to organize, to raise awareness for their cause, and to oppose the most egregious violations of wage theft by their employer. Yet, although rights mobilization was important in legitimating their struggle, it was not enough for them to exercise control in their working conditions. Therefore farmworkers drew on their litigative successes to politicize the value chain in which they worked, to form alliances with other constituencies, and to push for more radical transformation. Similarly, in chapter 5 we saw how food sovereignty activists mobilized the right to food in an effort to remind other participants in the Committee on World Food Security (CFS) about who were the rights holders (civil society), who were the stakeholders (corporations), and who was responsible for respecting and protecting the rights of citizens (states). Rights thus served to reanimate the antagonisms and frontiers between actors that were blurred by governance processes in the CFS. In both of these cases food sovereignty activists relied on liberal legality to open up political spaces through which they could then pursue more radical claims.

Dominant approaches to law, politics, and social change have not accounted for such practices because they often remain embedded in the ideology of liberal legality and its distinction between law and politics. In conceptualizing how social movements engage in transnational governance, Bronwen Morgan therefore argues that we need to expand our analyses past classic approaches of legal mobilization and disputing—"naming, blaming, claiming"—and also look at the way that movements engage in processes of "rulemaking, monitoring, and enforcement."[21] This framework is productive because it accounts for the necessity of both rights and regulation in challenging entrenched forms of power in neoliberal legality. But it also risks placing too much emphasis on the legal and regulatory institutions in which activists engage rather than on the autonomous prefigurative practices that remain at the heart of food sovereignty activists' efforts to create the conditions for new forms of world making. As Gianpaolo Baiocchi reminds us, "Institutions are not set up for popular sovereignty. They are designed for managing populations, protecting the social order, and defending private property. When activists engage in institutions they really do so in conditions not of their own choosing."[22]

In examining how food sovereignty movements engage with transnational governance, therefore, I chose instead to focus on the constitutive practices through which power is constructed and contested in transnational governance, what I call activists' social practices of translation. Analyzing how power operates in transnational governance, I contend, necessitates attending to the transcalar practices of translation through which competing actors constitute networks. Power is embedded in the ways that actors construct equivalences and in how they commensurate or manage difference—practices that are at the heart of translation. Hegemonic and counterhegemonic actors deploy different practices of translation; whereas hegemonic actors often seek to subsume difference in their efforts to promote a global market-based order, counterhegemonic movements endeavor to preserve social, cultural, and ecological difference. Rival actors and networks ultimately seek to institutionalize these practices of translation by encoding their communicative practices in formal arenas of governance. These arenas are thus critical not so much as instrumental processes of rule making but rather as part of a broader hegemonic struggle over the practices of representation, knowledge, and commensuration in transnational governance.

Food sovereignty activists' practices of translation therefore offer the most powerful democratic antidote to the social, economic, and ecological unsustainability of neoliberal capitalism. By constituting their claims and horizons of justice in relation to the postliberal landscape of transnational governance, activists have developed a radical democratic praxis that demands representation, resists epistemic enclosure by valuing alternative forms of local and Indigenous knowledge, and contests commensuration by developing new types of relationality that seek to embrace and preserve diversity. Through these practices, food sovereignty activists are producing autonomous forms of governance from below through which they are slowly shaping burgeoning institutions of regulatory governance.

THE TWO FACES OF TRANSNATIONAL GOVERNANCE

Participation in formal processes of transnational governance presents a paradox for food sovereignty movements. Given that transnational governance is a product of neoliberalism, many scholars see it as a technology of neoliberalism. Critics have argued that the turn to participatory networked forms of governance depoliticizes decision making, embeds sociomoral concerns in the market, promotes rule by experts, responsibilizes managed subjects, and disseminates neoliberal reason.[23] These critiques are not misguided. Arenas of transnational governance often draw on symbols familiar to social movements, such as participation and inclusion, but the rules and structures of these arenas are often already established by elites. These top-down forms of governance can suppress and co-opt resistance rather than decentralize democracy.

By engaging in transnational governance, food sovereignty activists therefore risk being co-opted by it. The blurred boundaries of transnational governance enable activists to press their claims for social and economic justice, but they can also be mobilized by powerful actors to represent the world as a global marketplace and thereby deepen neoliberal governmentality. Critical governance scholar Jonathan Davies argues that the problem with networked governance is not simply that it is a product of neoliberalism but that it also "relegates hierarchy to the background."[24] He contends that networks have become a hegemonic form through which capital has entrenched its power. Davies makes an important point. Transnational governance has not fundamentally transformed the relations of power at the heart of neoliberalism. Yet Davies's critique also comes close to suggesting that the network breeds false consciousness. It suggests that networks are inescapably imbued with capitalist meanings and power relations. His account therefore aligns with other narratives that see networked forms of capitalism as lacking any "outside" from which to challenge it.

Sociolegal scholarship offers important lessons in responding to such a critique. Long concerned with the relationship between formal and informal orders, sociolegal scholars have illuminated the productive and dialectical relationship between dominant and alternative normative orderings. For example, in his study of housing cooperatives in England, Stuart Henry illustrated how alternative economic and normative institutions "do not work transformations on capitalist structures and rule but instead interact with them in a dialectical way, such that both the alternative system and the capitalist order are vulnerable to incremental reformulations." He points out what feminists have long emphasized: that capitalism already relies on noncapitalist forms of care, social solidarity, and ecological processes and that it is by expanding and building these relations that transformations take place. Henry therefore suggests that the "greatest potential for transformation lies in these dialectical processes."[25]

Approached from this vantage, I read critiques of network governance as a warning that if food sovereignty movements do not protect their autonomy from transnational governance processes, they risk being absorbed into institutions that remain in the shadow of global hierarchies of power. This is something that movements are already aware of, and it is the reason that food sovereignty activists have cultivated their own autonomous meanings and practices of governance. However, it is also the reason that social movement activists find themselves in conflict with international NGOs, which are often much more willing to engage in governance processes. Analyses of co-optation and absorption into neoliberal governance thus need to attend more closely to the interactivist politics that shape engagement in governance. By refusing to delegate their voice and demand self-representation, food sovereignty movements seek to protect the autonomy of their own governance practices.

Transnational governance may therefore be a product of neoliberalism, but as food sovereignty activists construct their claims in relation to the networked form of governance, they are cultivating culturally constitutive claims that can shape society from the bottom up. Legal mobilization scholars have shown that social movements can resignify rights to shape social expectations of entitlements and thereby transform social relations of power, but so too can claims mobilized through transnational governance. Through the new alliances, relationships, and practices developed, food sovereignty activists are changing everyday expectations about representation, the value of local knowledge, and the importance of human and more-than-human diversity. Moreover, through their struggle, they have challenged the dominant productivist narrative on which the industrial food system is built. In doing so, they have raised critical questions about whether a new form of social, economic, and agrarian organization is necessary in our era of climate change and immense inequality. Ultimately, by reconstituting food sovereignty as a practice of translocal translation, food sovereignty movements have shown that another world and form of transnational governance is possible.

JUSTICE IN THE ERA OF POSTLIBERAL LEGALITY?

I began this project after the 2007–2008 global food and financial crises, when the failures of neoliberalism were laid bare before the world. It was a period of deep frustration and immense hope. Soon after the crisis, insurgent movements such as Occupy Wall Street, the Arab Spring, the student movement in Montreal, and the Indignados in Spain rose up to challenge neoliberal inequalities and demand a new political order. However, ten years later, the future looks grim. Across the world, right-wing populist leaders have been elected who are undermining the institutions of liberal democracy and backtracking on human rights obligations. Rather than seeing this as a break with neoliberalism, however, many simply see it as a metamorphosis of it—the ultimate realization of neoliberalism's antipathy toward democracy and social justice.[26] In this era, dismantling the liberal walls of separation has not led to a deepening of democracy as food sovereignty activists had hoped. Rather, it has given rise to an era of *illiberal* democracy in which transnational corporations have aligned with autocratic leaders.

In this current moment of "hyper-reactionary neoliberalism," as Nancy Fraser calls it, the short-term prospects of food sovereignty may look grim. Yet as inequalities deepen and the effects of climate change grow too apparent to ignore, hyperreactionary neoliberalism is unlikely to endure as the dominant national or transnational order. As Fraser argues, it "offers no prospect of secure hegemony."[27] Nor are we likely to simply return to the neoliberal or liberal legal order. What will eventually emerge is unknown. Fraser aptly draws on Gramsci's well-worn saying in this moment: "The old is dying and cannot be reborn." In the meantime, however, the network is likely to endure as the primary *form* of transnational governance. As Anne-Marie Slaughter argues, networked forms of governance are alluring because they offer a solution to the contemporary paradox of global governance, namely, that "we need more government on a global and a regional scale, but we don't want the centralization of decision-making power and coercive authority so far from the people actually to be governed."[28] The flexibility of the networked form thus makes it appealing to a wide variety of actors and enables what I have argued in this book is a critical terrain of contemporary hegemonic struggle.

Yet the network is also an unsatisfying metaphor for agrarian social relations. As a former leader of the International Planning Committee for Food Sovereignty told me (quoted in the introduction), the internet and digital networks are not a format of social organization that is appropriate for peasants, fisherfolk, and food-chain workers. Networks are decontextualized from the ecological relations between society and nature that have become so pressing a concern as we struggle to feed ourselves in a moment when climate change poses an existential threat. As humans grow increasingly cognizant of our role as the primary protagonists in planetary transformation, a new metaphor is needed to ground contemporary struggles over law, governance, and authority in the diverse global landscape. Just as food sovereignty activists have adopted the framework of agroecology as a template to cultivate new socioeconomic and socioecological relations, I want to suggest that a better metaphor for both describing and imagining the possibilities produced by transnational governance is a *patchwork*.

Scholars of international relations and transnational governance have drawn on the metaphor of the patchwork to describe transnational governance as a postmodern reconfiguration of political and legal space.[29] The description of transnational governance as a patchwork emphasizes that the global arrangements of law and power are a product of entangled actors that compete and collaborate across a fragmented and indeterminate terrain.[30] However, the real virtue of the patchwork metaphor lies in its connection to landscape. Agroecologists and anthropologists have developed the metaphor of the patchwork to analyze the relationships between humans and nature and as a guide for our collective future. From an ecological perspective, patchworks consist of fragmented matrices of cultivated and uncultivated land. Although the fragmentation of forestland into patches was once thought to be a major cause of the loss of biodiversity, Ivette Perfecto and her colleagues have found that better managing these patchworks can in fact *enhance* both human and more-than-human diversity. Rather than seeing agriculture and forests in conflict (or, we might say, humans and nature, more broadly), they suggest that a high-quality matrix of small-scale agricultural practices combined with well-coordinated conservation can enrich biodiversity as well as social and economic justice.[31] Anna Tsing and her colleagues build on this framework to describe what they call the "patchy Anthropocene." They argue that the metaphor of patchiness challenges universalizing visions of either emancipation or catastrophe: "Patchiness is hope's condition of possibility and its limit at the same time. Patchy hope operates on the acute awareness of its own limitation. Indeed, it operates on the acute likelihood of its own failure."[32]

Might patchiness provide a framework for thinking through the possibilities of transnational governance as well? Although a surfeit of analyses describe transnational governance as a sort of patchwork—a legally plural landscape—for legal scholars, pluralism and fragmentation are often framed as a problem. Patchiness creates uncertainty, the condition that modern law has been constructed to mitigate. Yet if we are reminded of the constitutive power of law—law's power not merely to regulate human relations but its role in producing contingent relations between humans and nature—then we might embrace the patchiness of transnational governance as a landscape of "diverse" legalities that might resist commensuration and allow human and ecological diversity to flourish.[33]

Following along similar lines, Fritjof Capra and Ugo Mattei have recently proposed a new approach to legal analysis, which they call the ecology of law. They argue that this approach does not "separate the law into a domain of facts—how the law *is*—and a domain of values—how the law *ought to be*"; nor does it "reduce law to a professionalized, preexisting objective framework 'out there,' separate from the behavior it regulates and tries to determine. Instead, law is always a process of '*commoning*,' a long-term collective action in which communities, sharing a common purpose and culture, institutionalize their collective will to maintain order and stability in the pursuit of social reproduction."[34]

An ecological perspective of transnational governance places analysts in the patchworked landscape of human and more-than-human relations rather than outside it or above it. It offers a way of seeing governance as a set of relations embedded in a web of life that needs diversity to sustain it. Such a perspective reveals that, rather than seeking to commensurate social, economic, and ecological contexts through liberal legality, we need diverse property regimes, forms of knowledge, and political practices of representation to be resilient in the face of the existential ecological crises of the Anthropocene. Put another way, viewing transnational governance from an ecological perspective of patchiness requires new ways of seeing that places us in the relational landscapes we inhabit.

Food sovereignty movements offer a glimpse into how we might begin to reimagine justice in an age of transnational governance. By starting with food—humans' most basic need and the primary productive process through which we transform our landscapes—activists have already built a powerful transnational movement. Through their practices of translocal translation, food sovereignty activists are not only shaping the standards and norms produced in existing institutional arenas but also cultivating new practices of representation, knowledge sharing, and relation making from the bottom up. Through their engagement across the postliberal transnational legal landscape, they reveal how this emergent regulatory order can serve to reconstitute more just and sustainable relations between communities, markets, and nature on a global scale.

Notes

INTRODUCTION

1. Coleman-Jensen et al. (2018); FAO et al. (2021).

2. Swinburn et al. (2019).

3. IPCC (2019).

4. Kelloway and Miller (2019); Hendrickson et al. (2021).

5. IPES-Food (2017a).

6. IPES-Food (2017a).

7. Fraser (2009).

8. See Handler (1978), Scheingold (2004), McCann (1994), Epp (1998), and Schmidt (2018).

9. Moyn (2012).

10. Sassen (2008).

11. Moyn (2014; 2018). See also Marks (2013), Fraser (2019), Whyte (2019), and Slobodian (2020).

12. For these critiques of rights, see Brown and Halley (2002) and Unger (2004).

13. Merry (2006).

14. De Sousa Santos and Martins (2021).

15. Mutua (2001).

16. Moyn (2018).

17. See, for example, Djelic and Sahlin-Andersson (2006), Morgan (2011), and Roger and Dauvergne (2016).

18. See, for example, Vogel (1996), Levi-Faur (2006), and Braithwaite (2008).

19. Davis et al. (2012).

20. As the political philosopher Michael Walzer (1984) observed, liberalism is premised on the construction of "walls of separation" between public and private, civil society and political community that separate the spheres of liberty and equality.

21. W. Brown (2015).

22. For example, in the national context, see McCann (1994), H. Silverstein (1996), and Vanhala (2010). In the international context, see Merry (2006), Goodale and Merry (2007), L. Allen (2013), and Chua (2018).

23. Brigham (1987).

24. Daw and Morales Opazo (2009);Vidal (2010).

25. Headey and Fan (2008).

26. See IPES-Food (2016).

27. Thompson (1971). See also Edelman (2008).

28. Paxson (2012, 4).

29. The formation of both capitalism and colonialism was premised on the extraction of surpluses from agricultural goods. Harriet Friedmann and Philip McMichael have described how successive food regimes—"rule-governed structure[s] of production and consumption of food on a world scale"—have been critical material processes through which shifting geopolitical relations have been organized (Friedmann 1993, 30). See also Friedmann (1982), Friedmann and McMichael (1989), Araghi (2009), McMichael (2013), Tilzey (2017), and Canfield (2018a; 2020).

30. John Locke drew on imagery of emerging forms of "scientific" commercial agricultural production as evidence for the necessity of private ownership over property to incentivize the "improvement" of land. Improvement was understood as a process of "putting into profit," of turning waste into value, and enclosing common land. The ethic of improvement provided a justification for colonial expansion and individual ownership that was based on commercial agricultural practices, racialized bodies, and an exploitative view of the environment. In turn, the liberal sovereign state was constructed to protect individual rights over property and to ensure the profitable and efficient development of land. See N. Wood (1984), Arneil (1994), Bhandar (2018), and Ince (2018).

31. Gonzalez (2004); Narula (2010); A. Cohen (2013; 2015; 2020); Fakhri (2014); Orford (2015); Saab (2018; 2019); Chadwick (2019); Canfield, Cohen, and Fakhri (2021).

32. Canfield (2021).

33. Many theories of governance have been developed, including network governance, collaborative governance, democratic experimentalism, and new governance. Lobel (2004) describes this paradigm as the "Renew Deal," an approach to governance that includes several features: anti-adversarialism, horizontal participation of "stakeholders," collaborative approaches to problem solving, self-regulation, and on-going learning and benchmarking. See also Dorf and Sabel (1998), J. Cohen and Sabel (2004), Birnngham et al. (2005), De Búrca and Scott (2006), Ansell and Gash (2008);De Búrca et al (2014).

34. Gereffi et al. (2005).

35. Bartley (2003); Roff (2008); Haedicke (2013).

36. Riles (2001).

37. Boltanski and Chiapello (2007).

38. Castells (1996, 500); Slaughter (2005).

39. Harrington and Merry (1988, 714).

40. As de Sousa Santos (2005a) reiterates, "The main features of the neoliberal governance matrix are also present in the insurgent governance matrix: voluntary participation, horizontality, autonomy, coordination, partnership, self-regulation, etc." (32).

41. https://víacampesina.org/en/peoples-food-sovereignty-wto-out-of-agriculture/; emphasis added.

42. See, for example, Held (1995), Hardt and Negri (2001), Slaughter (2005), and Sassen (2008).

43. Wittman (2011).

44. Claeys (2015) also identifies different networks that mobilize these claims. Whereas the food sovereignty movement has been led by transnational agrarian movements such as LVC, the right to food has been the focus of human rights organizations, rights-based development NGOs, and United Nations organizations. Although these networks are sometimes overlapping, Claeys emphasizes the distinctions between these discourses.

45. Claeys (2015, 25).

46. Ewick and Silbey (1998, 22).

47. Ewick and Silbey (1998, 23).

48. In the absence of the "solid" authority of the state, authority, as Nico Krisch (2017) argues, is more "liquid." See also Sassen (2008) and Barkan (2011).

49. Nicholson (2012, 3). Nicholson's paper was translated by Gail Hunter with the assistance of Nora Wintour, as "Food Sovereignty, a Basis for Transforming the Dominant Economic and Social Model: An Interview of Paul Nicholson, La Vía Campesina," https://www.cetim.ch/documents/food_sovereignty-Paul_Nicholson_interview.pdf (accessed May 20, 2020), p. 3.

50. Juris (2008a). Similarly, Maeckelbergh (2009) explains how the networked model provided activists with a framework to shift "from hierarchical power to non-hierarchical power" and thereby "reclaim control" (108–9).

51. Declaration of the International Forum for Agroecology, 2015, Nyéléni, Mali, https://viacampesina.org/en/declaration-of-the-international-forum-for-agroecology/ (accessed June 1, 2020).

52. In 2015 food sovereignty activists released the Declaration of the International Forum on Food Sovereignty, which affirmed that agroecology is "a key element in the construction of Food Sovereignty" and that it cannot be understood as "a mere set of technologies or production practices" but rather is a set of principles must be applied to local ecological and cultural contexts in different ways. See the Declaration of the International Forum for Agroecology (2015): https://www.foodsovereignty.org/wp-content/uploads/2015/02/Download-declaration-Agroecology-Nyeleni-2015.pdf (accessed July 15, 2020).

53. Wezel et al. (2009).

54. Gliessman (2013); HLPE (2019); Wezel et al. (2020).

55. De Sousa Santos and Rodríguez-Garavito (2005).

56. See, for example, Morgan (2007), Darian-Smith and Scott (2009), and Epp (2010).

57. Morgan (2011, 32). This framework also builds on Unger's (2004) notion of destabilization rights.

58. Grewal (2009, 171).

59. Iles and Montenegro de Wit (2015, 482).

60. Schiavoni (2017).

61. Morgan (2011, 29).

62. Merry (2006); Goodale and Merry (2007).

63. Shattuck et al. (2015, 429).

64. Grewal (2009); Castells (2013).

65. Braithwaite and Drahos (2000, 560).

66. Merry (2006).

67. Callon (1984); Burchell et al. (1991); Latour (2007).

68. Miller and Rose (2008) argue that power "is the outcome of the affiliation of persons, spaces, communications and inscriptions into a durable form." They contend that when actors are able to "translate the values of others into [their] own terms, such that they provide norms and standards for their own ambitions, judgements and conduct," they have constructed networks through which they exercise power (64–65).

69. Costa (2006, 63).

70. Gal (2015; 2016).

71. On the role of equivalences in political theory, see Laclau and Mouffe (1985).

72. For example, Michael Silverstein (2003) describes one practice of translation, which he describes as transduction. In contrast to Euro-American language ideologies that "expect maximal correspondence between word-labels and what is assumed to be a separately available real world" (Gal 2015, 233), transduction is a process of indexical mediation that aims to capture the energy or a term or phrase and translate it into something relevant or meaningful for the target language or culture. Silverstein argues that transduction operates like a hydroelectric generator, where "one form of organized energy . . . is asymmetrically converted into another kind of energy at an energetic transduction site . . . harnessing at least some of it across energetic frameworks" (23). This metaphor is fruitful because it recognizes the "friction" and "random contingent factors" that shape the process of translation. Thus, although the practice of translation expected by Euro-American language ideologies seek to *subsume* the words and texts of one language or discipline in another, transduction involves a recognition of difference.

73. De Sousa Santos (2005b, 21).

74. De Sousa Santos (2005b, 20).

75. Jessop (2016).

76. These metasemiotic practices operate as what Castells (2013) would call protocols of communication.

77. Harrington and Yngvesson (1990).

78. Alkon and Mares (2012); Brent et al. (2015); Figueroa (2015); Coté (2016);

Trauger (2017); Hoover (2017); Frisbie (2018); White (2018); D. Taylor (2018); Jones (2019); Reese (2019); Mihesuah and Hoover (2019).

79. Juris and Khasnabish (2013, 4).

80. De Sousa Santos (2018). Whereas Northern forms of knowledge have privileged what he describes as "knowing about," de Sousa Santos (2018, 14–15) argues for a model of "knowing-with" that echoes Juris and Khasnabish (2013). Importantly, however, de Sousa Santos notes that epistemologies of the South do not solely emerge from the geographic South; they derive from the epistemological South—the forms of knowing that dominant forms of science have sought to extinguish.

81. Boltanski and Chiapello (2007, xxiii).

82. See also Riles (2001).

83. See W. Brown (2015), Swyngedouw (2010), and Wilson and Swyngedouw (2015). See also Shamir (2008).

84. Others, such as Benedict Kingsbury, point out that networks are not always transparent and may not be publicly accountable. See Kingsbury et al. (2005) and Kingsbury (2009).

85. Gibson-Graham (2006, xxiii). J. K. Gibson-Graham is the pen name used by Julie Graham and Katherine Gibson.

86. As Amy Trauger (2017) reminds us, "Food sovereignty is a powerful narrative of alternative modernity (or antimodernity) that challenges the political practices that have failed to produce 'freedom from want'" (29). See also Capra and Mattei (2015).

87. Allison (2014, 18).

88. Tsing (2015, 20).

89. Halliday and Morgan (2013). See also Morgan and Kuch (2015; 2017; 2020).

90. Berry (2009, 292).

CHAPTER 1

1. Cookson Beecher, "Ag Summit Raises Questions About Globalization," *Capital Press*, December 17, 1999.

2. For a description of the alternative agricultural movement, see Youngberg (1978).

3. Thorelli (1986).

4. See, for example, P. Allen and Kovach (2000), Arcuri (2015), Obach (2015), and Haedicke (2016).

5. On past agrarian struggles, see Goodwyn (1978), Daniel (1982), Mooney and Majka (1995), D. Brown (2011), White (2018), and Montenegro de Wit et al. (2021).

6. Lappé (1971).

7. Belasco (2014, 27).

8. Friedmann and McMichael (1989).

9. FAO (2009b).

10. Rothschild (1976, 302).

11. Woertz (2013, 125).

12. Winders (2004).

13. The text of the speech can be found at http://tilthproducers.org/about-us/history/the-culture-of-agriculture.

14. Letter from Wendell Berry, http://tilthproducers.org/about-us/history/letter-from-wendell-berry/ (accessed August 18, 2021).

15. Poster, Tilth Association Papers, Washington State University.

16. Brand (1968, 34).

17. Turner (2006); Kirk (2001).

18. Letter from Mark Musick, October 23, 1980, Tilth Association Papers, Washington State University Libraries.

19. Letter from Mark Musick, October 23, 1980, Tilth Association Papers, Washington State University Libraries.

20. Letter from Mark Musick, October 23, 1980, Tilth Association Papers, Washington State University Libraries.

21. Guthman (2004).

22. Allen and Kovach (2000, 224).

23. Haedicke (2016).

24. Pollan (2006a, 159).

25. Powell (1990, 304).

26. King and Pearce (2010); McInerney (2014).

27. Piven and Cloward (1978); Hannah-Jones (2019).

28. McMichael (2011, 137).

29. Before the 1980s, "internationalist" agrarian organizations had existed. However, a new generation of transnational movements flourished in the 1980s and 1990s. For a brief history of peasant internationalism, see Edelman and Borras (2016).

30. Martinez-Torres and Rosset (2010, 155).

31. Routledge and Cumbers (2013).

32. Rajagopal (2005).

33. Desmarais (2002); Routledge and Cumbers (2013).

34. Keck and Sikkink (1998).

35. https://Víacampesina.org/en/managua-declaration/ (accessed October 6, 2020).

36. Desmarais (2007, 75–77).

37. Fraser (2009, 16).

38. Edelman (2013, 9).

39. Desmarais (2002, 92).

40. Marc Edelman points out that the language of food sovereignty has a longer history, including as part of the National Food Program in Mexico in 1983. Other scholars have pointed out that the term *food sovereignty* was used by agrarian movements in France before the LVC conference in Mexico. See Edelman (2014) and Heller (2013).

41. Rosset (2006, 9).

42. Although the linkages between hunger and global trade are far too complex to elaborate here, the reality of the Agreement on Agriculture is that it created an

uneven playing field that is a far cry from "free trade." States in the global North won legal sanction to protect their home markets, whereas states in the global South were required to dismantle theirs. As Jennifer Clapp (2015) notes, "The lack of balance in the agreement was a product of the ways in which politics mediated the application of two distinct norms. The industrialized countries were able to maintain policies that supported the idea that food is different at home, while painting them as compatible with liberalization in the WTO [World Trade Organization] context. At the same time, developing countries were forced to liberalize while their ability to enact policies that treated food differently in support of their own development needs was curtailed, with negative implications for food security" (119). For small-scale producers the results have been devastating. Lowering food prices has made it impossible for small-scale producers to compete in the global market and floods their markets with cheap food. Liberalization has thus bred increased market dependence in the global South. See De Schutter (2011), Margulis (2013; 2017), and Burnett and Murphy (2014).

43. Jarosz (2009; 2011); Duncan (2015).

44. "Statement by the NGO Forum to the World Food Summit," Annex III, http://www.fao.org/3/w3548e/w3548e00.htm.

45. Desmarais (2007, 101).

46. http://safsc.org.za/wp-content/uploads/2015/09/1996-Declaration-of-Food-Sovereignty.pdf (accessed October 22, 2020); emphasis added.

47. Clapp (2014).

48. https://viacampesina.org/en/peoples-food-sovereignty-wto-out-of-agriculture/ (accessed October 31, 2020); emphasis added.

49. Declaration of Nyéléni, February 27, 2007, http://nyeleni.org/spip.php?article290 (accessed May 7, 2020).

50. Claeys (2015, 91).

51. Boggs (1977); Polletta (2004).

52. Maeckelbergh (2011, 2).

53. Although many scholars have sought to parse the way power operates through networks, Manuel Castells has developed the most synthetic account that combines several approaches. According to Castells, power operates through communicative practices that seek to shape the values and interests that are "programmed" into networks. Power, he argues, is shaped by two types of actors and activities: programmers and switchers. Programmers operate to shape the values and interests embedded in networks, whereas switchers connect networks or fend off competition from other networks. What Castells describes as programming rests at the core of how food sovereignty activists seek to institutionalize their claims across global to local scales—by embedding their values and interests in networks. Programming is a cultural process. As Castells explains, "To be effective in programming the networks, they need to rely on a metaprogram that ensures that the recipients of the discourse internalize the categories through which they find meaning for their own actions in accordance with the programs of the networks" (Castells 2013, 52). However, the notion of a metaprogram suggests that networked actors such as food sovereignty

activists have a shared set of interests or ideological program. I argue instead that food sovereignty movements' metaprogram is embedded in their communicative practices.

54. Turem and Ballestero (2014, 3).

55. De Sousa Santos (2005b, 21).

56. Alvarez et al. (2014).

57. Blackwell (2014, 300).

58. http://www.fao.org/gender/resources/infographics/the-female-face-of-farming/en/ (accessed October 31, 2020).

59. https://nyeleni.org/spip.php?article290 (accessed October 31, 2020).

60. Zald (1996, 262).

61. On the role of representation in constituting politics and society, see Lefort (1986) and Lievens (2015).

62. Sørensen (2002, 698).

63. Some political theorists (e.g., Hardt and Negri 2005) have celebrated networked representations of society as the basis for a counterhegemonic multitude. Others have criticized the network as a political representation for failing to clearly represent where power lies (e.g., Laclau 1996).

64. https://www.nyeleni.org/spip.php?article290.

65. Pimbert (2006; 2015); Méndez et al (2013).

66. Holt-Giménez (2006); Rosset et al. (2011).

67. Martínez-Torres and Rosset (2014, 980).

68. Haas (2015).

69. Jasanoff (2011, 228).

70. See de Sousa Santos (2007) and Capra and Mattei (2015).

71. Daalgard et al. (2003) discuss agroecology in light of Robert Merton's definition of science. Although their discussion is useful, they also claim that agroecology is "disinterested," which many scholars disagree with. See, for example, Pimbert (2006), Wezel et al. (2009), and Gliessman (2013).

72. Shiva (1993); Coolsaet (2016).

73. Sending (2015).

74. One way powerful actors can enroll others into their networks is by offering conditional assistance, such as investment, based on countries' willingness to change certain laws and regulations. Another way that this can operate is by providing funding for conferences, scholarships, educational fellowships, and international travel.

75. https://www.nyeleni.org/spip.php?article290.

76. Gal (2015, 226).

77. See Espeland and Stevens (1998).

78. Espeland and Stevens (1998, 320).

79. Povinelli (2001).

80. De Sousa Santos (2005b, 20).

81. See Goux (1990), Finnis (1990), and Legrand (2009).

82. On the role of destabilizing regulatory arrangements, see Sabel and Simon (2004) and Unger (2004).

83. Nord et al. (2008).

84. Holt-Giménez and Patel (2012, 7).

85. Holt-Giménez and Patel (2012, 216–17).

86. This connection between the food banks and corporations has been well documented, as food banks rely on the donations from food processors and other corporations to maintain their operations, an alliance that Andrew Fisher terms "Big Hunger." See Poppendieck (1999) and Fisher (2017).

87. Felstiner et al. (1980).

88. M. Anderson and Cook (1999); P. Allen (2007).

89. Claeys (2015, 90–94).

90. The pamphlet is available at https://nffc.net/wp-content/uploads/REV-food_sovereignty_booklet.pdf (accessed June 1, 2020).

91. Food Sovereignty PMA Resolution, https://sites.google.com/a/usfoodsovereigntyalliance.org/www/foodsovereigntypma/food-sovereignty-pma-resolution (accessed May 2016).

92. Juris (2008b) explains that the organizers of the US Social Forum had a specific understanding of "grassroots" that differed from previous movements. In contrast "to the highly institutionalized politics of mainstream labor, environmental, and other large nonprofit organizations, as well as the 'personalized' politics of middle-class direct-action activists, anarchists, and radical environmentalists," the National Planning Committee was committed to "movement building" between working-class communities of color (360). Juris argues that this intentional privileging of grassroots organizations indicated a political approach to social change that intentionally excluded mainstream organizations that had long held the banner of social justice.

93. Although Michael Pollan (2010) has optimistically described a growing food movement in the United States, he has been criticized for lumping together a range of movements with different concerns and political goals. Alkon and Mares (2012) argue that even though many groups working on food today oppose the inequalities produced by neoliberalism, they nonetheless reproduce it in their policy prescriptions. School lunch programs, community gardening, and farmers markets all have been critiqued by food sovereignty scholars for cultivating neoliberal subjectivities and maintaining racial and class inequalities. See P. Allen and Guthman (2006), Pudup (2008), and Alkon and McCullen (2011). Giménez and Wang (2011) suggest that lumping together the different strands of food activism under the term *food movement* does not distinguish between ideologies and approaches. They argue that "the challenge for building a powerful food movement is to reach beyond the dominant (and depoliticizing) food-movement narrative to build strategic political alliances and construct a new narrative" (95).

94. https://viacampesina.org/en/statement-from-the-peoples-movement-assembly-on-food-sovereignty/ (accessed October 31, 2020).

95. Schiavoni (2015).

96. Turner (2006, 5).

CHAPTER 2

1. Bruni (2011).

2. King County Local Food Initiative, 2014, https://www.kingcounty.gov/elected/executive/constantine/initiatives/local-food-initiative/System.aspx (accessed August 11, 2020).

3. Borras et al. (2015); McMichael (2015); Roman-Alcalá (2015); Williams and Holt-Giménez (2017).

4. Swyngedouw (1997, 140). See also Harvey (1989).

5. Swyngedouw (2004).

6. Critics of localization and local food systems in North America argue that efforts to transform class and racial inequalities through the market narrow the political possibilities of social and economic transformation. For example, based on her research on the evolution of the organic movement and the contemporary formation of local food movements in California, Guthman (2008) argues that attempts to localize food systems are likely to reinforce neoliberal subjectivities by limiting what may have first been articulated as a mode of political transformation to a set of individual purchasing decisions in which the primary mode of citizenship is through consumption. See also Johnston (2008) and Busa and Garder (2015).

7. Purcell (2009); W. Brown (2015).

8. Poppendieck (1999, 87).

9. Sassen (2008); N. Smith (2008).

10. De Angelis (2006, 90).

11. Swyngedouw (2004).

12. Brenner (1999; 2019); Sassen (2002).

13. Healey (1997); Innes and Booher (2003); Innes (2004).

14. Hardt and Negri (2001, 45). See also Castells (1999) and Osterweil (2005).

15. Food studies scholars E. Melanie Dupuis and David Goodman (2005) caution that those promoting local food often adopt a romantic vision of localism that tends to be racially and economically exclusionary. They also argue that localism is not always associated with a more just food system or more ecological forms of production—the goals of localism are often ambiguous and contradictory. Rather than fetishize the local, they argue for a more "reflexive localism" that is attentive to the politics through which the meaning and the scale of the local are constructed. Similarly, Born and Purcell (2006) warn against the "local trap," which "conflates the scale of a food system with a desired outcome" (196). In a series of writings, Eric Holt-Giménez describes how different meanings and practices of localism can be located across different currents and ideologies of food activism, from reformist to progressive to radical. Each of these are identified with various organizations, movements, and discourses. Reformist movements are identified with the food security paradigm, progressive movements with food justice, and radical movements with food sovereignty. Holt-Giménez argues that "while the progressive trend focuses on local ownership of production and on improving the service and delivery aspects of the food system, the radical trend directs more of its

energy at structural changes to capitalist food systems. When taken together, both trends seek to change the rules and practices of food systems, locally, nationally, and internationally" (Holt-Giménez and Wang 2011, 94). Although reformists to radicals all support the ideal of localized food systems, the meaning and process by which localization occurs is highly contested. Ultimately, these struggles play out not only discursively—in the meanings attributed to localism—but through competing practices of networking.

16. Hadden and Tarrow (2007).

17. Community Alliance for Global Justice (1999).

18. Some scholars have challenged the discourse of resiliency for overlooking power asymmetries. See Mikulewicz (2019).

19. Yeatman (1994).

20. See Johns Hopkins Center for a Livable Future's Food Policy Networks (FPN) directory, http://www.foodpolicynetworks.org/councils/.

21. Fisher and Roberts (2011, 1).

22. Miller and Rose (2008, 88).

23. Miller and Rose (2008, 91). During this time sociologists also returned to the network metaphor for social and economic relationships; the proliferation of social network analysis in the 1980s was an effort to transcend the opposition between *Homo economicus* and *Homo sociologicus*, which itself was a product of liberalism.

24. De Sousa Santos and Rodríguez-Garavito (2005, 9). In their study of participatory policymaking, Baiocchi and Ganuza (2016) similarly find that many participatory policy arenas are created from the top down.

25. Benford and Snow (2000).

26. Callon (1998); Malloy (2003).

27. For a discussion on different theories of framing and their relation to collaborative governance, see Canfield (2018b).

28. Miller and Rose (2008, 62). See also Callon (1998, 17).

29. Goffman and Berger (1986); Callon (1998).

30. Sonntag (2008, 8).

31. Sonntag (2008, 60).

32. Sonntag (2008, 76).

33. Sonntag (2008, 36).

34. Gudeman (2013, 29).

35. As Gudeman (2005) explains, "The community realm offers security and a rampart against uncertainty, but it can be home to inequalities, the exercise of unconstrained power and exploitation. The market has proven to be a powerful solvent of community, because it breaks immutable bonds among people that are forged through material goods and services, and it permits and enforces a critique of unequal, if not Inefficient, connections" (97).

36. Gudeman (2013, 26).

37. This tension was evident in her report: "What is clear is that we can no longer assume that the material wealth generated through economic activity replaces natural

and social capital. At the same time, local economic transactions are seen to form a basis for relationships that generate natural and social wealth" (Sonntag 2008, 84).

38. Metropolitan planning organizations were originally established in the 1960s for the purposes of transportation planning after the Federal-Aid Highway Act of 1962. They were mandated under the Housing and Urban Development Act of 1965. For a history of metropolitan planning organizations, see Solof (1998).

39. Vision of the Puget Sound Regional Food Policy Council, established in 2011. On file with author.

40. PSRC Food Policy One Pager, http://www.psrc.org/assets/6436/FoodPolicy-OnePager.pdf (accessed May 2016).

41. Community Alliance for Global Justice (2012, 12).

42. For a representation of the consumer-centered approach to local food, see Pollan (2006b).

43. Holt-Giménez and Wang (2011, 85).

44. Seattle's Hmong population migrated to the United States in the 1980s. When they arrived, Seattle officials started a project to help them earn livelihoods through farming. Responding to the influx of migrants, Seattle officials worked with a range of local nonprofit organizations to develop the Seattle Indochinese Farm Project. Although the Hmong people who migrated were used to practicing swidden agriculture, Seattle officials thought that if they could help them learn farming skills appropriate to the region, they would be able to earn sustainable livelihoods. On a 22-acre plot of land in Woodinville, just northwest of the Snoqualmie Valley, the Hmong were trained in a new style of agriculture. The Hmong people who participated in the project were also offered training on buying and selling and were offered a space in the Pike Place Market. The project lasted for a few years but ended up collapsing. Today, instead of growing food, many Hmong farmers have decided to grow flowers, which has been highly successful in the downtown Pike Place Market.

45. Transcript of Puget Sound Food Policy Council Meeting, January 2013.

46. The link between food and tribal sovereignty has been clear since the first treaties were signed with settlers; Coast Salish tribes explicitly claimed rights to traditional fishing and gathering grounds. Article 5 of the Treaty of Point Elliott (1855) specifically designates access to fishing and hunting grounds. This right was reaffirmed in the now famous Boldt decision. *United States v. Washington*, 384 F. Supp. 312 (W.D. Wash. 1974).

47. Barker (2005).

48. Simpson (2017, 23).

49. Discussion item, Minutes of the Puget Sound Regional Food Policy Council, November 8, 2013, on file with author.

50. Graeber (2001, 88).

51. Hetherington (2014); Strathern (1996).

52. In the words of scholar Massimo De Angelis (2006), the market community frame "promote[d] a form of social cohesion that is compatible with capital accumulation," whereas the political community frame sought to create "a form of

social cohesion that sets a *limit* to capital accumulation and the colonization of life by capitalist markets" (92).

53. For this reason, the term *local* is a misnomer. Hardt and Negri (2001) suggest that contrasting the local with the global provides the false expectation that the local can be constructed outside of global flows of capitalism. They argue that "the better framework . . . to designate the distinction between the global and the local might refer to different networks of flows and obstacles in which the local moment or perspective gives priority to the reterritorializing barriers or boundaries and the global moment privileges the mobility of deterritorializing flows" (45). Although Hardt and Negri are right to point out the problem of localization, the solution they offer is far from elegant. It is unlikely to replace the struggle for the "local" anytime soon. Nevertheless, it emphasizes the depth to which networks are transforming the exercise, operation, and form of power.

CHAPTER 3

1. Gray (2013, 2).

2. Guthman (2004) traces how this narrative animated the organic movement in California.

3. Gereffi et al. (2005); Gibbon et al. (2008); Bair (2008). As Havice and Pickles (2019) point out, however, there is a wide variety of approaches to conceptualizing value.

4. S. Brown and Getz (2008).

5. Appleby (1982).

6. Lopez (2006).

7. Luna (1997).

8. Legal scholars have debated the impact of the NLRA and its subsequent reform and reinterpretation by the US Supreme Court. The legislation, which was sparked by labor unrest, sought to bring labor peace through a new deal between capital and labor. Although the immediate aftermath of the passage of the act prompted rapid growth of unionization, the law has also played a powerful role in constraining the labor movement—first through decisions by the Supreme Court to limit its interpretation, then through amendments that severely curtailed the ability of labor movements to challenge employers, and finally through the ossification of labor law. The labor movement has thus had a troubled history with law. Farmworkers' exclusion from the NLRA has meant that their right to collectively bargain has not been recognized, but it has also meant that they have not been subject to the pro-employer reforms of the NLRA that prohibit secondary boycotts and that they have not been wrapped up in the NLRA's slow-moving legalistic framework. See Klare (1977), Pope (1996), and Estlund (2002).

9. Martin (2003, 65).

10. Luna (1997); Schell (2002).

11. The Bracero Program is yet another example of labor legislation that served to facilitate an exploitable labor force. See Calavita (2010) and Loza (2016).

12. These alliances deeply enhanced the power of farmworkers. In 1965, when Mexican farmworkers went on strike alongside Filipino workers in the Agricultural Workers Organizing Committee (AWOC) led by Larry Itliong, Chavez not only supported striking workers but also initiated a rent strike in Delano and eventually organized the general public to boycott grapes. In 1966 the National Farm Workers Association and the AWOC merged to form the United Farm Workers Organizing Committee (UFWOC). These tactics were enormously successful. Throughout the late 1960s and early 1970s, 12% of Americans avoided eating table grapes as a result of the UFW's boycott (Martin 2003, 68). By 1970 the UFW had contracts with 85% of table-grape growers. Through their use of secondary boycotts and strong social movement orientation, the UFWOC successfully placed farmworkers on the national public stage, eventually renaming themselves the United Farm Workers when they joined the AFL-CIO in 1972.

13. Gordon (2005, 48).

14. Gordon (2005, 21).

15. Klare (1977).

16. R. Taylor (1971, 456).

17. As Willhoite (2012) notes, the AFL-CIO "saw all the UFW activity as disrupting and sapping of energy. For the AFL-CIO, victory was not defined in terms of changing social consciousness through a movement, it was defined in terms of winning contracts" (430).

18. Majka and Majka (2000, 162).

19. There are several accounts of Chavez's personal role in the UFW's decline. See Pawel (2009), Bardacke (2011), Garcia (2014), and Noah (2015).

20. Gordon (2005, 69).

21. See Fisk (2014), Andrias (2016), and Block (2020).

22. Barnett (2000).

23. Martin (2002).

24. Peck and Tickell (2002).

25. Regulatory governance scholars describe the shift of states from a "rowing" toward a "steering" role. See Horner (2017) and Horner and Alford (2019).

26. Humphrey and Schmitz (2001); Gereffi et al. (2005); Ponte and Gibbon (2005); Ponte and Sturgeon (2014).

27. Bartley (2003; 2007; 2018).

28. Suwandi (2019) explains that this "quest for valorization . . . is a strategy for both reducing necessary labor costs and maximizing the appropriation of surplus value. It extracts more out of workers through various means, including repressive work environments in periphery-economy factories, state-enforced bans on unionization, and quota systems or piece-rate work" (54).

29. S. Brown and Getz (2008, 1194).

30. Rodríguez-Garavito (2005).

31. Dias-Abey (2018); Mares (2018).

32. Holt-Giménez (2017, 70).

33. Holt-Giménez (2017, 71).

34. Espeland and Stevens (1998, 315).

35. Espeland and Stevens (1998, 320).

36. In GVCs value is primarily understood through the price system, or the forms of value promoted by capitalist markets. However, value has a much larger meaning. Anthropologists describe value as "the way people represent the importance of their own actions to themselves: normally, as reflected in one or another socially recognized form" (Graeber 2001, 47). People have a wide range of nonmonetary values that stem from their communities, religions, and beliefs about justice and the common good. These values play out in the context of labor through what Marx described as socially necessary labor time (SNLT). This approach emphasizes that, although the price of any good is a product of the labor exerted to create that good, the way that labor is valued is determined relationally. SNLT refers not only to the average time that is required to produce an object but also to cultural understandings of exertion and expectations about the reasonable amount of time to produce something. SNLT is therefore a set of shared meanings that communities, corporations, and other actors use to determine what is *socially necessary*. De Angelis (2006) argues that communities can "discipline firms to different norms, to different concepts of what is socially necessary" depending on the social forces that they are able to mobilize (187).

37. During World War II, the Sakuma family was evacuated from the West Coast and interned in California. After the war Atsusa and his family returned to Skagit County and continued to farm and expand their operation.

38. Holmes (2013).

39. Hansen and Donohoe (2003).

40. Zabin (1992).

41. Farmworker Justice (2014).

42. *Familias Unidas por la Justicia and Felimon Piñeda v. Sakuma Brothers* (2013), Order Granting Plaintiffs' Motion for Temporary Restraining Order and Order to Show Cause, Case #13-2-016441, Superior Court of the State of Washington in and for the County of Skagit.

43. Washington State's Agricultural Employment Standards (WAC 296-131-020(2)) provide that "every employee shall be allowed a rest period of at least ten minutes, on the employer's time, in each four-hour period of employment."

44. *Raul Marino Paz, individually and on behalf of similarly situated v. Sakuma Brothers Farms, Inc.* (2013), Class Action Complaint Demand for Jury Trial, Case 2:13-cv-01918-BJR, filed October 24, 2013.

45. The H-2A program was created through the Immigration Reform and Control Act (1986) to enable agricultural operations to apply for guest worker permits.

46. "We must ask why the very individuals who walked off the job last year because of alleged wage theft and mistreatment are now so eager to again work for Sakuma Brothers? The fact is that many of those who worked here last year have disqualified themselves. If they were part of the work disruptions, under the guest worker contract, they abandoned their jobs and are therefore not eligible to be rehired.

We have mailed letters to 379 employees who worked for us in 2013 to inform them that they abandoned their jobs and have disqualified themselves from working for Sakuma this year" (http://www.thestand.org/2014/05/sakuma-bros-aims-to-replac e-farm-workers-who-struck/ [accessed October 31, 2020]).

47. According to the Immigration and Nationality Act that authorizes the H-2A program, employers must comply with all applicable laws regarding pay and housing, and employers must not take action against workers who have filed complaints or engaged in labor disputes.

48. Richard M. Clark, "Decision and Order [ETA Case No. H-300-14115-379508, In the Matter of Washington Farm Labor Association, Sakuma Brothers Farms, Employer]," 2014, US Department of Labor, Office of Administrative Law Judges, San Francisco. https://www.oalj.dol.gov/DECISIONS/ALJ/TLC/2014/In_re_WASHING-TON_FARM_LABO_2014TLC00088_(MAY_20_2014)_134248_CADEC_SD.PD-F#search=Sakuma.

49. "Ceres and WWF Add World's Largest Berry Company to AgWater Challenge," October 16, 2019, https://www.driscolls.com/about/in-the-news/ceres-and-ww f-add-worlds-largest-berry-company-to-agwater-challenge (accessed October 31, 2020).

50. Goodyear (2017).

51. Christina Babbitt, "How Driscoll's, the World's Largest Berry Company, Is Becoming a Leader in Water Conservation," Environmental Defense Fund, January 23, 2019, http://blogs.edf.org/growingreturns/2019/01/23/ driscolls-berry-company-water-conservation/#:~:text=Driscoll's%20works%20 with%20approximately%20750,harvest%20on%20their%20own%20farms (accessed October 31, 2020).

52. Lee et al. (2012, 12,327).

53. DFTA, "Mission and History," http://www.thedfta.org/about/mission-and-his-tory/ (accessed October 31, 2020).

54. Reiter Affiliated Companies, https://www.berry.net/company/#:~:tex-t=With%20a%20family%20legacy%20of,in%20all%20of%20North%20America (accessed October 31, 2020).

55. Orleck (2018).

56. Letter to Miles Reitner, CEO of Driscoll's, from the Fair World Project, signed by nearly 10,000 concerned consumers, https://fairworldproject.org/wp-content/ uploads/2012/08/driscoll-binder.pdf (accessed October 31, 2020).

57. "U.S.: Union Negotiations Off the Table for Sakuma Brothers Farms," Fresh Fruit Portal, April 3, 2015, https://www.freshfruitportal.com/news/2015/04/03/u-s-union-negotiations-off-the-table-for-sakuma-brothers-farms/ (accessed October 31, 2020).

58. "Labor Standards," https://www.driscolls.com/about/thriving-workforce/ standards (accessed May 19, 2021).

59. "Driscoll's Underscores Commitment to Worker Welfare," Fresh Plaza,

February 1, 2016, www.freshplaza.com/article/2152786/driscoll-s-underscore s-commitment-to-worker-welfare/ (accessed July 26, 2019).

60. Mayer and Phillips (2017, 136).

61. Rodriguez-Garavito (2005); Esbenshade (2012).

62. Fransen and LeBaron (2019).

63. Egels-Zandén and Merk (2014).

64. Shamir (2008, 3).

65. Workers in San Quintín tried to establish an independent union—the National Independent Democratic Union of Farm Workers—but Driscoll's Worker Welfare Program does not address interunion struggles. In fact, workers in San Quintín faced direct police violence when they challenged state-sanctioned unions, which they argued failed to represent the interest of workers. In addition, BerryMex and Driscoll's close ties may have made Driscoll's less willing to put pressure on Berry-Mex. However, the expansion of fair-trade-certified berries in San Quintín is a significant change that has had some positive impact on the working conditions of farmworkers in Baja California. See Zlolniski (2019).

66. Bartley (2018).

CHAPTER 4

1. The Gates Foundation's efforts to transform US educational systems have been notorious for their failures. For example, in 2011 the Gates Foundation provided $100 million to inBloom, which was meant to gather and analyze student data to improve education. It ended after only one year because of public backlash over the use of student data. Similarly, Gates provided $1 billion to the Intensive Partnership for Effective Teaching Initiative, which sought to improve the training, hiring, and evaluation of teachers through data-based instruments; that program also failed (https://www.rand.org/pubs/research_reports/RR2242.html). The Gates Foundation's small-schools initiative, which provided millions of dollars for large schools to be broken up into smaller schools to create smaller class sizes, also failed to provide any substantive improvements. But the greatest failure was the Common Core Initiative, which the federal government incentivized states to adopt, only to see forty-five states withdraw because of complaints from parents, students, teachers, and state policy-makers that the standards were not only inappropriate but also required schools to purchase corporately developed content that cost $16 billion by some estimates. See Ravitch (2013).

2. Le Marre et al. (2007).

3. Haas (1992).

4. Sending (2015).

5. Jasanoff (2006, 287).

6. N. Wood (1984); Polanyi (2001); E. M. Wood (2016).

7. Bhandar (2018).

8. C. Anderson et al. (2017).

9. https://www.gatesfoundation.org/Who-We-Are/General-Information/Financials (accessed July 15, 2020).

10. Navdanya International (2020).

11. The seeds of the Green Revolution in Africa were planted in 1997, when Gordon Conway, the newly elected president of the Rockefeller Foundation published his book *The Doubly Green Revolution: Food for All in the 21st Century*. The Rockefeller Foundation had been at the helm of the Green Revolution in Latin America and Asia in the 1950s. At that time, they promoted a program of increasing food production through a package of hybrid seeds and chemical inputs. This program was also funded by the US government who saw the "green" revolution as a way of averting a "red" revolution. Conway celebrated the Green Revolution for contributing to the mitigation of hunger, but he also acknowledged some of the shortcomings of the Green Revolution, namely, that the chemical package that the Green Revolution introduced had contributed to some environmental problems and that it had missed a large swath of the population. He evaded other critiques of the Green Revolution about its contribution to economic inequality. Conway argued that a new Green Revolution was needed in places that the first wave had "missed," namely, in Africa. Africa, however, had not been missed by the Green Revolution. The Rockefeller Foundation and Northern governments had tried to implement the same program in Africa. They failed because the one-size-fits-all approach of the Green Revolution was not appropriate to the diverse tapestry of sub-Saharan farming. Africa was also a lesser strategic concern for the Green Revolution's anticommunist program. Nevertheless, Conway argued that a "new" Green Revolution was needed to address hunger in Africa, but this time with a greater focus on sustainability and small-scale farmers. In 1999 the Rockefeller Foundation decided to concentrate its agricultural development funding in Africa, developing the new Green Revolution in Africa. However, it was not until 2006 that the Green Revolution really made it onto the international agenda. It was then that the Bill & Melinda Gates Foundation decided to join the effort. Together, the Gates Foundation and the Rockefeller Foundation founded the Alliance for a Green Revolution in Africa (AGRA) with the Gates Foundation offering an initial $100 million and the Rockefeller Foundation $50 million. Although both foundations have remained involved, the Gates Foundation has eclipsed the Rockefeller Foundation. In the ten years since its first commitment, the Gates Foundation poured more than $5 billion into African agriculture. Of this, AGRA has received only a small portion.

12. Eddens (2017).

13. Shiva (1991).

14. Perkins (1997); Patel (2013, 38).

15. For example, Stone (2019).

16. McArthur and Rasmussen (2017).

17. Before Gates established Microsoft, a vibrant free and open-source software movement had advocated for the free sharing of code. In his now famous "Open Letter to Hobbyists," Gates called hobbyists thieves, rejecting the free and open-source software movement's view that sharing information could lead to innovation. See Kelty (2008), Coleman (2013), and Dizon (2017). Gates also pioneered the use of

"independent contractors" to miscategorize workers and exclude them from benefits. See Klein (2010, 249).

18. Egan (2020).

19. For example, INCITE! (2007).

20. Kiviat and Gates (2008).

21. Gates (2021, 199).

22. For example, Edwards (2009), Bishop and Green (2010), and McGoey (2015).

23. T. Schwab (2020). For analyses of philanthrocapitalism, see Edwards (2009), Ramdas (2011), and McGoey (2015).

24. Pingali (2012, 1).

25. Although the Gates Foundation has provided approximately two-thirds of the funding to AGRA, its funding for African agricultural development far exceeds their contributions to AGRA. See GRAIN (2014) and Wise (2020).

26. Navdanya International (2020).

27. IPES-Food (2020).

28. Schurman (2018, 181).

29. The Gates Foundation provides funding for agricultural biotechnology, but AGRA claims that it does not. Most of AGRA's budget goes to funding its staff rather than to grant making. Through its advocacy, AGRA has focused largely on securing an enabling environment for the adoption of commercial agricultural inputs, particularly non-GMO improved seeds and fertilizer.

30. Only seven countries currently have commercialized genetically modified crops: Ethiopia, Malawi, Nigeria, South Africa, Kenya, Sudan, and eSwatini (Akinbo et al. 2021, 7). As Rock and Schurman (2020) note, however, "only South Africa and Nigeria have embraced agricultural biotechnology in a significant way" (2).

31. This does not include funding directed to AGRA. See IPES-Food (2020).

32. Schurman (2017, 442). The African Agricultural Technology Foundation works to facilitate partnerships for the sharing of proprietary genetic modification technologies on the African continent, engages in policy advocacy to promote biotechnology, and encourages public demand for biotechnology.

33. Schnurr (2019, 13).

34. Heim and O'Hagan (2010).

35. Zaitchik et al. (2021).

36. Although CAGJ has kept the name AGRA Watch for its program, AGRA Watch is really focused on all of the Gates Foundation's funding for African agricultural development.

37. Kloppenburg (2004).

38. Critiques of GMOs are discussed by Shiva (1993), Nestle (2010), and Schurman and Munro (2010).

39. It is estimated that 75% of processed food in the United States contains genetically modified ingredients. See Center for Food Safety, "About Genetically Modified Foods," https://www.centerforfoodsafety.org/issues/311/ge-foods/about-ge-foods (accessed October 31, 2020).

40. Fitzgerald (2010).

41. For an analysis of the "pro-poor" discourse developed to promote agricultural biotechnology, see Glover (2010).

42. Proponents of agricultural biotechnology tend to portray genetic engineering as an extension of the long history of plant modification, a natural process that builds on conventional forms of plant breeding, the mechanisms of which humans have only recently been able to understand and precisely develop. For example, a pamphlet titled *10 Myths About GMOs* distributed by the Bill & Melinda Gates Foundation–funded Cornell Alliance for Science seeks to counter the "myth" that "GMOs are unnatural" by explaining that "humans have been selectively breeding plants and animals for countless millennia, so all domesticated plant species—and even your pet dogs and cats—are technically genetically modified. Genetic engineering replicates a process that has been occurring in nature for millions of years as bacteria and viruses regularly shuttle genes between different species" (https://allianceforscience.cornell.edu/wp-content/uploads/2018/03/mythsFINAL.pdf [accessed May 20, 2021]). Critics of biotechnology suggest that this portrayal of genetic engineering is disingenuous on a number of accounts. Agricultural biotechnology often takes genes from other plants, bacteria, and animals and inserts them into a foreign species to achieve particular features and traits. For example, one of the most popular varieties of genetically modified corn, Bt Corn, has a gene inserted in it from the toxin *Bacillus thuringiensis* to provide insecticidal properties. Still, scientists argue that because they are inserting segments of DNA (which is made of the same subunits in all organisms), this should not make any difference. For an explanation of this, see Marion Nestle's easy-to-understand description in Nestle (2010, 299–304).

43. La Via Campesina (2013, [iii]).

44. Peschard and Randeria (2020).

45. Although plants had been excluded from intellectual property rights since their development in the fifteenth century, the US Supreme Court decided that technology enabled humans to create novel creations from genetic resources. In 1980 the Supreme Court ruled in *Diamond v. Chakrabarty* (1980) that a bacterium that had been genetically engineered by Ananda Chakrabarty to eat crude oil could be patented under law. Before *Chakrabarty* the Supreme Court maintained a doctrine that intellectual property rights could not be extended to "products of nature." However, the US Congress had allowed patents on plants through the Plant Patent Act of 1930, which enabled plant breeders to claim patents on plants produced asexually, and then extended these protections to plants produced sexually in the Plant Variety Protection Act (1970). As a result, the US Patent Office soon approved the patents on 114 pending applications involving the use of biotechnology.

46. Soon after the Supreme Court's recognition that intellectual property rights could be claimed over biotechnology, the US Congress passed the Bayh-Dole Act (1980), which allowed US universities to own intellectual property rights and patents, even when products were funded by the federal government. The law incentivized greater collaboration between universities and for-profit firms. Combined, these laws provided the legal architecture that incentivized the development of genetically modified crops.

47. For example, Raustiala and Victor (2004) and Pechlaner (2012).

48. The Union for the Protection of New Varieties of Plants was adopted in 1961 and revised in 1972, 1978, and 1991.

49. The TRIPS Agreement specifically requires that parties to the agreement create a system for patenting microorganisms, although it allows for some flexibility in the system that states develop to do so. It also allows states to exclude some "essentially" biological processes. See Article 27.3(b) of the TRIPS Agreement.

50. Article 2(2) of the Cartagena Protocol on Biosafety to the Convention on Biological Diversity.

51. Nestle (2010, 142).

52. Peekhaus (2010); Glenna et al. (2015).

53. Newell (2009, 38).

54. Pollack and Shaffer (2009).

55. Jasanoff (2014, 288).

56. As Rock and Schurman (2020) make clear, the regulation of biotechnology in Africa must be understood contextually. Any given struggle is shaped by a contingent set of actors, products of biotechnology, and national and international regulatory agencies.

57. Gödecke et al. (2018).

58. Paul et al. (2018, 21).

59. Rubongoya (2007); Weigratz (2010).

60. These crops include "Water Efficient Maize for Africa," cotton, rice, cassava, sweet potato, cowpeas, and three different types of banana. The bananas—the staple *matooke* (East African Highland Banana), sweet bananas, and roasting bananas—are primarily being developed to resist pathogens and pests, such as bacterial wilt disease, Black Sigatoka, Panama disease, and nematodes. See Schnurr and Gore (2015).

61. Wambugu and Kamanga (2014, 161).

62. Breasley and Tickell (2014).

63. See Mgbeoji (2004).

64. Paul et al. (2018).

65. Schnurr and Gore (2015, 65).

66. Schnurr (2013).

67. For example, Schubert (2008).

68. See the Cornell Alliance for Science website: https://allianceforscience.cornell.edu/about/mission/ (accessed April 23, 2018).

69. Jasanoff (2006, 288).

70. Paul et al. (2018).

71. Schnurr and Gore (2015).

72. "Open Letter from AFSA Opposing Human Feeding Trials with GM Bananas," December 9, 2014, https://foodfirst.org/open-letter-from-the-alliance-for-food-sovereignty-in-africa-opposing-human-feeding-trials-with-gm-bananas (accessed August 20, 2021).

73. Tripp (2004); Rubongoya (2007).

74. Karamura et al. (2012).

75. "Nakitembe Banana" (n.d.).

76. Musoke (2018).

77. Agba (2018).

78. Anker (2009, 116).

79. Wise (2020).

80. Holt-Giménez and Altieri (2013, 95).

CHAPTER 5

1. Although the meaning and definition of land grabs are still being debated, in general land grabs refer to the foreign acquisition of large tracts of land for crop production, resource extraction, or speculation. See Hall (2013).

2. "Why We Oppose the Principles for Responsible Agricultural Investment (RAI)," October 12, 2010, https://viacampesina.org/en/why-we-oppose-the-principles-for-responsible-agricultural-investment-rai/ (accessed May 4, 2021).

3. This is how the CFS describes itself on its website: http://www.fao.org/cfs/en (accessed August 22, 2021).

4. Saward (2010).

5. Candel (2014); Barling and Duncan (2015); McKeon (2015); Canfield (2021).

6. Friedmann and McMichael (1989); McMichael (2013).

7. Shaw (2007).

8. Fakhri (forthcoming).

9. Canfield (2020).

10. FAO (1975).

11. Some nations favored the creation of a "World Food Authority," an institution that would be equipped with significantly more authority to monitor grain surpluses and supplies. However, the United States ultimately prevailed in proposing a pared-back World Food Council. See Shaw (2007).

12. Slobodian (2020).

13. Jarosz (2009; 2011).

14. Immediately after the voluntary guidelines were completed, the NGO Caucus of the Intergovernmental Working Group on the voluntary guidelines published "No Masterpiece of Political Will," noting that, although the working group did take several steps forward, it ultimately did not display the political will to substantively end hunger, by refusing to address issues such as international trade and the right to food during conflict and the overall weak language and voluntary nature of the guidelines. Scholars' assessments of these guidelines differ. McKeon (2009) claims that the voluntary guidelines were beneficial, particularly in strengthening the legal mechanism of the right to food. Although they are voluntary, she suggests that "they provide both valuable support to governments that are interested in implementing the right to food and a powerful lobbying instrument for civil society actors in countries where the government is less proactive" (76). Similarly, Oshaug (2005) notes that the existence of the voluntary guidelines valorizes the concept of human rights to food. He argues that they transformed the right to food from a moral imperative into a policy goal. He explains that the guidelines were meant to "serve to guide

administrative and legislative agendas and systematically identify legal and policy measures and programs to achieve the realization of the right to adequate food" (253).

15. Gitz and Meybeck (2011).

16. https://www.wikileaks.org/plusd/cables/09UNROME49_a.html (accessed May 22, 2020).

17. Initially the CSM was called the Civil Society Mechanism; however, in 2018 it changed its name to the Civil Society and Indigenous Peoples' Mechanism for Relations with the Committee on World Food Security. Nevertheless, it is still commonly referred to as the CSM.

18. FAO (2009a).

19. Getachew (2020).

20. For example, see Commission on Global Governance (1995).

21. Freeman (1984).

22. Bäckstrand (2006, 470).

23. World Economic Forum (2010, 7); McKeon (2017, 387).

24. K. Schwab (2021, 57).

25. W. Brown (2015, 128).

26. For example, Ranciere (2004), Lievens (2015), and Wilson and Swyngedouw (2015).

27. HLPE (2018, 16).

28. MSI Integrity (2020, 4).

29. For example, Cheyns (2011), Cheyns and Riisgaard (2014), McKeon (2017), Bartley (2018), and Gleckman (2018).

30. J. Smith (2007).

31. For example, Held (1995), Sklair (2001), and Scholte (2014).

32. Catlaw (2009, 482).

33. Sørensen (2002, 701).

34. Sørensen is not alone in arguing that networked governance can provide a framework to deepen democracy. Scholte (2014) proposes the concept of "postmodern global democracies"—a pluralistic framework of global democracy—which he develops around the principles of transscalar geographies, plural solidarities, transculturality, egalitarian distribution, and ecocentric rights and responsibilities. Scholte's framework is but one approach through which democratic theorists have sought to transcend the confines of statist approaches to democracy, without reifying liberal, Western visions of global cosmopolitanism that are inattentive to pluralism and power asymmetries.

35. Sørensen (2002, 698).

36. Pitkin (1967) describes this form of representation as "acting for" others.

37. Saward (2005; 2010).

38. Claeys (2015).

39. Shue (1980).

40. Lambek and Claeys (2015).

41. De Schutter (2014, 231).

42. De Schutter (2014, 231).

43. FAO (2014, 8).

44. De Schutter (2014, 233–34).

45. The same is also true for the right to water, which, as Morgan (2011) notes, "has acquired an open political texture that belies any simply dichotomy" (10).

46. Sociolegal scholars of legal mobilization have long emphasized the symbolic function of rights claiming in the national context. See McCann (1994) and Scheingold (2004).

47. Gaarde (2017) has written an excellent book examining the role of La Vía Campesina in developing this space.

48. Committee on World Food Security, "Proposal for an International Food Security and Nutrition Civil Society Mechanism for Relations with the CFS," October 2010, http://www.csm4cfs.org/wp-content/uploads/2016/03/Proposal-for-an-international-civil-society-mechanism.pdf.

49. Committee on World Food Security, "Proposal for an International Food Security and Nutrition Civil Society Mechanism for Relations with the CFS," October 2010. http://www.csm4cfs.org/wp-content/uploads/2016/03/Proposal-for-an-international-civil-society-mechanism.pdf.

50. McKeon (2015, 109).

51. See Maeckelbergh (2009) for an analysis of representation in the context of the alter-globalization movement.

52. McKeon (2015, 109).

53. Claeys and Duncan (2019a, 3).

54. Claeys and Duncan (2019a, 3).

55. Committee on World Food Security, "Proposal for an International Food Security and Nutrition Civil Society Mechanism for Relations with the CFS," October 2010, http://www.csm4cfs.org/wp-content/uploads/2016/03/Proposal-for-an-international-civil-society-mechanism.pdf.

56. "Draft Guidelines for Facilitating Common Policy Positions and Messages Through the Civil Society Mechanism," http://www.csm4cfs.org/wp-content/uploads/2016/03/draft_guidelines_on_common_policy_positions_en.pdf (accessed May 25, 2021).

57. CSM Facilitation Working Group, "Common Understanding of Facilitation in Principle and Practice," January 2020, http://www.csm4cfs.org/wp-content/uploads/2018/02/Common-understanding-of-Facilitation_English_21.1.20.pdf (accessed May 22, 2020).

58. Brem-Wilson (2015).

59. "Draft Guidelines for Facilitating Common Policy Positions and Messages Through the Civil Society Mechanism," http://www.csm4cfs.org/wp-content/uploads/2016/03/draft_guidelines_on_common_policy_positions_en.pdf (accessed May 25, 2021).

60. Claeys and Duncan (2019b).

61. See the 2018 evaluation of the CSM developed by Priscilla Claeys and Jessica Duncan at http://www.csm4cfs.org/wp-content/uploads/2018/02/CSM-Evaluation-Report-2018-ilovepdf-compressed.pdf (accessed May 5, 2021).

62. Claeys and Duncan (2019a, 9).

63. Zoomers (2010); Cotula (2013).

64. Michelle Dobrovolny, "Open Data Reveal Extent of Land Grabbing," June 13, 2021, http://www.scidev.net/global/data/news/open-data-land-grabbing.html (accessed October 31, 2020).

65. Narula (2013); Canfield (2018b).

66. McMichael (2014, 35).

67. CFS work products vary in the time they take. In general, the more controversial issues take a longer time to negotiate. However, the length of negotiations also depends on the status of the documents being negotiated. Documents that are described as "principles" or "guidelines" generally take longer to develop than do "policy recommendations."

68. Intervention by the Civil Society Mechanism, on file with the author.

69. Intervention by the Civil Society Mechanism, on file with the author.

70. "Connecting Smallholders to Markets: An Analytical Guide," http://www.fao.org/fileadmin/templates/cfs/Docs1516/cfs43/CSM_Connecting_Smallholder_to_Markets_EN.pdf (accessed May 5, 2021).

71. On the legitimacy of the CFS, see Brem-Wilson (2019).

72. "It's Time to Recommit: CSM Statement Towards CFS 45," October 2018, https://www.csm4cfs.org/wp-content/uploads/2018/10/EN-CSM-statement-towards-CFS-45-October-2018.pdf (accessed August 22, 2021).

73. Tom (2020).

74. Canfield, Anderson, and McMichael (2021).

75. https://foodsovereignty.org/wp-content/uploads/2020/02/EN_Edited_draft-letter-UN-food-systems-summit_070220-4.pdf (accessed August 22, 2021).

76. Sabel and Simon (2004, 1020). See also Unger (2004).

77. Morgan (2011, 173).

CONCLUSIONS

1. FAO et al. (2021, xii).

2. Sen (1983, 1); emphasis added.

3. Sen (1983, 166).

4. This is how Foucault describes the primary ideology of neoliberalism. See Foucault (2010, 117).

5. See, for example, Morgan (2011) and McCallum (2013).

6. See Kautsky (1988), Bernstein (1996), and Akram-Lodhi and Kay (2010a; 2010b).

7. Moore (1993).

8. Wolf (1969).

9. Fakhri (2020, 9).

10. Sassen (2008, 415).

11. As agrarian scholar Philip McMichael (2008) explains, in "reformulating questions of rights, social reproduction and sustainability, the peasant movement poses an 'agrarian question of food,' where food embodies social, cultural and ecological values over and above its material value" (218).

12. Edelman (2008, 377).

13. Thompson (1993, 337).

14. IPES-Food (2017b, 48).

15. FAO (2017).

16. Of course, the cultural meanings of food are not simply endogenous. As Mintz (1986) famously illustrated in his study of the global sugar trade, the cultural meanings of food are responsive to wider relations of power. Yet these do not diminish the importance of these meanings in shaping everyday social relations.

17. "The Culture of Agriculture," http://tilthproducers.org/about-us/history/the-culture-of-agriculture/ (accessed September 29, 2020).

18. See, for example, Scoones et al. (2018) and Montenegro de Wit et al. (2021).

19. Parker and Johnson (2019, 219).

20. For example, Moyn (2018).

21. Morgan (2011, 29).

22. Baiocchi (2018, 85).

23. See, for example, Shamir (2008), Wilson and Swyngedouw (2015), W. Brown (2015), and Kennedy (2016).

24. Davies (2012, 2687).

25. Henry (1985, 324).

26. Wendy Brown (2020) argues that "instead of insulated from and thus capable of steering the economy, the state has been openly politicized as an instrument serving big capital and at the same time broken off from democratic representativeness, accountability, and the common good" (50). See also Peck and Theodore (2019).

27. Fraser (2017).

28. Slaughter (2005, 8).

29. See Ruggie (1993).

30. Djelic and Sahlin-Andersson (2006) explain that "'patchwork' political structures mean interdependence and entanglement. Actors converge across fluid boundaries in the ways they structure themselves, connect with others and pursue their interests" (4). More recently, Thérien and Pouliot (2020, 2) have built on this concept to suggest that this recognition of transnational governance is assembled as "a contingent combination of governance practices and competing values" (2).

31. Perfecto et al. (2009).

32. Tsing et al. (2019, S193).

33. Morgan and Kuch (2020).

34. Capra and Mattei (2015, 14).

References

Agba, John. 2018. "Ugandan Scientists Skeptical of Revised GMO Bill." *Alliance for Science*, November 29. https://allianceforscience.cornell.edu/blog/2018/11/ugandan-scientists-skeptical-revised-gmo-bill/.

Akinbo, Olalekan, Silas Obukosia, Jeremy Ouedraogo, Woldeyesus Sinebo, Moussa Savadogo, Samuel Timpo, Ruth Mbabazi, Karim Maredia, Diran Makinde, and Aggrey Ambali. 2021. "Commercial Release of Genetically Modified Crops in Africa: Interface Between Biosafety Regulatory Systems and Varietal Release Systems." *Frontiers in Plant Science* 12 (March): art. 314. https://doi.org/10.3389/fpls.2021.605937.

Akram-Lodhi, A. Haroon, and Cristóbal Kay. 2010a. "Surveying the Agrarian Question (Part 1): Unearthing Foundations, Exploring Diversity." *Journal of Peasant Studies* 37 (1): 177–202.

———. 2010b. "Surveying the Agrarian Question (Part 2): Current Debates and Beyond." *Journal of Peasant Studies* 37 (2): 255–84.

Alkon, Alison Hope, and Teresa Marie Mares. 2012. "Food Sovereignty in US Food Movements: Radical Visions and Neoliberal Constraints." *Agriculture and Human Values* 29 (3): 347–59.

Alkon, Alison Hope, and Christie Grace McCullen. 2011. "Whiteness and Farmers Markets: Performances, Perpetuations . . . Contestations?" *Antipode* 43 (4): 937–59.

Allen, Lori. 2013. *The Rise and Fall of Human Rights: Cynicism and Politics in Occupied Palestine*. Stanford, CA: Stanford University Press.

Allen, Patricia. 2007. *Together at the Table: Sustainability and Sustenance in the American Agrifood System*. University Park, PA: Penn State University Press.

Allen, Patricia, and Julie Guthman. 2006. "From 'Old School' to 'Farm-to-School': Neoliberalization from the Ground Up." *Agriculture and Human Values* 23 (4): 401–15.

Allen, Patricia, and Martin Kovach. 2000. "The Capitalist Composition of Organic: The Potential of Markets in Fulfilling the Promise of Organic Agriculture." *Agriculture and Human Values* 17 (3): 221–32.

Allison, Anne. 2014. *Precarious Japan*. Durham, NC: Duke University Press.

Alvarez, Sonia E., Claudia de Lima Costa, Verónica Feliu, Rebecca J. Hester, Norma Klahn, Millie Thayer, and Cruz Caridad Bueno. 2014. *Translocalities/Translocalidades: Feminist Politics of Translation in the Latin/a Américas*. Durham, NC: Duke University Press.

Anderson, Colin, Christabel Buchanan, Tom Wakeford, Marina Chang, and Javier Sanchez Rodriguez. 2017. *Everyday Experts: How People's Knowledge Can Transform the Food System*. Coventry, UK: Coventry University.

Anderson, Molly D., and John T. Cook. 1999. "Community Food Security: Practice in Need of Theory?" *Agriculture and Human Values* 16 (2): 141–50.

Andrias, Kate. 2016. "The New Labor Law." *Yale Law Journal* 126 (1): 2–101.

Anker, Peder. 2009. *Imperial Ecology: Environmental Order in the British Empire, 1895–1945*. Cambridge, MA: Harvard University Press.

Ansell, Chris, and Alison Gash. 2008. "Collaborative Governance in Theory and Practice." *Journal of Public Administration Research and Theory* 18 (4): 543–71.

Appleby, Joyce. 1982. "Commercial Farming and the 'Agrarian Myth' in the Early Republic." *Journal of American History* 68 (4): 833–49.

Araghi, Farshad. 2009. "Accumulation by Displacement: Global Enclosures, Food Crisis, and the Ecological Contradictions of Capitalism." *Review (Fernand Braudel Center)* 32 (1): 113–46.

Arcuri, Alessandra. 2015. "The Transformation of Organic Regulation: The Ambiguous Effects of Publicization." *Regulation and Governance* 9 (2): 144–59.

Arneil, Barbara. 1994. "Trade, Plantations, and Property: John Locke and the Economic Defense of Colonialism." *Journal of the History of Ideas* 55 (4): 591–609.

Bäckstrand, Karin. 2006. "Democratizing Global Environmental Governance? Stakeholder Democracy After the World Summit on Sustainable Development." *European Journal of International Relations* 12 (4): 467–98.

Baiocchi, Gianpaolo. 2018. *We, the Sovereign*. Medford, MA: Polity Press.

Baiocchi, Gianpaolo, and Ernesto Ganuza. 2016. *Popular Democracy: The Paradox of Participation*. Stanford, CA: Stanford University Press.

Bair, Jennifer. 2008. "Analysing Global Economic Organization: Embedded Networks and Global Chains Compared." *Economy and Society* 37 (3): 339–64.

Bardacke, Frank. 2011. *Trampling Out the Vintage: Cesar Chavez and the Two Souls of the United Farm Workers*. New York: Verso.

Barkan, Joshua. 2011. "Law and the Geographic Analysis of Economic Globalization." *Progress in Human Geography* 35 (5): 589–607.

Barker, Joanne. 2005. *Sovereignty Matters: Locations of Contestation and Possibility in Indigenous Struggles for Self-Determination*. Lincoln: University of Nebraska Press.

Barling, David, and Jessica Duncan. 2015. "The Dynamics of the Contemporary Governance of the World's Food Supply and the Challenges of Policy Redirection." *Food Security* 7 (2): 415–24.

Barnett, Barry J. 2000. "The U.S. Farm Financial Crisis of the 1980s." *Agricultural History* 74 (2): 366–80.

Bartley, Tim. 2003. "Certifying Forests and Factories: States, Social Movements, and the Rise of Private Regulation in the Apparel and Forest Products Fields." *Politics and Society* 31 (3): 433–64.

———. 2007. "Institutional Emergence in an Era of Globalization: The Rise of Transnational Private Regulation of Labor and Environmental Conditions." *American Journal of Sociology* 113 (2): 297–351.

———. 2018. *Rules Without Rights: Land, Labor, and Private Authority in the Global Economy*. Oxford, UK: Oxford University Press.

Belasco, Warren J. 2014. *Appetite for Change: How the Counterculture Took on the Food Industry*. Ithaca, NY: Cornell University Press.

Benford, Robert D., and David A. Snow. 2000. "Framing Processes and Social Movements: An Overview and Assessment." *Annual Review of Sociology* 26 (1): 611–39.

Bernstein, Henry. 1996. "Agrarian Questions Then and Now." *Journal of Peasant Studies* 24 (1–2): 22–59.

Berry, Wendell. 2009. *Bringing It to the Table: On Farming and Food*. Berkeley, CA: Counterpoint Press.

Bhandar, Brenna. 2018. *Colonial Lives of Property: Law, Land, and Racial Regimes of Ownership*. Durham, NC: Duke University Press.

Bingham, Lisa Blomgren, Tina Nabatchi, and Rosemary O'Leary. 2005. "The New Governance: Practices and Processes for Stakeholder and Citizen Participation in the Work of Government." *Public Administration Review* 65 (5): 547–58.

Bishop, Matthew, and Michael Green. 2010. *Philanthrocapitalism: How Giving Can Save the World*. New York: Bloomsbury.

Blackwell, Maylei. 2014. "Translenguas: Mapping the Possibilities and Challenges of Transnational Women's Organizing Across Geographies of Difference." In *Translocalities/Translocalidades: Feminist Politics of Translation in the Latin/a Américas*, ed. Sonia E. Alvarez, Claudia de Lima Costa, Verónica Feliu, Rebecca Hester, Norma Klahn, and Millie Thayer, 299–320. Durham, NC: Duke University Press.

Block, Sharon. 2020. "Go Big or Go Home: The Case for Clean Slate Labor Law Reform." *Berkeley Journal of Employment and Labor Law* 41 (1): 167–86.

Boggs, Carl. 1977. "Revolutionary Process, Political Strategy, and the Dilemma of Power." *Theory and Society* 4 (3): 359–93.

Boltanski, Luc, and Eve Chiapello. 2007. *The New Spirit of Capitalism*, trans. Gregory Elliott. London: Verso.

Born, Branden, and Mark Purcell. 2006. "Avoiding the Local Trap Scale and Food Systems in Planning Research." *Journal of Planning Education and Research* 26 (2): 195–207.

Borras, Saturnino M., Jr., Jennifer C. Franco, and Sofía Monsalve Suárez. 2015. "Land and Food Sovereignty." *Third World Quarterly* 36 (3): 600–617.

Braithwaite, John. 2008. *Regulatory Capitalism: How It Works, Ideas for Making It Work Better.* Northampton, MA: Edward Elgar.

Braithwaite, John, and Peter Drahos. 2000. *Global Business Regulation.* Cambridge, UK: Cambridge University Press.

Brand, Stewart. 1968. *Whole Earth Catalogue: Access to Tools.* Menlo Park, CA: Portola Institute.

Breasley, Adam, and Adam Tickell. 2014. "Why Is Bill Gates Backing GMO Red Banana 'Biopiracy'?" *The Ecologist*, November 24. http://www.theecologist.org/News/news_analysis/2648196/why_is_bill_gates_backing_gmo_red_banana_biopiracy.html.

Brem-Wilson, Josh. 2015. "Towards Food Sovereignty: Interrogating Peasant Voice in the United Nations Committee on World Food Security." *Journal of Peasant Studies* 42 (1): 73–95.

———. 2019. "Legitimating Global Governance: Publicisation, Affectedness, and the Committee on World Food Security." *Third World Thematics: A TWQ Journal* 3 (5–6): 605–25. doi: 10.1080/23802014.2018.1552536.

Brenner, Neil. 1999. "Globalisation as Reterritorialisation: The Re-Scaling of Urban Governance in the European Union." *Urban Studies* 36 (3): 431–51.

———. 2019. *New Urban Spaces: Urban Theory and the Scale Question.* Oxford, UK: Oxford University Press.

Brent, Zoe W., Christina M. Schiavoni, and Alberto Alonso-Fradejas. 2015. "Contextualising Food Sovereignty: The Politics of Convergence Among Movements in the USA." *Third World Quarterly* 36 (3): 618–35.

Brigham, John. 1987. "Right, Rage, and Remedy: Forms of Law in Political Discourse." *Studies in American Political Development* 2: 303–16.

Brown, Dona. 2011. *Back to the Land: The Enduring Dream of Self-Sufficiency in Modern America.* Madison: University of Wisconsin Press.

Brown, Sandy, and Christy Getz. 2008. "Privatizing Farm Worker Justice: Regulating Labor Through Voluntary Certification and Labeling." *Geoforum* 39 (3): 1184–96.

Brown, Wendy. 2015. *Undoing the Demos: Neoliberalism's Stealth Revolution.* Cambridge, MA: MIT Press.

———. 2020. "Neoliberalism's Scorpion Tail." In *Mutant Neoliberalism*, ed. William Callison and Zachary Manfredi, 39–60. New York: Fordham University Press.

Brown, Wendy, and Janet E. Halley. 2002. *Left Legalism/Left Critique.* Durham, NC: Duke University Press.

Bruni, Frank. 2011. "Eating In and Around Seattle." *New York Times*, June 10. http://www.nytimes.com/2011/06/12/travel/eating-in-and-around-seattle.html.

Burchell, Graham, Colin Gordon, and Peter Miller, eds. 1991. *The Foucault Effect: Studies in Governmentality*. Chicago: University of Chicago Press.

Burnett, Kim, and Sophia Murphy. 2014. "What Place for International Trade in Food Sovereignty?" *Journal of Peasant Studies* 41 (6): 1065–84.

Busa, Julianne H., and Rebekah Garder. 2015. "Champions of the Movement or Fair-Weather Heroes? Individualization and the (A)Politics of Local Food." *Antipode* 47 (2): 323–41.

Calavita, Kitty. 2010. *Inside the State: The Bracero Program, Immigration, and the I.N.S.* New Orleans, LA: Quid Pro Books.

Callon, Michel. 1984. "Some Elements of a Sociology of Translation: Domestication of the Scallops and the Fishermen of St. Brieuc Bay." *Sociological Review* 32 (May): 196–233.

———, ed. 1998. *Laws of the Markets*. Malden, MA: Wiley-Blackwell.

Candel, Jeroen J. L. 2014. "Food Security Governance: A Systematic Literature Review." *Food Security* 6 (4): 585–601.

Canfield, Matthew C. 2018a. "Compromised Collaborations: Food, Fuel, and Power in Transnational Food Security Governance." *Transnational Legal Theory* 9 (3–4): 272–87.

———. 2018b. "Disputing the Global Land Grab: Claiming Rights and Making Markets Through Collaborative Governance." *Law and Society Review* 52 (4): 994–1025.

———. 2019. "Banana Brokers: Communicative Labor, Translocal Translation, and Transnational Law." *Public Culture* 31 (1): 69–92.

———. 2020. "From Colonialism to Collaboration: Disputing Biofuels in the Age of the Anthropocene." Working Paper no. 201. Halle, Germany: Max Planck Institute for Social Anthropology. https://pure.mpg.de/rest/items/item_3243842/component/file_3244455/content.

———. 2021. "Transnational Food Law." In *Oxford Handbook on Transnational Law*, ed. Peer Zumbansen, 269–90. Oxford, UK: Oxford University Press.

Canfield, Matthew C., Molly D. Anderson, and Philip McMichael. 2021. "UN Food Systems Summit 2021: Dismantling Democracy and Resetting Corporate Control of Food Systems." *Frontiers in Sustainable Food Systems* 5. https://www.frontiersin.org/article/10.3389/fsufs.2021.661552.

Canfield, Matthew, Amy J. Cohen, and Michael Fakhri. 2021. "Agriculture, Law, and the State." In *Routledge Handbook of Law and Society*, 69–73. New York: Routledge.

Capra, Fritjof, and Ugo Mattei. 2015. *The Ecology of Law: Toward a Legal System in Tune with Nature and Community*. Oakland, CA: Berrett-Koehler.

Castells, Manuel. 1996. *Rise of the Network Society*. Malden, MA: Wiley-Blackwell.

———. 1999. "Grassrooting the Space of Flows." *Urban Geography* 20 (4): 294–302.

———. 2013. *Communication Power*. New York: Oxford University Press.

Catlaw, Thomas J. 2009. "Governance and Networks at the Limits of Representation." *American Review of Public Administration* 39 (5): 478–98.

Chadwick, Anna. 2019. *Law and the Political Economy of Hunger*. Oxford, UK: Oxford University Press.

Cheyns, Emmanuelle. 2011. "Multi-Stakeholder Initiatives for Sustainable Agriculture: Limits of the 'Inclusiveness' Paradigm." In *Governing Through Standards: Origins, Drivers, and Limitations*, ed. Stefano Ponte, Jakob Vestergaard, and Peter Gibbon, 210–35. London: Palgrave McMillan.

Cheyns, Emmanuelle, and Lone Riisgaard. 2014. "Introduction to the Symposium: The Exercise of Power Through Multi-Stakeholder Initiatives for Sustainable Agriculture and Its Inclusion and Exclusion Outcomes." *Agriculture and Human Values* 31 (3): 409–23.

Chua, Lynette J. 2018. *The Politics of Love in Myanmar: LGBT Mobilization and Human Rights as a Way of Life*. Stanford, CA. Stanford University Press.

Claeys, Priscilla. 2015. *Human Rights and the Food Sovereignty Movement: Reclaiming Control*. New York: Routledge.

Claeys, Priscilla, and Jessica Duncan. 2019a. "Do We Need to Categorize It? Reflections on Constituencies and Quotas as Tools for Negotiating Difference in the Global Food Sovereignty Convergence Space." *Journal of Peasant Studies* 46 (7): 1477–98.

———. 2019b. "Food Sovereignty and Convergence Spaces." *Political Geography* 75 (November): 102045.

Clapp, Jennifer. 2014. "Food Security and Food Sovereignty: Getting Past the Binary." *Dialogues in Human Geography* 4 (2): 206–11.

———. 2015. "Food Security and Contested Agricultural Trade Norms." *Journal of International Law and International Relations* 11 (2): 104–15.

Cohen, Amy J. 2013. "Supermarkets in India: Struggles over the Organization of Agricultural Markets and Food Supply Chains." *University of Miami Law Review* 68 (1): 19–86.

———. 2015. "The Law and Political Economy of Contemporary Food: Some Reflections on the Local and the Small." *Law and Contemporary Problems* 78 (1): 101–45.

———. 2020. "Negotiating the Value Chain: A Study of Surplus and Distribution in Indian Markets for Food." *Law and Social Inquiry* 45 (2): 460–92.

Cohen, Joshua, and Charles F. Sabel. 2004. "Global Democracy." *New York University Journal of International Law and Politics* 37 (4): 763–97.

Coleman, E. Gabriella. 2013. *Coding Freedom: The Ethics and Aesthetics of Hacking*. Princeton, NJ: Princeton University Press.

Coleman-Jensen, Alisha, Matthew P. Rabbitt, Christian A. Gregory, and Anita Singh. 2018. *Household Food Security in the United States in 2017*. Economic Research Report no. ERR-270. Washington, DC: US Department of Agriculture, Economic Research Service.

Commission on Global Governance. 1995. *Our Global Neighbourhood: The Report*. Oxford, UK: Oxford University Press.

Community Alliance for Global Justice. 1999. "Report on Day 2 of Community

Food Security Coalition Conference." https://cagj.org/2009/10/report-on-day-2-of-community-food-security-coalition-conference/ (accessed May 16, 2020).

———. 2012. *Our Food, Our Right: Recipes for Food Justice*, 2nd ed. Seattle: Community Alliance for Global Justice.

Coolsaet, Brendan. 2016. "Towards an Agroecology of Knowledges: Recognition, Cognitive Justice, and Farmers' Autonomy in France." *Journal of Rural Studies* 47 (October): 165–71.

Costa, Claudia de Lima. 2006. "Lost (and Found?) in Translation: Feminisms in Hemispheric Dialogue." *Latino Studies* 4 (1–2): 62–78.

Coté, Charlotte. 2016. "'Indigenizing' Food Sovereignty: Revitalizing Indigenous Food Practices and Ecological Knowledges in Canada and the United States." *Humanities* 5 (3): 57.

Cotula, Lorenzo. 2013. *The Great African Land Grab? Agricultural Investments and the Global Food System*. New York: Zed Books.

Dalgaard, Tommy, Nicholas J. Hutchings, and John R. Porter. 2003. "Agroecology, Scaling, and Interdisciplinarity." *Agriculture, Ecosystems, and Environment* 100 (1): 39–51.

Daniel, Cletus E. 1982. *Bitter Harvest: A History of California Farmworkers, 1870–1941*. Berkeley: University of California Press.

Darian-Smith, Eve, and Colin Scott. 2009. "Regulation and Human Rights in Socio-Legal Scholarship." *Law and Policy* 31 (3): 271–81.

Davies, Jonathan S. 2012. "Network Governance Theory: A Gramscian Critique." *Environment and Planning A: Economy and Space* 44 (11): 2687–2704.

Davis, Kevin E., Benedict Kingsbury, and Sally Engle Merry. 2012. "Indicators as a Technology of Global Governance." *Law and Society Review* 46 (1): 71–104.

Dawe, David, and Cristian Morales-Opazo. 2009. "How Much Did Developing Country Domestic Staple Food Prices Increase During the World Food Crisis? How Much Have They Declined?" ESA Working Paper no. 09-09. Rome: Agricultural Development Economics Division, Food and Agriculture Organization of the United Nations.

De Angelis, Massimo. 2006. *The Beginning of History: Value Struggles and Global Capital*. London: Pluto Press.

De Búrca, Gráinne, Robert O. Keohane, and Charles Sabel. 2014. "Global Experimentalist Governance." *British Journal of Political Science* 44 (3): 477–86.

De Búrca, Gráinne, and Joanne Scott. 2006. *Law and New Governance in the EU and the U.S.* Portland, OR: Hart.

De Schutter, Olivier. 2011. *The World Trade Organization and the Post-Global Food Crisis Agenda: Putting Food Security First in the International Trade System*. Geneva: World Trade Organization.

———. 2014. "The Reform of the Committee on World Food Security: The Quest for Coherence in Global Governance." In *Rethinking Food Systems: Structural Challenges, New Strategies, and the Law*, ed. Nadia C. S. Lambek, Priscilla Claeys, Adrienna Wong, and Lea Brilmayer, 219–38. Dordrecht, Netherlands: Springer.

Desmarais, Annette Aurelie. 2002. "Peasants Speak—The Vía Campesina: Consolidating an International Peasant and Farm Movement." *Journal of Peasant Studies* 29 (2): 91–124.

———. 2007. *La Via Campesina: Globalization and the Power of Peasants.* Ann Arbor, MI: Pluto Press.

De Sousa Santos, Boaventura. 2005a. "Beyond Neoliberal Governance: The World Social Forum as Subaltern Cosmopolitan Politics and Legality." In *Law and Globalization from Below: Towards a Cosmopolitan Legality,* ed. Boaventura de Sousa Santos and Rodriguez-Garavito, 29–63. Cambridge, UK: Cambridge University Press.

———. 2005b. "The Future of the World Social Forum: The Work of Translation." *Development* 48 (2): 15–22.

———. 2007. *Cognitive Justice in a Global World: Prudent Knowledges for a Decent Life.* Lanham, MD: Lexington Books.

———. 2018. *The End of the Cognitive Empire: The Coming of Age of Epistemologies of the South.* Durham, NC: Duke University Press.

De Sousa Santos, Boaventura, and César A. Rodríguez-Garavito. 2005. *Law and Globalization from Below: Towards a Cosmopolitan Legality.* Cambridge, UK: Cambridge University Press.

De Sousa Santos, Boaventura, and Bruno Sena Martins. 2021. *The Pluriverse of Human Rights: The Diversity of Struggles for Dignity.* New York: Routledge.

Dias-Abey, Manoj. 2018. "Justice on Our Fields: Can Alt-Labor Organizations Improve Migrant Farm Workers' Conditions." *Harvard Civil Rights–Civil Liberties Law Review* 53: 167–211.

Dizon, Michael Anthony C. 2017. *A Socio-Legal Study of Hacking: Breaking and Remaking Law and Technology.* New York: Routledge.

Djelic, Marie-Laure, and Kerstin Sahlin-Andersson. 2006. *Transnational Governance: Institutional Dynamics of Regulation.* Cambridge, UK: Cambridge University Press.

Dorf, Michael C., and Charles F. Sabel. 1998. "A Constitution of Democratic Experimentalism." *Columbia Law Review* 98 (2): 267–473.

Duncan, Jessica. 2015. *Global Food Security Governance: Civil Society Engagement in the Reformed Committee on World Food Security.* New York: Routledge.

DuPuis, E. Melanie, and David Goodman. 2005. "Should We Go 'Home' to Eat? Toward a Reflexive Politics of Localism." *Journal of Rural Studies* 21 (3): 359–71.

Eddens, Aaron. 2017. "White Science and Indigenous Maize: The Racial Logics of the Green Revolution." *Journal of Peasant Studies* 46 (3): 653–73.

Edelman, Marc. 2008. "Bringing the Moral Economy Back in . . . to the Study of 21st-Century Transnational Peasant Movements." *American Anthropologist* 107 (3): 331–45.

———. 2013. "What Is a Peasant? What Are Peasantries? A Briefing Paper on Issues of Definition." Paper prepared for the First Session of the Intergovernmental Working Group on a United Nations Declaration on the Rights of Peasants and

Other People Working in Rural Areas, Geneva, July 15–19. City University of New York, Graduate Center.

———. 2014. "Food Sovereignty: Forgotten Genealogies and Future Regulatory Challenges." *Journal of Peasant Studies* 41 (6): 959–78.

Edelman, Marc, and Saturnino M. Borras. 2016. *Political Dynamics of Transnational Agrarian Movements*. Black Point, Canada: Fernwood.

Edwards, Michael. 2009. "Gates, Google, and the Ending of Global Poverty: Philanthrocapitalism and International Development." *Brown Journal of World Affairs* 15 (2): 35–42.

Egan, Timothy. 2020. "Bill Gates Is the Most Interesting Man in the World." *New York Times*, May 22. https://www.nytimes.com/2020/05/22/opinion/bill-gates-coronavirus.html.

Egels-Zandén, Niklas, and Jeroen Merk. 2014. "Private Regulation and Trade Union Rights: Why Codes of Conduct Have Limited Impact on Trade Union Rights." *Journal of Business Ethics* 123 (3): 461–73.

Epp, Charles R. 1998. *The Rights Revolution: Lawyers, Activists, and Supreme Courts in Comparative Perspective*. Chicago: University of Chicago Press.

———. 2010. *Making Rights Real: Activists, Bureaucrats, and the Creation of the Legalistic State*. Chicago: University of Chicago Press.

Esbenshade, Jill. 2012. "A Review of Private Regulation: Codes and Monitoring in the Apparel Industry." *Sociology Compass* 6 (7): 541–56.

Espeland, Wendy, and Mitchell L. Stevens. 1998. "Commensuration as a Social Process." *Annual Review of Sociology* 24 (1): 313–43.

Estlund, Cynthia L. 2002. "The Ossification of American Labor Law." *Columbia Law Review* 102 (6): 1527–1612.

Ewick, Patricia, and Susan S. Silbey. 1998. *The Common Place of Law: Stories from Everyday Life*. Chicago: University of Chicago Press.

Fakhri, Michael. 2014. "The Institutionalisation of Free Trade and Empire: A Study of the 1902 Brussels Convention." *London Review of International Law* 2 (1): 49–76.

———. Forthcoming. "The International Political Economy of the Right to Food." In *Human Rights and Global Governance*, ed. Nehal Bhuta. Oxford, UK: Oxford University Press. https://www.academia.edu/40614188/The_International_Political_Economy_of_the_Right_to_Food.

———. 2020. *The Right to Food in the Context of International Trade Law and Policy*. Report A/75/219. New York: United Nations General Assembly. https://undocs.org/A/75/219.

FAO (UN Food and Agriculture Organization). 1975. *The State of Food and Agriculture 1974*. Rome: UN Food and Agriculture Organization. www.fao.org/3/f3350e/f3350e.pdf.

———. 2009a. *Reform of the Committee on World Food Security: Final Version*. Report CFS:2009/2 Rev.2. Rome: Committee on World Food Security, UN Food and Agriculture Organization. http://www.fao.org/tempref/docrep/fao/meeting/018/k7197e.pdf.

———. 2009b. *The State of Agricultural Commodity Markets 2009*. Rome: UN Food and Agriculture Organization. http://www.fao.org/3/i0854e/i0854e.pdf.

———. 2014. *The Right to Food and the Responsible Governance of Tenure: A Dialogue Towards Interpretation*. Rome: UN Food and Agriculture Organization.

———. 2017. *Migration, Agriculture, and Climate Change: Reducing Vulnerabilities and Enhancing Resistance*. Rome: UN Food and Agriculture Organization. http://www.fao.org/3/I8297EN/i8297en.pdf.

FAO, IFAD, UNICEF, WFP, and WHO. 2021. *The State of Food Security and Nutrition in the World 2020: Transforming Food Systems for Affordable Healthy Diets*. Rome: UN Food and Agriculture Organization.

Farmworker Justice. 2014. "Selected Statistics on Farmworkers." https://www.farmworkerjustice.org/sites/default/files/NAWS%20data%20factsht%201-13-15FINAL.pdf.

Felstiner, William L. F., Richard L. Abel, and Austin Sarat. 1980. "The Emergence and Transformation of Disputes: Naming, Blaming, Claiming . . ." *Law and Society Review* 15 (3–5): 631–54.

Figueroa, Meleiza. 2015. "Food Sovereignty in Everyday Life: Toward a People-Centered Approach to Food Systems." *Globalizations* 12 (4): 498–512.

Finnis, John. 1990. "Natural Law and Legal Reasoning." *Cleveland State Law Review* 38 (1): art. 4. https://engagedscholarship.csuohio.edu/clevstlrev/vol38/iss1/4.

Fisher, Andrew. 2017. *Big Hunger: The Unholy Alliance Between Corporate America and Anti-Hunger Groups*. Cambridge, MA: MIT Press.

Fisher, Andrew, and Susan Roberts. 2011. *Community Food Security Coalitions Recommendation for Food Systems Policy in Seattle*. http://foodsecurity.org/pub/Food_System_Policy_Recommendations-Seattle.pdf (accessed August 18, 2020).

Fisk, Catherine L. 2014. "Reimagining Collective Rights in the Workplace." *UC Irvine Law Review* 4 (2): 523–38.

Fitzgerald, Deborah. 2010. *Every Farm a Factory: The Industrial Ideal in American Agriculture*. New Haven, CT: Yale University Press.

Foucault, Michel. 2010. *The Birth of Biopolitics: Lectures at the Collège de France, 1978–1979*. New York: Palgrave Macmillan.

Fransen, Luc, and Genevieve LeBaron. 2019. "Big Audit Firms as Regulatory Intermediaries in Transnational Labor Governance." *Regulation and Governance* 13 (2): 260–79.

Fraser, Nancy. 2009. *Scales of Justice: Reimagining Political Space in a Globalizing World*. New York: Columbia University Press.

———. 2017. "From Progressive Neoliberalism to Trump—and Beyond." *American Affairs* 1 (4): 46–64. https://americanaffairsjournal.org/2017/11/progressive-neoliberalism-trump-beyond/.

———. 2019. *The Old Is Dying and the New Cannot Be Born*. New York: Verso Books.

Freeman, R. Edward. 1984. *Strategic Management: A Stakeholder Approach*. Boston: Pitman.

Friedmann, Harriet. 1982. "The Political Economy of Food: The Rise and Fall of the Postwar International Food Order." *American Journal of Sociology* 88 (January): S248–S286.

———. 1993. "The Political Economy of Food: A Global Crisis." *New Left Review* 1 (197): 29–57.

Friedmann, Harriet, and Philip McMichael. 1989. "Agriculture and the State System: The Rise and Decline of National Agricultures, 1870 to Present." *Sociologica Ruralis* 29 (2): 93–117.

Frisbie, Charlotte J. 2018. *Food Sovereignty the Navajo Way: Cooking with Tall Woman*. Albuquerque: University of New Mexico Press.

Gaarde, Ingeborg. 2017. *Peasants Negotiating a Global Policy Space: La Vía Campesina in the Committee on World Food Security*. New York: Routledge.

Gal, Susan. 2015. "Politics of Translation." *Annual Review of Anthropology* 44 (1): 225–40.

———. 2016. "Part Two Commentary: Processes of Translation and Demarcation in Legal Worlds." In *Translating the Social World for Law: Linguistic Tools for a New Legal Realism*, ed. Elizabeth Mertz, William K. Ford, and Gregory M. Matoesian, 216–34. New York: Oxford University Press.

Garcia, Matthew. 2014. *From the Jaws of Victory: The Triumph and Tragedy of Cesar Chavez and the Farm Worker Movement*. Berkeley: University of California Press.

Gates, Bill. 2021. *How to Avoid a Climate Disaster: The Solutions We Have and the Breakthroughs We Need*. New York: Knopf.

Gereffi, Gary, John Humphrey, and Timothy Sturgeon. 2005. "The Governance of Global Value Chains." *Review of International Political Economy* 12 (1): 78–104.

Getachew, Adom. 2020. *Worldmaking After Empire: The Rise and Fall of Self-Determination*. Princeton, NJ: Princeton University Press.

Gibbon, Peter, Jennifer Bair, and Stefano Ponte. 2008. "Governing Global Value Chains: An Introduction." *Economy and Society* 37 (3): 315–38.

Gibson-Graham, J. K. 2006. *The End of Capitalism (As We Knew It): A Feminist Critique of Political Economy*. Minneapolis: University of Minnesota Press.

Gitz, Vincent, and Alexandre Meybeck. 2011. "The Establishment of the High Level Panel of Experts on Food Security and Nutrition (HLPE): Shared, Independent, and Comprehensive Knowledge for International Policy Coherence in Food Security and Nutrition." CIRED Working Paper n2011-30.g. Nogent sur Marne, France: Centre International de Recherches sur l'Environnement et le Développement.

Gleckman, Harris. 2018. *Multistakeholder Governance and Democracy: A Global Challenge*. New York: Routledge.

Glenna, Leland, Sally Shortall, and Barbara Brandl. 2015. "Neoliberalism, the University, Public Goods, and Agricultural Innovation." *Sociologia Ruralis* 55 (4): 438–59.

Gliessman, Steve. 2013. "Agroecology: Growing the Roots of Resistance." *Agroecology and Sustainable Food Systems* 37 (1): 19–31.

Glover, Dominic. 2010. "The Corporate Shaping of GM Crops as a Technology for the Poor." *Journal of Peasant Studies* 37 (1): 67–90.

Gödecke, Theda, Alexander J. Stein, and Matin Qaim. 2018. "The Global Burden of Chronic and Hidden Hunger: Trends and Determinants." *Global Food Security* 17 (June): 21–29.

Goffman, Erving, and Bennett Berger. 1986. *Frame Analysis: An Essay on the Organization of Experience.* Boston: Northeastern University Press.

Gonzalez, Carmen G. 2004. "Trade Liberalization, Food Security, and the Environment: The Neoliberal Threat to Sustainable Rural Development." *Transnational Law and Contemporary Problems* 14: 419–98.

Goodale, Mark, and Sally Engle Merry. 2007. *The Practice of Human Rights: Tracking Law Between the Global and the Local.* New York: Cambridge University Press.

Goodwyn, Lawrence. 1978. *The Populist Moment: A Short History of the Agrarian Revolt in America.* Oxford, UK: Oxford University Press.

Goodyear, Dana. 2017. "How Driscoll's Reinvented the Strawberry." *The New Yorker,* August 14. http://www.newyorker.com/magazine/2017/08/21/how-driscolls-reinvented-the-strawberry.

Gordon, Jennifer. 2005. "Law, Lawyers, and Labor: The United Farm Workers' Legal Strategy in the 1960s and 1970s and the Role of Law in Union Organizing Today." *University of Pennsylvania Journal of Labor and Employment Law* 8: 1–72.

Goux, Jean-Joseph. 1990. *Symbolic Economies: After Marx and Freud.* Ithaca, NY: Cornell University Press.

Graeber, David. 2001. *Toward an Anthropological Theory of Value: The False Coin of Our Own Dreams.* New York: Palgrave Macmillan.

GRAIN. 2014. "How Does the Gates Foundation Spend Its Money to Feed the World?" GRAIN, November 4. https://www.grain.org/article/entries/5064-how-does-the-gates-foundation-spend-its-money-to-feed-the-world.

Gray, Margaret. 2013. *Labor and the Locavore: The Making of a Comprehensive Food Ethic.* Berkeley: University of California Press.

Grewal, David Singh. 2009. *Network Power: The Social Dynamics of Globalization.* New Haven, CT: Yale University Press.

Gudeman, Stephen. 2005. "Community and Economy: Economy's Base." In *A Handbook of Economic Anthropology,* ed. James Carrier, 94–106. Northampton, MA: Edward Elgar.

———. 2013. *Economy's Tension: The Dialectics of Community and Market.* New York: Berghahn.

Guthman, Julie. 2004. *Agrarian Dreams: The Paradox of Organic Farming in California.* Berkeley: University of California Press.

———. 2008. "Neoliberalism and the Making of Food Politics in California." *Geoforum* 39 (3): 1171–83.

Haas, Peter M. 1992. "Introduction: Epistemic Communities and International Policy Coordination." *International Organization* 46 (1): 1–35.

———. 2015. *Epistemic Communities, Constructivism, and International Environmental Politics.* New York: Routledge.

Hadden, Jennifer, and Sidney Tarrow. 2007. "Spillover or Spillout? The Global Justice Movement in the United States After 9/11." *Mobilization: An International Quarterly* 12 (4): 359–76.

Haedicke, Michael A. 2013. "From Collective Bargaining to Social Justice Certification: Workers' Rights in the American Meatpacking Industry." *Sociological Focus* 46 (2): 119–37.

———. 2016. *Organizing Organic: Conflict and Compromise in an Emerging Market.* Stanford, CA: Stanford University Press.

Hall, Derek. 2013. "Primitive Accumulation, Accumulation by Dispossession, and the Global Land Grab." *Third World Quarterly* 34 (9): 1582–1604.

Halliday, Simon, and Bronwen Morgan. 2013. "I Fought the Law and the Law Won? Legal Consciousness and the Critical Imagination." *Current Legal Problems* 66 (1): 1–32.

Handler, Joel F. 1978. *Social Movements and the Legal System: A Theory of Law Reform and Social Change.* New York: Academic Press.

Hannah-Jones, Nikole. 2019. "America Wasn't a Democracy, Until Black Americans Made It One." *New York Times,* August 14, 2019. https://www.nytimes.com/interactive/2019/08/14/magazine/black-history-american-democracy.html.

Hansen, Eric, and Martin Donohoe. 2003. "Health Issues of Migrant and Seasonal Farmworkers." *Journal of Health Care for the Poor and Underserved* 14 (2): 153–64.

Hardt, Michael, and Antonio Negri. 2001. *Empire.* Cambridge, MA: Harvard University Press.

———. 2005. *Multitude: War and Democracy in the Age of Empire.* New York: Penguin.

Harrington, Christine B., and Sally Engle Merry. 1988. "Ideological Production: The Making of Community Mediation." *Law and Society Review* 22 (4): 709–36.

Harrington, Christine B., and Barbara Yngvesson. 1990. "Interpretive Sociolegal Research." *Law and Social Inquiry* 15 (1): 135–48.

Harvey, David. 1989. "From Managerialism to Entrepreneurialism: The Transformation in Urban Governance in Late Capitalism." *Geografiska Annaler, ser. B, Human Geography* 71 (1): 3–17.

Havice, Elizabeth, and John Pickles. 2019. "On Value in Value Chains." In *Handbook on Global Value Chains,* ed. Stefano Ponte, Gary Gereffi, and Gale Raj-Reichert, 169–82. Northampton, MA: Edward Elgar.

Headey, Derek, and Shenggen Fan. 2008. "Anatomy of a Crisis: The Causes and Consequences of Surging Food Prices." *Agricultural Economics* 39 (suppl. 1): 375–91.

Healey, Patsy. 1997. *Collaborative Planning: Shaping Places in Fragmented Societies.* Vancouver, Canada: UBC Press.

Heim, Kristi, and Maureen O'Hagan. 2010. "Gates Foundation Ties with Monsanto Under Fire from Activists." *Seattle Times*, August 28. https://www.seattletimes.com/seattle-news/gates-foundation-ties-with-monsanto-under-fire-from-activists/.

Held, David. 1995. *Democracy and the Global Order: From the Modern State to Cosmopolitan Governance*. Stanford, CA: Stanford University Press.

Heller, Chaia. 2013. *Food, Farms, and Solidarity: French Farmers Challenge Industrial Agriculture and Genetically Modified Crops*. Durham, NC: Duke University Press.

Hendrickson, Mary K., Philip H. Howard, Emily M. Miller, and Douglas H. Constance. 2021. *The Food System: Concentration and Its Impacts*. Mexico, MO: Family Farm Action Alliance. https://farmactionalliance.org/wp-content/uploads/2021/05/Hendrickson-et-al.-2020.-Concentration-and-Its-Impacts_FINAL_Addended.pdf.

Henry, Stuart. 1985. "Community Justice, Capitalist Society, and Human Agency: The Dialectics of Collective Law in the Cooperative." *Law and Society Review* 19 (2): 303–27.

Hetherington, Kregg. 2014. "Regular Soybeans: Translation and Framing in the Ontological Politics of a Coup." *Indiana Journal of Global Legal Studies* 21 (1): 55–78.

HLPE. 2018. *Multi-Stakeholder Partnerships to Finance and Improve Food Security and Nutrition in the Framework of the 2030 Agenda*. Rome: High Level Panel of Experts on Food Security and Nutrition, Committee on World Food Security.

———. 2019. *Agroecological and Other Innovative Approaches for Sustainable Agriculture and Food Systems That Enhance Food Security and Nutrition*. Rome: High Level Panel of Experts on Food Security and Nutrition, Committee on World Food Security.

Holmes, Seth. 2013. *Fresh Fruit, Broken Bodies: Migrant Farmworkers in the United States*. Berkeley: University of California Press.

Holt-Giménez, Eric. 2006. *Campesino a Campesino: Voices from Latin America's Farmer to Farmer Movement for Sustainable Agriculture*. Oakland, CA: Food First Books.

———. 2017. *A Foodie's Guide to Capitalism*. New York: NYU Press.

Holt-Giménez, Eric, and Miguel A. Altieri. 2013. "Agroecology, Food Sovereignty, and the New Green Revolution." *Agroecology and Sustainable Food Systems* 37 (1): 90–102.

Holt-Giménez, Eric, and Raj Patel. 2012. *Food Rebellions: Crisis and the Hunger for Justice*. Oakland, CA: Food First Books.

Holt-Giménez, Eric, and Yi Wang. 2011. "Reform or Transformation? The Pivotal Role of Food Justice in the U.S. Food Movement." *Race/Ethnicity: Multidisciplinary Global Contexts* 5 (1): 83–102.

Hoover, Elizabeth. 2017. "'You Can't Say You're Sovereign If You Can't Feed Yourself':

Defining and Enacting Food Sovereignty in American Indian Community Gardening." *American Indian Culture and Research Journal* 41 (3): 31–70.

Horner, Rory. 2017. "Beyond Facilitator? State Roles in Global Value Chains and Global Production Networks." *Geography Compass* 11 (2): e12307.

Horner, Rory, and Matthew Alford. 2019. "The Roles of the State in Global Value Chains." In *Handbook on Global Value Chains*, ed. Stefano Ponte, Gary Gereffi, and Gale Raj-Reichert, 555–69. Northampton, MA: Edward Elgar.

Humphrey, John, and Hubert Schmitz. 2001. "Governance in Global Value Chains." *IDS Bulletin* 32 (3): 19–29.

Iles, Alastair, and Maywa Montenegro de Wit. 2015. "Sovereignty at What Scale? An Inquiry into Multiple Dimensions of Food Sovereignty." *Globalizations* 12 (4): 481–97.

Ince, Onur Ulas. 2018. *Colonial Capitalism and the Dilemmas of Liberalism*. Oxford, UK: Oxford University Press.

INCITE! 2007. *The Revolution Will Not Be Funded: Beyond the Non-Profit Industrial Complex*. Durham, NC: Duke University Press.

Innes, Judith E. 2004. "Consensus Building: Clarifications for the Critics." *Planning Theory* 3 (1): 5–20.

Innes, Judith E., and David E. Booher. 2003. "Collaborative Policymaking: Governance Through Dialogue." In *Deliberative Policy Analysis: Understanding Governance in the Network Society*, ed. M. Hajer and H. Wagenaar, 33–59. Cambridge, UK: Cambridge University Press.

IPCC (Intergovernmental Panel on Climate Change). 2019. *Climate Change and Land: An IPCC Special Report on Climate Change, Desertification, Land Degradation, Sustainable Land Management, Food Security, and Greenhouse Gas Fluxes in Terrestrial Ecosystems*. Geneva: Intergovernmental Panel on Climate Change.

IPES-Food. 2016. *From Uniformity to Diversity: A Paradigm Shift from Industrial Agriculture to Diversified Agroecological Systems*. Brussels: International Panel of Experts on Sustainable Food Systems. http://www.ipes-food.org/_img/upload/files/UniformityToDiversity_FULL.pdf.

———. 2017a. "Too Big to Feed: Exploring the Impacts of Mega-Mergers, Consolidation and Concentration of Power in the Agri-Food Sector." GRAIN, October 16. https://grain.org/en/article/5821-too-big-to-feed-exploring-the-impacts-of-mega-mergers-consolidation-and-concentration-of-power-in-the-agri-food-sectorb.

———. 2017b. *Unravelling the Food-Health Nexus: Addressing Practices, Political Economy, and Power Relations to Build Healthier Food Systems*. Brussels: Global Alliance for the Future of Food and IPES-Food. http://www.ipes-food.org/_img/upload/files/Health_FullReport(1).pdf.

———. 2020. *Money Flows: What Is Holding Back Investment in Agroecological Research for Africa?* Brussels: Biovision Foundation for Ecological Development and International Panel of Experts on Sustainable Food Systems. http://www.ipes-food.org/_img/upload/files/Money%20Flows_Full%20report.pdf.

Jarosz, Lucy. 2009. "The Political Economy of Global Governance and the World Food Crisis: The Case of the FAO." *Review (Fernand Braudel Center)* 32 (1): 37–60.

———. 2011. "Defining World Hunger: Scale and Neoliberal Ideology in International Food Security Policy Discourse." *Food, Culture, and Society* 14: 117–39.

Jasanoff, Sheila. 2006. "Biotechnology and Empire: The Global Power of Seeds and Science." *Osiris* 21 (1): 273–92.

———. 2011. *Designs on Nature: Science and Democracy in Europe and the United States.* Princeton, NJ: Princeton University Press.

———. 2014. "Biotechnology and Empire: The Global Power of Seeds and Science." In *The Global Politics of Science and Technology,* ed. Maximilian Mayer, Mariana Carpes, and Ruth Knoblich, 1: 201–25. Berlin: Springer.

Jessop, Bob. 2016. "Territory, Politics, Governance, and Multispatial Metagovernance." *Territory, Politics, Governance* 4 (1): 8–32.

Johnston, Josée. 2008. "The Citizen-Consumer Hybrid: Ideological Tensions and the Case of Whole Foods Market." *Theory and Society* 37 (3): 229–70.

Jones, Naya. 2019. "(Re)Visiting the Corner Store: Black Youth, Gentrification, and Food Sovereignty." In *Race in the Marketplace: Crossing Critical Boundaries,* ed. Guillaume D. Johnson, Kevin D. Thomas, Anthony Kwame Harrison, and Sonya A. Grier, 55–72. Cham, Switzerland: Springer International.

Juris, Jeffrey S. 2008a. *Networking Futures: The Movements Against Corporate Globalization.* Durham, NC: Duke University Press.

———. 2008b. "Spaces of Intentionality: Race, Class, and Horizontality at the United States Social Forum." *Mobilization: An International Quarterly* 13 (4): 353–72.

Juris, Jeffrey S., and Alexander Khasnabish. 2013. *Insurgent Encounters: Transnational Activism, Ethnography, and the Political.* Durham, NC: Duke University Press.

Karamura, D. A., E. Karamura, and W. Tinzaara. 2012. *Banana Cultivar Names, Synonyms, and Their Usage in Eastern Africa.* Kampala, Uganda: Biodiversity International. http://banana-networks.org/barnesa/files/2013/07/Banana-cultivar-names-synonyms-and-their-usage-in-East-Africa.pdf.

Kautsky, Karl. 1988. *The Agrarian Question.* London: Pluto Press.

Keck, Margaret E., and Kathryn Sikkink. 1998. *Activists Beyond Borders: Advocacy Networks in International Politics.* Ithaca, NY: Cornell University Press.

Kelloway, Claire, and Sarah Miller. 2019. *Food and Power: Addressing Monopolization in America's Food System.* Washington, DC: Open Markets Institute. https://www.openmarketsinstitute.org/publications/food-power-addressing-monopolization-americas-food-system.

Kelty, Christopher M. 2008. *Two Bits: The Cultural Significance of Free Software.* Durham, NC: Duke University Press.

Kennedy, David. 2016. *A World of Struggle: How Power, Law, and Expertise Shape Global Political Economy*. Princeton, NJ: Princeton University Press.

King, Brayden G., and Nicholas A. Pearce. 2010. "The Contentiousness of Markets: Politics, Social Movements, and Institutional Change in Markets." *Annual Review of Sociology* 36 (1): 249–67.

Kingsbury, Benedict. 2009. "The Concept of 'Law' in Global Administrative Law." *European Journal of International Law* 20 (1): 23–57.

Kingsbury, Benedict, Nico Krisch, and Richard B. Stewart. 2005. "The Emergence of Global Administrative Law." *Law and Contemporary Problems* 68 (3–4): 15–61.

Kirk, Andrew. 2001. "Appropriating Technology: The Whole Earth Catalog and Counterculture Environmental Politics." *Environmental History* 6 (3): 374–94.

Kiviat, Barbara, and Bill Gates. 2008. "Making Capitalism More Creative." *Time Magazine*, July 31.

Klare, Karl E. 1977. "Judicial Deradicalization of the Wagner Act and the Origins of Modern Legal Consciousness, 1937–1941." *Minnesota Law Review* 62: 265–339.

Klein, Naomi. 2010. *No Logo: 10th Anniversary Edition*. New York: Picador.

Kloppenburg, Jack Ralph. 2004. *First the Seed: The Political Economy of Plant Biotechnology, 1492–2000*. Madison: University of Wisconsin Press.

Krisch, Nico. 2017. "Liquid Authority in Global Governance." *International Theory* 9 (2): 237–60.

Laclau, Ernesto. 1996. *Emancipation(s)*. New York: Verso.

Laclau, Ernesto, and Chantal Mouffe. 1985. *Hegemony and Socialist Strategy: Towards a Radical Democratic Politics*. London: Verso.

Lambek, Nadia, and Priscilla Claeys. 2015. "Institutionalizing a Fully Realized Right to Food: Progress, Limitations, and Lessons Learned from Emerging Alternative Policy Models." *Vermont Law Review* 40: 743–90.

Lappe, Frances Moore. 1971. *Diet for a Small Planet*. New York: Ballantine Books.

Latour, Bruno. 2007. *Reassembling the Social: An Introduction to Actor-Network-Theory*. New York: Oxford University Press.

La Via Campesina. 2013. *La Via Campesina: Our Seeds, Our Future*. Notebook no. 6. Jakarta, Indonesia: La Via Campesina. https://viacampesina.org/en/wp-content/uploads/sites/2/2013/06/EN-notebook6cover.pdf.

Lee, Joonkoo, Gary Gereffi, and Janet Beauvais. 2012. "Global Value Chains and Agrifood Standards: Challenges and Possibilities for Smallholders in Developing Countries." *Proceedings of the National Academy of Sciences* 109 (31): 12,326–331.

Lefort, Claude. 1986. *The Political Forms of Modern Society: Bureaucracy, Democracy, Totalitarianism*. Cambridge, MA: MIT Press.

Legrand, Pierre. 2009. "Econocentrism." *University of Toronto Law Journal* 59 (2): 215–22.

Le Marre, Klervi N., Carl L. Witte, Timothy J. Burkink, Marko Grünhagen, and Gary J. Wells. 2007. "A Second Generation of Genetically Modified Food." *Journal of Food Products Marketing* 13 (1): 81–100.

Levi-Faur, David. 2006. "Regulatory Capitalism: The Dynamics of Change Beyond Telecoms and Electricity." *Governance* 19 (3): 497–525.

Lievens, Matthias. 2015. "From Government to Governance: A Symbolic Mutation and Its Repercussions for Democracy." *Political Studies* 63 (1, suppl.): 2–17.

Lobel, Orly. 2004. "Renew Deal: The Fall of Regulation and the Rise of Governance in Contemporary Legal Thought." *Minnesota Law Review* 89: 262–390.

Lopez, Ian Haney. 2006. *White by Law: The Legal Construction of Race.* New York: NYU Press.

Loza, Mireya. 2016. *Defiant Braceros: How Migrant Workers Fought for Racial, Sexual, and Political Freedom.* Chapel Hill: University of North Carolina Press.

Luna, Guadalupe T. 1997. "An Infinite Distance: Agricultural Exceptionalism and Agricultural Labor." *University of Pennsylvania Journal of Labor and Employment Law* 1 (2): 487–510.

Maeckelbergh, Marianne. 2009. *The Will of the Many: How the Alterglobalisation Movement Is Changing the Face of Democracy.* London: Pluto Press.

———. 2011. "Doing Is Believing: Prefiguration as Strategic Practice in the Alterglobalization Movement." *Social Movement Studies* 10 (1): 1–20.

Majka, Linda C., and Theo J. Majka. 2000. "Organizing U.S. Farm Workers: A Continuous Struggle." In *Hungry for Profit: The Agribusiness Threat to Farmers, Food, and the Environment*, ed. Fred Magdoff, John Bellamy Foster, and Frederick H. Buttel, 161–74. New York: NYU Press and Monthly Review Press.

Malloy, Robin Paul. 2003. "Framing the Market: Representations of Meaning and Value in Law, Markets, and Culture." *Buffalo Law Review* 51: 1–126.

Mares, Teresa. 2018. "Cultivating Comida: Dignity and Devastation in Vermont's Dairy Industry." *Journal of Agriculture, Food Systems, and Community Development* 8 (3): 5–8.

Margulis, Matias E. 2013. "The Regime Complex for Food Security: Implications for the Global Hunger Challenge." *Global Governance* 19: 53–67.

———. 2017. "The Forgotten History of Food Security in Multilateral Trade Negotiations." *World Trade Review* 16 (1): 25–57.

Marks, Susan. 2013. "Four Human Rights Myths." In *Human Rights: Old Problems, New Possibilities*, ed. David Kinley, Wojciech Sadurski, and Walton Kevin, 217–35. Northampton, MA: Edward Elgar.

Martin, Philip L. 2002. "Mexican Workers and U.S. Agriculture: The Revolving Door." *International Migration Review* 36 (4): 1124–42.

———. 2003. *Promise Unfulfilled: Unions, Immigration, and the Farm Workers.* Ithaca, NY: Cornell University Press.

Martinez-Torres, Maria Elena, and Peter M. Rosset. 2010. "La Vía Campesina: The Evolution of a Transnational Movement." Global Policy Forum, February 7. https://www.globalpolicy.org/social-and-economic-policy/world-hunger/land-ownership-and-hunger/48733-la-via-campesina-the-evolution-of-a-transnational-movement.html.

———. 2014. "Diálogo de Saberes in La Vía Campesina: Food Sovereignty and Agroecology." *Journal of Peasant Studies* 41 (6): 979–97.

Mayer, Frederick W., and Nicola Phillips. 2017. "Outsourcing Governance: States and the Politics of a 'Global Value Chain World.'" *New Political Economy* 22 (2): 134–52.

McArthur, John, and Krista Rasmussen. 2017. "Who Funds Which Multilateral Organizations?" Blog post, *Brookings*, December 20. https://www.brookings.edu/research/who-funds-which-multilateral-organizations/.

McCallum, Jamie K. 2013. *Global Unions, Local Power: The New Spirit of Transnational Labor Organizing*. Ithaca, NY: Cornell University Press.

McCann, Michael W. 1994. *Rights at Work: Pay Equity Reform and the Politics of Legal Mobilization*. Chicago: University of Chicago Press.

McGoey, Linsey. 2015. *No Such Thing as a Free Gift: The Gates Foundation and the Price of Philanthropy*. New York: Verso Books.

McInerney, Paul-Brian. 2014. *From Social Movement to Moral Market: How the Circuit Riders Sparked an IT Revolution and Created a Technology Market*. Stanford, CA: Stanford University Press.

McKeon, Nora. 2009. *The United Nations and Civil Society: Legitimating Global Governance—Whose Voice?* London: Zed Books.

———. 2015. *Food Security Governance: Empowering Communities, Regulating Corporations*. New York: Routledge.

———. 2017. "Are Equity and Sustainability a Likely Outcome When Foxes and Chickens Share the Same Coop? Critiquing the Concept of Multistakeholder Governance of Food Security." *Globalizations* 14 (3): 379–98.

McMichael, Philip. 2008. "Peasants Make Their Own History, but not Just as They Please . . ." *Journal of Agrarian Change* 8 (2–3): 205–28.

———. 2011. *Development and Social Change: A Global Perspective*, 5th ed. Los Angeles: SAGE.

———. 2013. *Food Regimes and Agrarian Questions*. Rugby, UK: Practical Action.

———. 2014. "Rethinking Land Grab Ontology." *Rural Sociology* 79 (1): 34–55.

———. 2015. "The Land Question in the Food Sovereignty Project." *Globalizations* 12 (4): 434–51.

Méndez, V. Ernesto, Christopher M. Bacon, and Roseann Cohen. 2013. "Agroecology as a Transdisciplinary, Participatory, and Action-Oriented Approach." *Agroecology and Sustainable Food Systems* 37 (1): 3–18.

Merry, Sally Engle. 2006. *Human Rights and Gender Violence: Translating International Law into Local Justice*. Chicago: University of Chicago Press.

Mgbeoji, Ikechi. 2004. "Beyond Rhetoric: State Sovereignty, Common Concern, and the Inapplicability of the Common Heritage Concept to Plant Genetic Resources." *Leiden Journal of International Law* 16 (4): 821–37.

Mihesuah, Devon A., and Elizabeth Hoover, eds. 2019. *Indigenous Food Sovereignty in the United States: Restoring Cultural Knowledge, Protecting Environments, and Regaining Health*. Norman: University of Oklahoma Press.

Mikulewicz, Michael. 2019. "Thwarting Adaptation's Potential? A Critique of Resilience and Climate-Resilient Development." *Geoforum* 104 (August): 267–82.

Miller, Peter, and Nikolas Rose. 2008. *Governing the Present: Administering Economic, Social, and Personal Life.* London: Polity.

Mintz, Sidney W. 1986. *Sweetness and Power: The Place of Sugar in Modern History.* New York: Penguin.

Montenegro de Wit, Maywa, Antonio Roman-Alcalá, Alex Liebman, and Siena Chrisman. 2021. "Agrarian Origins of Authoritarian Populism in the United States: What Can We Learn from 20th-Century Struggles in California and the Midwest?" *Journal of Rural Studies* 82 (February): 518–30.

Mooney, Patrick H., and Theo J. Majka. 1995. *Farmers' and Farm Workers' Movements: Social Protest in American Agriculture.* New York: Twayne.

Moore, Barrington. 1993. *Social Origins of Dictatorship and Democracy: Lord and Peasant in the Making of the Modern World.* Boston: Beacon Press.

Morgan, Bronwen. 2007. *The Intersection of Rights and Regulation: New Directions in Sociolegal Scholarship.* Farnham, UK: Ashgate.

———. 2011. *Water on Tap: Rights and Regulation in the Transnational Governance of Urban Water Services.* New York: Cambridge University Press.

Morgan, Bronwen, and Declan Kuch. 2015. "Radical Transactionalism: Legal Consciousness, Diverse Economies, and the Sharing Economy." *Journal of Law and Society* 42 (4): 556–87.

———. 2017. "Sharing Subjects and Legality: Ambiguities in Moving Beyond Neoliberalism." In *Assembling Neoliberalism: Expertise, Practices, Subjects,* ed. Vaughan Higgins and Wendy Larner, 219–41. New York: Palgrave Macmillan.

———. 2020. "Diverse Legalities: Pluralism and Instrumentalism." In *The Handbook of Diverse Economies,* ed. J. K. Gibson-Graham and Kelly Dombroski, 323–30. Northampton, MA: Edward Elgar.

Moyn, Samuel. 2012. *The Last Utopia.* Cambridge, MA: Harvard University Press.

———. 2014. "A Powerless Companion: Human Rights in the Age of Neoliberalism Law and Neoliberalism." *Law and Contemporary Problems* 77: 147–70.

———. 2018. *Not Enough: Human Rights in an Unequal World.* Cambridge, MA: Harvard University Press.

MSI Integrity. 2020. *Not Fit-for-Purpose: The Grand Experiment of Multi-Stakeholder Initiatives in Corporate Accountability, Human Rights, and Global Governance.* Berkeley, CA: MSI Integrity. https://www.msi-integrity.org/wp-content/uploads/2020/07/MSI_Not_Fit_For_Purpose_FORWEBSITE.FINAL_.pdf.

Musoke, Ronald. 2018. "GMO Law Fight not Over." Blog post, *The Independent Uganda,* December 17. https://www.independent.co.ug/gmo-law-fight-not-over/.

Mutua, Makau. 2001. "Savages, Victims, and Saviors: The Metaphor of Human Rights." *Harvard International Law Journal* 42 (1): 201–46.

"Nakitembe Banana." n.d. Blog post, *Slow Food Foundation.* https://www.fondazioneslowfood.com/en/ark-of-taste-slow-food/nakitembe-banana/ (accessed July 9, 2020).

Narula, Smita. 2010. "Reclaiming the Right to Food as a Normative Response to the Global Food Crisis." *Yale Human Rights and Development Law Journal* 13: 403–20.

———. 2013. "The Global Land Rush: Markets, Rights, and the Politics of Food." *Stanford Journal of International Law* 49: 101–75.

Navdanya International. 2020. *Gates to a Global Empire: Over Seed, Food, Health, Knowledge . . . and the Earth.* Florence, Italy: Navdanya International.

Nestle, Marion. 2010. *Safe Food: The Politics of Food Safety.* Berkeley: University of California Press.

Newell, Peter. 2009. "Bio-Hegemony: The Political Economy of Agricultural Biotechnology in Argentina." *Journal of Latin American Studies* 41 (1): 27–57.

Nicholson, Paul. 2012. *Terre et liberté! A la conquête de la souveraineté alimentaire.* Geneva: Centre Europe Tiers-Monde.

Noah, Timothy. 2015. "The Myths of Cesar Chavez." *New York Review*, October 8. https://www.nybooks.com/articles/2015/10/08/myths-cesar-chavez/.

Nord, Mark, Margaret Andrews, and Steven Carlson. 2008. *Household Food Security in the United States, 2007.* Economic Research Report no. 66. Washington, DC: US Department of Agriculture, Economic Research Service.

Obach, Brian K. 2015. *Organic Struggle: The Movement for Sustainable Agriculture in the United States.* Cambridge, MA: MIT Press.

Orford, Anne. 2015. "Food Security, Free Trade, and the Battle for the State." *Journal of International Law and International Relations* 11 (2): 1–67.

Orleck, Annelise. 2018. *We Are All Fast-Food Workers Now: The Global Uprising Against Poverty Wages.* Boston: Beacon Press.

Oshaug, Arne. 2005. "Developing Voluntary Guidelines for Implementing the Right to Adequate Food: Anatomy of an Intergovernmental Process." In *Food and Human Rights in Development*, vol. 1, *Legal and Institutional Dimensions and Selected Topics*, ed. Wenche Barth Eide and Uwe Kracht, 259–82. Oxford, UK: Intersentia.

Osterweil, Michal. 2005. "Place-Based Globalism: Theorizing the Global Justice Movement." *Development* 48 (2): 23–28.

Parker, Christine, and Hope Johnson. 2019. "From Food Chains to Food Webs: Regulating Capitalist Production and Consumption in the Food System." *Annual Review of Law and Social Science* 15 (1): 205–25.

Patel, Raj. 2013. "The Long Green Revolution." *Journal of Peasant Studies* 40 (1): 1–63.

Paul, Jean-Yves, Robert Harding, Wilberforce Tushemereirwe, and James Dale. 2018. "Banana21: From Gene Discovery to Deregulated Golden Bananas." *Frontiers in Plant Science* 9 (April): art. 558.

Pawel, Miriam. 2009. *The Union of Their Dreams: Power, Hope, and Struggle in Cesar Chavez's Farm Worker Movement.* New York: Bloomsbury.

Paxson, Heather. 2012. *The Life of Cheese: Crafting Food and Value in America.* Berkeley: University of California Press.

Pechlaner, Gabriela. 2012. *Corporate Crops: Biotechnology, Agriculture, and the Struggle for Control*. Austin: University of Texas Press.

Peck, Jamie, and Nik Theodore. 2019. "Still Neoliberalism?" *South Atlantic Quarterly* 118 (2): 245–65.

Peck, Jamie, and Adam Tickell. 2002. "Neoliberalizing Space." *Antipode* 34 (3): 380–404.

Peekhaus, Wilhelm. 2010. "The Neoliberal University and Agricultural Biotechnology: Reports from the Field." *Bulletin of Science, Technology, and Society* 30 (6): 415–29.

Perfecto, Ivette, John H. Vandermeer, and Angus Lindsay Wright. 2009. *Nature's Matrix: Linking Agriculture, Conservation, and Food Sovereignty*. London: Earthscan.

Perkins, John. 1997. *Geopolitics and the Green Revolution: Wheat, Genes, and the Cold War*. New York: Oxford University Press.

Peschard, Karine, and Shalini Randeria. 2020. "'Keeping Seeds in Our Hands': The Rise of Seed Activism." *Journal of Peasant Studies* 47 (4): 613–47.

Pimbert, Michel. 2006. *Transforming Knowledge and Ways of Knowing for Food Sovereignty*. London: International Institute for Environment and Development.

———. 2015. "Agroecology as an Alternative Vision to Conventional Development and Climate-Smart Agriculture." *Development* 58 (2–3): 286–98.

Pingali, Prabhu. 2012. *Scaling Up in Agriculture, Rural Development, and Nutrition: The Bill and Melinda Gates Foundation—Catalyzing Agricultural Innovation*. Washington, DC: International Food Policy Research Institute. https://www.ifpri.org/publication/scaling-agriculture-rural-development-and-nutrition-bill-melinda-gates-foundation.

Pitkin, Hanna F. 1967. *The Concept of Representation*. Berkeley: University of California Press.

Piven, Frances Fox, and Richard Cloward. 1978. *Regulating the Poor: The Functions of Public Welfare*. New York: Vintage.

Polanyi, Karl. 2001. *The Great Transformation: The Political and Economic Origins of Our Time*. Boston: Beacon Press.

Pollack, Mark A., and Gregory C. Shaffer. 2009. *When Cooperation Fails: The International Law and Politics of Genetically Modified Foods*. New York: Oxford University Press.

Pollan, Michael. 2006a. *The Omnivore's Dilemma: A Natural History of Four Meals*. New York: Penguin Press.

———. 2006b. "Voting with Your Fork." Blog post, May 7. https://pollan.blogs.nytimes.com/2006/05/07/voting-with-your-fork/.

———. 2010. "The Food Movement, Rising." *New York Review of Books*, June 10. http://www.nybooks.com/articles/archives/2010/jun/10/food-movement-rising/.

Polletta, Francesca. 2004. *Freedom Is an Endless Meeting: Democracy in American Social Movements*. Chicago: University of Chicago Press.

Ponte, Stefano, and Peter Gibbon. 2005. "Quality Standards, Conventions, and the Governance of Global Value Chains." *Economy and Society* 34 (1): 1–31.

Ponte, Stefano, and Timothy Sturgeon. 2014. "Explaining Governance in Global Value Chains: A Modular Theory-Building Effort." *Review of International Political Economy* 21 (1): 195–223.

Pope, James Gray. 1996. "Labor's Constitution of Freedom." *Yale Law Journal* 106 (4): 941–1031.

Poppendieck, Janet. 1999. *Sweet Charity? Emergency Food and the End of Entitlement.* New York: Penguin Books.

Povinelli, Elizabeth A. 2001. "The Anthropology of Incommensurability and Inconceivability." *Annual Review of Anthropology* 30: 319–34.

Powell, Walter. 1990. "Neither Market nor Hierarchy: Network Forms of Organization." *Research in Organizational Behavior* 12: 295–336.

Pudup, Mary Beth. 2008. "It Takes a Garden: Cultivating Citizen-Subjects in Organized Garden Projects." *Geoforum* 39 (3): 1228–40.

Purcell, Mark. 2009. "Resisting Neoliberalization: Communicative Planning or Counter-Hegemonic Movements?" *Planning Theory* 8 (2): 140–65.

Rajagopal, Balakrishnan. 2005. "The Role of Law in Counter-Hegemonic Globalization and Global Legal Pluralism: Lessons from the Narmada Valley Struggle in India." *Leiden Journal of International Law* 18 (3): 345–87.

Ramdas, Kavita N. 2011. "Philanthrocapitalism: Reflections on Politics and Policy Making." *Society* 48 (5): 393–96.

Ranciere, Jacques. 2004. "Who Is the Subject of the Rights of Man." *South Atlantic Quarterly* 103 (2–3): 297–310.

Raustiala, Kal, and David G. Victor. 2004. "The Regime Complex for Plant Genetic Resources." *International Organization* 58 (2): 277–309.

Ravitch, Diane. 2013. *Reign of Error: The Hoax of the Privatization Movement and the Danger to America's Public Schools.* New York: Knopf Doubleday.

Reese, Ashanté M. 2019. *Black Food Geographies: Race, Self-Reliance, and Food Access in Washington, D.C.* Chapel Hill: University of North Carolina Press.

Riles, Annelise. 2001. *The Network Inside Out.* Ann Arbor: University of Michigan Press.

Rock, Joeva, and Rachel Schurman. 2020. "The Complex Choreography of Agricultural Biotechnology in Africa." *African Affairs* 119 (477): 499–525.

Rodríguez-Garavito, César A. 2005. "Nike's Law: The Anti-Sweatshop Movement, Transnational Corporations, and the Struggle over International Labor Rights in the Americas." In *Law and Globalization from Below: Towards a Cosmopolitan Legality,* ed. Cesar Rodriguez-Garavito and Boaventura de Sousa Santos, 64–91. Cambridge, UK: Cambridge University Press.

Roff, Robin Jane. 2008. "No Alternative? The Politics and History of Non-GMO Certification." *Agriculture and Human Values* 26 (4): 351–63.

Roger, Charles, and Peter Dauvergne. 2016. "The Rise of Transnational Governance as a Field of Study." *International Studies Review* 18 (3): 415–37.

Roman-Alcalá, Antonio. 2015. "Broadening the Land Question in Food Sovereignty to Northern Settings: A Case Study of Occupy the Farm." *Globalizations* 12 (4): 545–58.

Rosset, Peter. 2006. *Food Is Different: Why the WTO Should Get Out of Agriculture.* London: Zed Books.

Rosset, Peter Michael, Braulio Machín Sosa, Adilén María Roque Jaime, and Dana Rocío Ávila Lozano. 2011. "The Campesino-to-Campesino Agroecology Movement of ANAP in Cuba: Social Process Methodology in the Construction of Sustainable Peasant Agriculture and Food Sovereignty." *Journal of Peasant Studies* 38 (1): 161–91.

Rothschild, Emma. 1976. "Food Politics." *Foreign Affairs* 54 (2): 285–307.

Routledge, Paul, and Andrew Cumbers. 2013. *Global Justice Networks: Geographies of Transnational Solidarity.* Oxford, UK: Oxford University Press.

Rubongoya, Joshua B. 2007. *Regime Hegemony in Museveni's Uganda: Pax Musevenica.* New York: Palgrave Macmillan.

Ruggie, John Gerard. 1993. "Territoriality and Beyond: Problematizing Modernity in International Relations." *International Organization* 47 (1): 139–74.

Saab, Anne. 2018. "An International Law Approach to Food Regime Theory." *Leiden Journal of International Law* 31 (2): 251–65.

———. 2019. *Narratives of Hunger in International Law: Feeding the World in Times of Climate Change.* Cambridge, UK: Cambridge University Press.

Sabel, Charles F., and William H. Simon. 2004. "Destabilization Rights: How Public Law Litigation Succeeds." *Harvard Law Review* 117 (4): 1015–1101.

Sassen, Saskia. 2002. *Global Networks, Linked Cities.* London: Psychology Press.

———. 2008. *Territory, Authority, Rights: From Medieval to Global Assemblages.* Princeton, NJ: Princeton University Press.

Saward, Michael. 2005. "Governance and the Transformation of Political Representation." In *Remaking Governance: Peoples, Politics, and the Public Sphere*, ed. Janet Newman, 179–96. Bristol, UK: Policy Press.

———. 2010. *The Representative Claim.* Oxford, UK: Oxford University Press.

Scheingold, Stuart A. 2004. *The Politics of Rights: Lawyers, Public Policy, and Political Change.* Ann Arbor: University of Michigan Press.

Schell, Greg. 2002. "Farmworker Exceptionalism Under the Law: How the Legal System Contributes to Farmworker Poverty and Powerlessness." In *The Human Cost of Food: Farmworkers' Lives, Labor, and Advocacy*, ed. Charles D. Thompson and Melinda F. Wiggins, 139–68. Austin: University of Texas Press.

Schiavoni, Christina M. 2015. "Competing Sovereignties, Contested Processes: Insights from the Venezuelan Food Sovereignty Experiment." *Globalizations* 12 (4): 466–80.

———. 2017. "The Contested Terrain of Food Sovereignty Construction: Toward a Historical, Relational, and Interactive Approach." *Journal of Peasant Studies* 44 (1): 1–32.

Schmidt, Christopher W. 2018. *The Sit-Ins: Protest and Legal Change in the Civil Rights Era.* Chicago: University of Chicago Press.

Schnurr, Matthew A. 2013. "Biotechnology and Bio-Hegemony in Uganda: Unraveling the Social Relations Underpinning the Promotion of Genetically Modified Crops into New African Markets." *Journal of Peasant Studies* 40 (4): 639–58.

———. 2019. *Africa's Gene Revolution: Genetically Modified Crops and the Future of African Agriculture*. Montreal: McGill-Queen's University Press.

Schnurr, Matthew A., and Christopher Gore. 2015. "Getting to 'Yes': Governing Genetically Modified Crops in Uganda." *Journal of International Development* 27 (1): 55–72.

Scholte, Jan Aart. 2014. "Reinventing Global Democracy." *European Journal of International Relations* 20 (1): 3–28.

Schubert, David R. 2008. "The Problem with Nutritionally Enhanced Plants." *Journal of Medicinal Food* 11 (4): 601–5.

Schurman, Rachel. 2017. "Building an Alliance for Biotechnology in Africa." *Journal of Agrarian Change* 17 (3): 441–58.

———. 2018. "Micro(Soft) Managing a 'Green Revolution' for Africa: The New Donor Culture and International Agricultural Development." *World Development* 112 (December): 180–92.

Schurman, Rachel, and William A. Munro. 2010. *Fighting for the Future of Food: Activists Versus Agribusiness in the Struggle over Biotechnology*. Minneapolis: University of Minnesota Press.

Schwab, Klaus. 2021. *Stakeholder Capitalism: A Global Economy That Works for Progress, People, and Planet*. New York: Wiley.

Schwab, Tim. 2020. "Bill Gates Gives to the Rich (Including Himself)." *The Nation*, March 17. https://www.thenation.com/article/society/bill-gates-foundation-philanthropy/.

Scoones, Ian, Marc Edelman, Saturnino M. Borras Jr., Ruth Hall, Wendy Wolford, and Ben White. 2018. "Emancipatory Rural Politics: Confronting Authoritarian Populism." *Journal of Peasant Studies* 45 (1): 1–20.

Sen, Amartya. 1983. *Poverty and Famines: An Essay on Entitlement and Deprivation*. Oxford, UK: Oxford University Press.

Sending, Ole Jacob. 2015. *The Politics of Expertise: Competing for Authority in Global Governance*. Ann Arbor: University of Michigan Press.

Shamir, Ronen. 2008. "The Age of Responsibilization: On Market-Embedded Morality." *Economy and Society* 37 (1): 1–19.

Shattuck, Annie, Christina M. Schiavoni, and Zoe VanGelder. 2015. "Translating the Politics of Food Sovereignty: Digging into Contradictions, Uncovering New Dimensions." *Globalizations* 12 (4): 421–33.

Shaw, D. John. 2007. *World Food Security: A History Since 1945*. Basingstoke, UK: Palgrave Macmillan.

Shiva, Vandana. 1991. *The Violence of Green Revolution: Third World Agriculture, Ecology, and Politics*. London: Zed Books.

———. 1993. *Monocultures of the Mind: Perspectives on Biodiversity and Biotechnology*. New York: Palgrave Macmillan.

Shue, Henry. 1980. *Basic Rights: Subsistence, Affluence, and U.S. Foreign Policy.* Princeton, NJ: Princeton University Press.

Silverstein, Helena. 1996. *Unleashing Rights: Law, Meaning, and the Animal Rights Movement.* Ann Arbor: University of Michigan Press.

Silverstein, Michael. 2003. "Translation, Transduction, Transformation: Skating 'Glossando' on Thin Semiotic Ice." In *Translating Cultures: Perspectives on Translation and Anthropology,* ed. Paula G. Rubel and Abraham Rosman, 75–105. Oxford, UK: Berg.

Simpson, Leanne Betasamosake. 2017. *As We Have Always Done: Indigenous Freedom Through Radical Resistance.* Minneapolis: University of Minnesota Press.

Sklair, Leslie. 2001. *The Transnational Capitalist Class.* New York: Wiley.

Slaughter, Anne-Marie. 2005. *A New World Order.* Princeton, NJ: Princeton University Press.

Slobodian, Quinn. 2020. *Globalists: The End of Empire and the Birth of Neoliberalism.* Cambridge, MA: Harvard University Press.

Smith, Jackie. 2007. *Social Movements for Global Democracy.* Baltimore: Johns Hopkins University Press.

Smith, Neil. 2008. *Uneven Development: Nature, Capital, and the Production of Space.* Athens: University of Georgia Press.

Solof, Mark. 1998. *History of Metropolitan Planning Organizations.* Newark, NJ: North Jersey Transportation Planning Authority.

Sonntag, Viki. 2008. *Why Local Linkages Matter: Findings from the Local Food Economy Survey.* Seattle: Sustainable Seattle.

Sørensen, Eva. 2002. "Democratic Theory and Network Governance." *Administrative Theory and Praxis* 24 (4): 693–720.

Stone, Glenn Davis. 2019. "Commentary: New Histories of the Indian Green Revolution." *Geographical Journal* 185 (2): 243–50.

Strathern, Marilyn. 1996. "Cutting the Network." *Journal of the Royal Anthropological Institute* 2 (3): 517–35.

Suwandi, Intan. 2019. *Value Chains: The New Economic Imperialism.* New York: Monthly Review Press.

Swinburn, Boyd A., Vivica I. Kraak, Steven Allender, Vincent J. Atkins, Phillip I. Baker, Jessica R. Bogard, Hannah Brinsden et al. 2019. "The Global Syndemic of Obesity, Undernutrition, and Climate Change: The Lancet Commission Report." *The Lancet* 393 (10173): 791–846.

Swyngedouw, Erik. 1997. "Neither Global nor Local: 'Glocalization' and the Politics of Scale." In *Spaces of Globalization: Reasserting the Power of the Local,* ed. Kevin R. Cox, 137–66. London: Guilford Press.

———. 2004. "Globalisation or 'Glocalisation'? Networks, Territories and Rescaling." *Cambridge Review of International Affairs* 17 (1): 25–48.

———. 2010. "Apocalypse Forever? Post-Political Populism and the Spectre of Climate Change." *Theory, Culture, and Society* 27 (2–3): 213–32.

Taylor, Dorceta E. 2018. "Black Farmers in the USA and Michigan: Longevity,

Empowerment, and Food Sovereignty." *Journal of African American Studies* 22 (1): 49–76.

Taylor, Ronald B. 1971. "Why Chavez Spurns the Labor Act." *Nation* 212 (15): 454–56.

Thérien, Jean-Philippe, and Vincent Pouliot. 2020. "Global Governance as Patchwork: The Making of the Sustainable Development Goals." *Review of International Political Economy* 27 (3): 612–36.

Thompson, E. P. 1971. "The Moral Economy of the English Crowd in the Eighteenth Century." *Past and Present* 50 (1): 76–136.

———. 1993. *Customs in Common*. London: Penguin Books.

Thorelli, Hans B. 1986. "Networks: Between Markets and Hierarchies." *Strategic Management Journal* 7 (1): 37–51.

Tilzey, Mark. 2017. *Political Ecology, Food Regimes, and Food Sovereignty: Crisis, Resistance, and Resilience*. Cham, Switzerland: Springer.

Tom, Kip. 2020. "The UN Should Learn That Ideology Won't Stop a Plague of Locusts." RealClearWorld, August 5. https://www.realclearworld.com/articles/2020/08/05/the_un_should_learn_that_ideology_wont_stop_a_plague_of_locusts_501134.html.

Trauger, Amy. 2017. *We Want Land to Live: Making Political Space for Food Sovereignty*. Athens: University of Georgia Press.

Tripp, Aili Mari. 2004. "The Changing Face of Authoritarianism in Africa: The Case of Uganda." *Africa Today* 50 (3): 3–26.

Tsing, Anna Lowenhaupt. 2015. *The Mushroom at the End of the World: On the Possibility of Life in Capitalist Ruins*. Princeton, NJ: Princeton University Press.

Tsing, Anna Lowenhaupt, Andrew S. Mathews, and Nils Bubandt. 2019. "Patchy Anthropocene: Landscape Structure, Multispecies History, and the Retooling of Anthropology—An Introduction to Supplement 20." *Current Anthropology* 60 (suppl. 20): S186–S197.

Turem, Ziya Umut, and Andrea Ballestero. 2014. "Regulatory Translations: Expertise and Affect in Global Legal Fields (Symposium Introduction)." *Indiana Journal of Global Legal Studies* 21 (1): 1–26.

Turner, Fred. 2006. *From Counterculture to Cyberculture: Stewart Brand, the Whole Earth Network, and the Rise of Digital Utopianism*. Chicago: University of Chicago Press.

Unger, Roberto Mangabeira. 2004. *False Necessity: Anti-Necessitarian Social Theory in the Service of Radical Democracy—From Politics, a Work in Constructive Social Theory*. New York: Verso.

Vanhala, Lisa. 2010. *Making Rights a Reality? Disability Rights Activists and Legal Mobilization*. Cambridge, UK: Cambridge University Press.

Vidal, John. 2010. "UN Warned of Major New Food Crisis at Emergency Meeting in Rome." *The Guardian*, September 24. https://www.theguardian.com/environment/2010/sep/24/food-crisis-un-emergency-meeting-rome.

Vogel, Steven Kent. 1996. *Freer Markets, More Rules: Regulatory Reform in Advanced Industrial Countries*. Ithaca, NY: Cornell University Press.

Walzer, Michael. 1984. "Liberalism and the Art of Separation." *Political Theory* 12 (3): 315–30.

Wambugu, Florence, and Daniel Kamanga. 2014. *Biotechnology in Africa: Emergence, Initiatives, and Future.* Cham, Switzerland: Springer.

Wezel, A., S. Bellon, T. Dore, C. Francis, D. Vallod, and C. David. 2009. "Agroecology as a Science, a Movement, and a Practice: A Review." *Agronomy for Sustainable Development* 29 (4): 503–15.

Wezel, Alexander, Barbara Gemmill Herren, Rachel Bezner Kerr, Edmundo Barrios, André Luiz Rodrigues Gonçalves, and Fergus Sinclair. 2020. "Agroecological Principles and Elements and Their Implications for Transitioning to Sustainable Food Systems: A Review." *Agronomy for Sustainable Development* 40 (6): 1–13.

White, Monica M. 2018. *Freedom Farmers: Agricultural Resistance and the Black Freedom Movement.* Chapel Hill: University of North Carolina Press.

Whyte, Jessica. 2019. *The Morals of the Market: Human Rights and the Rise of Neoliberalism.* New York: Verso.

Wiegratz, Jörg. 2010. "Fake Capitalism? The Dynamics of Neoliberal Moral Restructuring and Pseudo-Development: The Case of Uganda." *Review of African Political Economy* 37 (124): 123–37.

Willhoite, David. 2012. "The Story of the California Agricultural Labor Relations Act: How Cesar Chavez Won the Best Labor Law in the Country and Lost the Union (UC Hastings College of the Law Student Symposium: California Aspects of the Rise and Fall of Legal Liberalism)." *California Legal History* 7: 409–44.

Williams, Justine M., and Eric Holt-Giménez. 2017. *Land Justice: Re-Imagining Land, Food, and the Commons.* Oakland, CA: Food First Books.

Wilson, Japhy, and Erik Swyngedouw, eds. 2015. *The Post-Political and Its Discontents: Spaces of Depoliticization, Spectres of Radical Politics.* Edinburgh: Edinburgh University Press.

Winders, Bill. 2004. "Sliding Toward the Free Market: Shifting Political Coalitions and U.S. Agricultural Policy, 1945–1975." *Rural Sociology* 69 (4): 467–89.

Wise, Timothy. 2020. "Failing Africa's Farmers: An Impact Assessment of the Alliance for a Green Revolution in Africa." Working Paper no. 20–01. Boston: Global Development and Environment Institute, Tufts University.

Wittman, Hannah. 2011. "Food Sovereignty: A New Rights Framework for Food and Nature?" *Environment and Society: Advances in Research* 2 (1): 87–105.

Woertz, Eckart. 2013. *Oil for Food: The Global Food Crisis and the Middle East.* Oxford, UK: Oxford University Press.

Wolf, Eric R. 1969. *Peasant Wars of the Twentieth Century.* Norman: University of Oklahoma Press.

Wood, Ellen Meiksins. 2016. *The Origin of Capitalism: A Longer View.* New York: Verso.

Wood, Neal. 1984. *John Locke and Agrarian Capitalism*. Berkeley: University of California Press.

World Economic Forum. 2010. *Everybody's Business: Strengthening International Cooperation in a More Interdependent World*. Geneva: World Economic Forum.

Yeatman, Heather. 1994. "Food Policy Councils in North America: Observations and Insights." In *Final Report on a World Health Organization's Traveling Fellowship*, by Heather Yeatman. Wollongong, Australia: University of Wollongong. https://documents.uow.edu.au/content/groups/public/@web/@health/documents/doc/uow025389.pdf.

Youngberg, Garth. 1978. "The Alternative Agricultural Movement." *Policy Studies Journal* 6 (4): 524–30.

Zabin, Carol. 1992. *Mixtec Migrant Farmworkers in California Agriculture: A Dialogue Among Mixtec Leaders, Researchers, and Farm Labor Advocates*. Davis: California Institute for Rural Studies.

Zaitchik, Alexander. 2021. "How Bill Gates Impeded Global Access to Covid Vaccines." *The New Republic*, April 12. https://newrepublic.com/article/162000/bill-gates-impeded-global-access-covid-vaccines.

Zald, Mayer N. 1996. "Culture, Ideology, and Strategic Framing." In *Comparative Perspectives on Social Movements: Political Opportunities, Mobilizing Structures, and Cultural Framings*, ed. Doug McAdam, John D. McCarthy, and Mayer N. Zald, 261–74. Cambridge, UK: Cambridge University Press.

Zlolniski, Christian. 2019. *Made in Baja: The Lives of Farmworkers and Growers Behind Mexico's Transnational Agricultural Boom*. Berkeley: University of California Press.

Zoomers, Annelies. 2010. "Globalisation and the Foreignisation of Space: Seven Processes Driving the Current Global Land Grab." *Journal of Peasant Studies* 37 (2): 429–47.

Index

Tilth: Tilth Association, 30, 34–42,
62, Tilth Newsletter, 35, 38; Tilth
Producers Cooperative, 37, 40–41
trade: See GATT; WTO
translation: as the practice of food
sovereignty, 7–8, 17–19, 48–54;
hegemonic practices of, 136, 137–40;
theories of, 17–19, 49–50, 206n68,
206n72; translocal forms of, 28–29,
48–54
transnational governance: concept
and forms of, 6–7, 11–12; in relation
to neoliberalism, 6–7, 11–12, 21-25,
161–65, 188–91, 194–202; in relation
to international law, 15–17, 194–96
TRIPS (Agreement on Trade-Related
Aspects of Intellectual Property), 45,
134, 145, 148, 223n49. See also WTO

UFW (United Farm Workers), 61, 97–
99, 102–3, 216n12
Uganda: biotechnology regulation in,
137–50, Green Revolution in 124,
136–37

UN Food Systems Summit, 184–85
USFSA (US Food Sovereignty Alliance),
59–61, 102, 113, 149
US Food Sovereignty National
Assembly, 1–5, 60, 93, 102
US Working Group on the Food Crisis,
55–59

worker-driven social responsibility, 101.
See also GVCs
WEF (World Economic Forum), 162,
184–85
World Food Conference, 32–33, 155
World Food Council, 155–56, 224n11
World Food Summit, 45, 156–57
WTO (World Trade Organization):
and global food governance,
156, 166, 191; as an expression of
neoliberal regulation, 99–100;
effects of on food security, 209n42;
mobilization in opposition to, 2, 11,
20, 26–27, 60. See also Agreement
on Agriculture; Battle in Seattle;
TRIPS

The authorized representative in the EU for product safety and compliance is:
Mare Nostrum Group
B.V Doelen 72
4831 GR Breda
The Netherlands

www.ingramcontent.com/pod-product-compliance
Lightning Source LLC
Chambersburg PA
CBHW020844270326
41928CB00006B/533

9 781503 631304